The Carmack-Cooper
Shooting

The Carmack-Cooper Shooting

Tennessee Politics Turns Violent, November 9, 1908

JAMES SUMMERVILLE

McFarland & Company, Inc., Publishers

Jefferson, North Carolina

The present work is a reprint of the library bound edition of The Carmack-Cooper Shooting: Tennessee Politics Turns Violent, November 9, 1908, *first published in 1994 by McFarland.*

LIBRARY OF CONGRESS CATALOGUING-IN-PUBLICATION DATA

Summerville, James, 1947–
    The Carmack-Cooper shooting : Tennessee politics turns violent, November 9, 1908 / by James Summerville.
        p.   cm.
    Includes bibliographical references and index.

ISBN 978-0-7864-9386-9 (softcover : acid free paper) ∞

    1. Carmack, Edward Ward, 1858–1908.   2. Cooper, Duncan Brown.
3. Cooper, Robin, d. 1919.   4. Vendetta—Tennessee—History—19th century.   5. Murder—Tennessee—History—19th century.
6. Tennessee—Politics and government—1865–1950.   I. Title.
E664.C28S86 2014
976.8'051—dc20   94-10807

BRITISH LIBRARY CATALOGUING DATA ARE AVAILABLE

On the cover: *insets top to bottom* Edward Ward Carmack, 1902 (Library of Congress); Robin J. Cooper, 1908 (Current Literature); Duncan B. Cooper, 1908 (Current Literature); *background* Tennessee State Capitol © 2014 iStock/Thinkstock

Printed in the United States of America

McFarland & Company, Inc., Publishers
    Box 611, Jefferson, North Carolina 28640
        www.mcfarlandpub.com

This book is in loving memory of
Mrs. James Mapheus Smith (1890–1986)

CONTENTS

PREFACE

THE AUTHOR OWES A SPECIAL DEBT to Nashville attorney Gary Blackburn, who proposed this study but was hindered from coauthoring it by the demands of his full and accomplished professional life. Gary imparted insights in conversation, read portions of the manuscript, and arranged those interviews with which his name appears in the notes and the works cited. He is a peer of the Tennessee lawyers of stature in these pages, Guston Fitzhugh and Jeff McCarn, Charles T. Cates, Jr., and John M. Anderson.

Every one of my friends bore with, or was bored by, my long obsession with this story and patiently listened as I told it time and again. Some actually had to endure being led to the spot on Seventh Avenue where Carmack fell and were made to stand in the place of victim or witness, killer or utility pole. They included Lea McIntosh, Jill Haydel, Jerry George, Charlie Phillips, Libby Fryer, Dana Lowe, Sheila Riley, Currey Courtney Cobble, Cynthia Ogorek, and Priscilla Juchemich. I also thank members of the local post of the American Legion, the Cumberland Chapter of the Daughters of the American Revolution, and the Rutherford County Historical Society, who listened with greater or lesser patience to talks drawn from the book. Among those who read and commented on portions of the manuscript were Lucius Burch, Jr., Mrs. Frank Fletcher, Ridley Wills, II, Ward DeWitt, Jr., and Randal Whittington. Not all of these necessarily agree with my conclusions and interpretations.

Many more gave me encouragement, assistance, or example, sometimes unawares. I thank Public Service Commissioner Steve Hewlett for reprinting Carmack's masterful essay, "Character; Or, the Making of the Man"; former district attorney general Paul Bumpus for collecting and publishing all the senator's speeches and writings; Mrs. Lowe Watkins, niece of Kate Eastman; Mary Glenn Hearne of the Nashville Room, Public Library of Nashville and Davidson County; Virginia Lyle, Margaret Shea, and the staff of the archives of the Metropolitan Government of Nashville and Davidson County; the late State Senator E. E. Loftin; John Burch, descendant of Colonel Cooper; Mrs. Lesbia Word Roberts, whose study of the Cooper family is a model of industry, care for detail, and thoroughness; Dr. James High; Dr. Joseph F. Jacobs; coworkers at the American Association for State and Local History; Arthur Ben Chitty; Mark B. McKenney; Larrye J. Kelly; Peter Taylor; Dr. Miller McDonald; Dr. Samuel McSeveney; Louis Torres; Dr. Sherman Paul; Mary Louise Tidwell; Charles A. Howell, III; Sherwood B. Seeley; Patty Hall; Candace Floyd; Mimi Phillips, granddaughter of Governor Patterson; Professor James A. Hodges of the College of Wooster; Professor Emeritus Robert E. Corlew of Middle Tennessee State University; friends on the Vanderbilt University history faculty, professors Dewey Grantham and Jacque Voegeli; archivists at the U.S. Department of Justice, the Pinkerton Company, and Washington and Jefferson College; librarians at the public libraries of Indianapolis, Indiana, Washington, D.C., Memphis, Tennessee, and Onandaga County, New York; and their colleagues at the Jean and Alexander Heard Library of Vanderbilt University.

I have examined the causes and consequences of the killing of Carmack with no preconceived opinion about the guilt or innocence of the Coopers. My interpretations, sometimes implicit, sometimes boldly stated, rest on a disinterested review of the evidence, including the thousand pages of transcript from their trial for murder. The other chief sources for this book were the papers of Edward Ward Carmack and those of Duncan Brown Cooper, the last having never been examined by a student of this minor Southern epic. The transcripts and the principals' papers repose in the Tennessee State Library and Archives, the Carmack Papers in photocopied form.

The staff of that institution were endlessly helpful and courteous, and I mention with particular gratitude Ruth Jarvis, Bob DePriest, Ann Alley, Genella Oakley, Marylin Hughes, and Wayne Moore. The General Assembly can insure preservation of the people's history of Tennessee, during this its bicentennial era, by adequately funding our state library.

Daughter Laurel Means retyped Chapter Three after the computer lost it again and again, glitched no doubt by the shade of Edward Carmack. Daughter Leigh Bizaillon, a young woman who always has morning in her face, often asked, in utter amazement, "Are you *still* working on that?" John Means after awhile stopped inquiring about how the book was going, to kindly avoid embarrassing me. John Carter claims to doubt everything he reads and so ought to become a historian rather than the mathematician he aspires to be. This household has also been shared by my four-footed feline children and three-legged keeshond. The textual scholar who peruses the original manuscript and research files in the State Library will find pawprints on a good many pages.

And this book is for Linda Andersen Summerville, who has fallen asleep many nights to the thickety-thickety-thick of the keyboard keys. With unfailing grace and cheerfulness and faith, when I have had only grim determination, she has seen it, and me, and us through. For the six years of the book's composition, I took great pleasure in the company of Edward, Dunc, Ham, Harvey, Ned, and Katrina. This is my understanding of their days and lives, and I am pleased to share it with as many as care to remember them.

Nashville, February 1994

—— INTRODUCTION ——

*T*ENNESSEE PEOPLE WHO STILL possess a sense of the past often come to their history through stories to which they have a personal connection. A whole generation became involved in the Cooper-Carmack affair. Many of them revered the dead man's memory. Wrote Mrs. Guston Fitzhugh of Memphis, "Like the martyrs of early Christendom, he stood facing with royal courage the powers of darkness, bearing in his hand the staff of temperance." Others shared the view of J. L. C. Kerr of Decatur, Georgia, who called Duncan Cooper a "gallant old Confederate hero that had the manhood and true Southern courage to defend himself from the defamation and abuse of a crank." An anonymous newspaper columnist of the time, "Old Politician," summarized their deadly encounter well: "Edward Ward Carmack was not an angel, and Colonel Duncan Cooper hasn't any wings to speak of, as far as known. These men were political gladiators, they played the game all their lives, they were arrogant and ambitious, and neither could brook opposition."

The purpose of this book is simply to tell again one of the great stories from Tennessee's past, the political and personal feud among the state's most prominent men of the early twentieth century. It is a story of pride and honor, ambition and revenge.

Edward L. Ayers, in *Vengeance and Justice*, notes that well into the twentieth century, many Southern men lived by honor, "a system of values within which you have exactly as much worth as others confer upon you." If a man did not respond to insult, the code of honor marked him as less than a man. Duncan Cooper embraced that view of life, according to his friends. "I scarcely met anybody but who asked me why [Carmack's] attacks on me," he told the jury in his trial for murder. Hours before the encounter, he asked his daughter, who was pleading for peace, "Do you want me to lay down my manhood?"

Cooper personifies the Southerner, described by Bertram Wyatt-Brown in *Southern Honor; Ethics and Behavior in the Old South,* who justifies his

1

behavior by the consensus of the community. Only it was his private interpretation of that consensus that really determined his action and subsequently justified it. As John Shelton Reed has observed, it was almost
impossible to convict a man of murder when the jury believed that his
honor had been injured. By the prevailing standards of justice in the late
nineteenth century South, the Coopers should have walked out of the
courtroom free men. Instead this jury imposed a fierce and dramatic
punishment.

The reasons why shed light on the changes that were coming to the
old code. Sheldon Hackney has noted how the absence of the institutions
of law enforcement on the frontier contributed to Southerners' inclination
to settle private disputes through violence. But in the jurors' community,
the forces of "progress" had recently made the disposition of justice, even
in cases of personal honor, a monopoly of the constabulary and judiciary.
Colonel Cooper took to the stand honor's cardinal principle, that mortal
insult had justified him. But he testified before a jury whose community
was being transformed by bureaucracy, complexity, legal refinement. The
code was yielding to the courts, and ancient honor to community consensus over the justification of a given act of violence.

Within the short space of eight years, three Southern reformers in
politics met violent deaths, and it was people acting through instruments
of the state, not individuals driven by honor, who worked justice. Governor
William Goebels of Kentucky, an enemy of the L & N Railroad, was felled
near the Capitol at Frankfort by an unknown gunman in January 1900. Nar-
ciso G. Gonzales, editor of the Columbia, South Carolina, *Herald,* met his
end when shot by the lieutenant governor of the state, James Tillman,
whom his newspaper had called a liar, defaulter, gambler, and drunkard
during the campaign of 1902. Like Carmack, Goebels and Gonzales were,
according to Professor Dewey Grantham, "aggressive, unrelenting, crusading men," skilled polemicists ever ready to flail their enemies with in-
vective and sarcasm. Grantham notes that each courted his own martyrdom
in those days when people often answered violent words with violent
deeds. Each man's death inflamed public opinion in his state and, fairly or
not, the people drove from office those they blamed for the crimes. Citing
Carmack's memory, a majority of Tennessee Democrats took up his causes
and forced their party, at the price of retaining power, to adopt them, too:
the outlawing of liquor in Tennessee, the curbing of gubernatorial power
over the election machinery, and the dilution of the influence of the L & N.

Carmack's crusade for prohibition should be seen as part of the era of
Southern progressivism, and it stands squarely in the American reform
tradition. Southern progressivism, says Dewey Grantham, stressed ration-
ality, order, and the search for a sense of stability amid the disturbing ac-
celeration of social change, exactly the goals sought by those who wanted

to rid the world of alcohol. As Norman H. Clark points out, the prohibitionists' ranks included many who were also working for laws to regulate giant corporations, insure pure food and drugs, and give women the right to vote. And both progressives and prohibitionists wished for a cleansing of society, including an end to corruption in politics and business. When that stalwart friend of the L & N, Duncan Cooper, and Governor Malcolm "Ham" Patterson joined forces to fight prohibition, it became easy, in the words of C. Vann Woodward, to identify "demon rum and the railroad monster as an enemy of the people."

Out of the letters he left behind rides Dunc Cooper, a colonel in the Confederate army at age twenty, harassing the occupation forces trying to hold middle Tennessee. Scion of an old Maury County family, he mined for silver, bought and sold newspapers, directed operations for the Astor interests in Central America, and served as a legislator and railroad lobbyist. Like a Richard Harding Davis character, he was equally at home in the jungle and on New York's Park Avenue. Cooper espoused laissez-faire, businessman's government, and above all an untrammeled personal liberty. During the administration of Malcolm Patterson, the colonel became the most powerful man in Tennessee politics.

The colonel had plucked Edward Carmack from the obscurity of a country law practice and set him up as editorial writer on the Nashville *American,* the leading voice of the state Democratic Party. From there, the fiery, articulate Carmack attained an influence in the public life of the state for twenty years, until he fell under the fusillade fired by the colonel's son.

There followed the most noted murder trial in the history of the South, wherein attorneys performed "feats of erudition," in the time-honored tradition recognized by Wyatt-Brown. The case split the Tennessee Democracy and cleaved the social and political elite of the state: Carmack's friends cursed the Coopers and their friends in high places defended their good name. Despite widespread charges of political assassination directed from the executive chambers, the prosecution brought forward no evidence that Governor Patterson, Duncan Cooper, and Robin Cooper plotted Carmack's death; such a plot never existed. But the Coopers' friends did conspire so that they would never suffer because of the colonel's rage and his supremely careless, threatening approach to Carmack. The pardon from the governor, arriving as the judges of the Supreme Court were stepping down from the bench after upholding his conviction, put an end to Patterson's political career, a gifted man more loyal to his friends than driven by his ambitions.

Austin Peay, regarded as one of the great governors in Tennessee history, began his public life as an aide to Governor Patterson, who is unjustly underrated. (Portraits of two of the seven former governors from West Tennessee hang in the Capitol; Malcolm Patterson's hangs in the basement of a state office building.) Peay acutely observed that the first trial had a powerful cathartic effect on public opinion. It cleared the air, he told the colonel; and from that point, the door opened for separating Robin Cooper's case from that of his father and allowing Robin's plea of self-defense to be heard. At the same time, no one believed he would ever be convicted; everyone knew Patterson had a second pardon ready if he were. Most accounts report, erroneously, that Robin Cooper's case was dismissed for failure to prosecute; actually, he was acquitted, by collusion.

So Carmack was killed with impunity, but that did not directly cause the election of Tennessee's second Republican governor. As my analysis shows, the Democratic Party had long been vulnerable before the strongest Republican organization in the South. Voting studies of the Tennessee electorate at the turn of the century, sorely needed, will show that Ben Hooper's election in 1910 can be forecast in trends visible ten years before.

The triumph of prohibition might have been the end of this story, but it was not. In the summer of 1919, as American culture veered toward the edge of madness, Robin Cooper was murdered. He was bludgeoned to death and his body thrown into a rain-swollen creek near his home in the posh Belle Meade section of Nashville. All his life, Edward Carmack, Jr., the senator's son, claimed to have done that horrible work. The last chapter of this book evaluates Ned Carmack's confession and, based on the most thorough investigation of the crime in seventy years, suggests what may have happened to Robin Cooper.

By the popular will, Ned Carmack should have taken his seat as United States Senator from Tennessee in January 1943. Instead, Mr. Crump of Memphis counted him out. He nonetheless helped prepare the way for the defeat of the Crump machine and the senatorial careers of Estes Kefauver and Albert Gore, Sr. Ned's story, briefly reviewed in the epilogue, brings this tale down to our time.

The one biography of Edward Carmack, William Majors' *Editorial Wild Oats*, is widely admired for its portrait of Carmack's public life against the background of Tennessee politics at the turn of the century. (But Majors doesn't like Carmack very much.) While tangential to that work, this book replies to it on one key point. Majors takes the modern viewpoint of Richard Hofstader, arguing that Southern progressivism became sidetracked into the fight for prohibition. Carmack, so Majors says, distracted serious reform in the state by harping on whiskey. But no evidence shows that Carmack was less "progressive" on the issues of the day than his political opponents. His defense of the traditional society—of honor—took the form, in the years before his death, of a crusade for prohibition. Was prohibition reform? Yes, it was, Hofstader and Majors notwithstanding. Was Carmack both a prohibitionist and a reformer? Yes, he was.

Carmack's evolving views on prohibition are treated in Chapter Two. But there is no basis to take at face value the charge of hypocrisy made by a political opponent, as Don H. Doyle does in *Nashville in the New South*. Majors regards "occasional rumors" that Carmack drank as confirmation that he was "no teetotaler." This is not evidence, but common gossip. A reasonable man in politics may change his mind on issues over time as new conditions arise and as public opinion itself changes. Based on the sources that survive, we must in fairness assume that Carmack's eventual embrace of the prohibitionist position was a matter of intellectual honesty. If many voters had already taken up that position and supported him in consequence, it is simply another example of the people leading and the leaders following.

Majors is indisputably correct when he concludes that Carmack's public stances often had a strong cast of resentment. Hackney regards resentment as explaining much about Southern identity. Men of modest background, like Carmack, coveted the respect due the high stations they won, Ayers notes; thus politics raised the stakes of honor. In the gubernatorial election of 1908 his enemies brought him down, through means that his own community, the evangelical moralists, disapproved. He saw his honor assailed, and he appealed in the fateful editorials for the true majority and consensus of Democrats to win—at law and through the power of the state—the golden prize of reform, prohibition. And they did so, by hardscrabble politics in the legislative races that year, not by Carmack's martyrdom. Tennessee would have gone dry, even if the editor had been delayed from setting out on his walk home by a few minutes or if Robin Cooper had steered his father by another way to the governor's mansion.

Loved and hated, it has come to the same for Carmack; he is forgotten, largely because his cause is. Not even the Tennesseeans who marched to protest the Vietnam War quoted his brilliant speeches against an earlier American misadventure in Asia. The neo–Agrarians and the religious fundamentalists in the public life of today might acknowledge him as a beloved predecessor, if they knew who he was.

Despite Edward Carmack's oblivion, his statue occupies the most prominent place on the grounds of the State Capitol, above the tunnel named for Motlow, the whiskey maker. The senator's noble and romantic countenance looks out from the Capitol grounds onto a city that day by day grows more like many other American cities—bigger, noisier, more dangerous, less civil—because emptier of historical memory and sense of home and place. It serves the corporation and the state that we forget names like Carmack, and Sequoyah, Anne Dallas Dudley, and Cordell Hull. If we don't remember them, we shall certainly forget the possibilities in ourselves for exercising our sovereignty over our government and leading our communities with imagination and energy. The quality of our public life depends on people knowing and passing on such stories. Did I think the Carmack statue ought to be moved to a less prominent place? asked a questioner who clearly did. No, I answered; it's our finest monument to our collective amnesia, the neglect of our history, and the catastrophic condition of democracy in Tennessee.

CHAPTER ONE

The Killing

AUTUMN CAME TO NASHVILLE in 1908 as it comes no more, with the whistle of trains carrying for miles on the air at dawn and yellow leaves clattering over the granite pavements of Broad Street.

The city was small, crowded, noisy, and dirty. Cows and horses were kept in town, sometimes breaking free from the stable lots behind their owners' homes and wandering onto the streetcar tracks. Animal-drawn buggies and wagons rattled over the narrow thoroughfares, with flying hooves and whirring steel-shod wheels. Every Saturday morning on the courthouse square, people came in from the country to hawk souse, crack-lings, eggs, butter, live chickens, and sausage wrapped in cornshuck.

His produce sold and cash money in his pocket, the visiting farmer might be tempted to wash the week's dust from his throat with a glass of whiskey at one of the hundred and seventy bars crowded within a few square blocks. Henry Goodpasture recalled walking with his father along the south side of the Public Square, after they had left their horse and buggy at Sandy Brown's livery stable on Front Street. "It seems to me there was a solid block of saloons. It was a rather wide sidewalk, and I can remember men staggering about...."[1]

The yeoman and the townsman at his elbow had to drink up before midnight, else they would hear themselves and other violators of the law against Sunday tippling denounced from the pulpits of the Protestant churches. Worse, they risked arrest in a raid directed by Jeff McCarn, the fiery attorney general of Davidson County.

For the gentlemen the city offered still more diversions. A game of poker, faro, or craps was usually available in one of the saloons along Fourth Avenue, and a betting man could lay down money on the horses. Men of affairs like Colonel Duncan Brown Cooper passed the time and gathered the political intelligence of the hour at the Tulane Hotel, the Maxwell House, or the Watauga Club, all within an easy walk of the Capitol office of his friend and political ally, Governor Malcolm Patterson.

The colonel gambled, drank good whiskey, made money and gave it away indifferently. Cooper's roots sank deep into Tennessee soil. Two ancestral mansions, Riverwood in east Nashville, and Mulberry Hill, his birthplace near Columbia, attached to the family name. In Edwardian fashion he favored butterfly collars and sported a handlebar mustache. Bald and portly, he was a man at home in the world. "Colonel Cooper has shrewd mentality," a contemporary observed, "[and] the suave manners and culture of a gentleman of the old school. He has mingled freely and on equal terms with the leading men of his time."[2] The colonel's detractors were legion; but his keen sense of personal honor and dignity caused them to speak softly behind their hands whenever he passed down the peacock row of Washington's Willard Hotel or through the stands at Saratoga.

The colonel's son Robin, and most of the other members of the bar, maintained offices on Church, Union, or the Public Square, near the courts of state and city. Those in the twenty-seven year old attorney's set favored Stumb's, on Fourth Avenue two doors north of Church, as a gathering place. They could carry their colas from the pink marble fountain out to the sidewalk in front to watch laborers raising the beams for the Third National Bank and playing pitch and catch with red hot rivets.

To leave this teeming center of town for the supposedly virtuous and peaceful countryside was no great undertaking. Harold Wickliffe Rose recalled his family's move just beyond the city limits to Convent Place, two miles south of the courthouse, in 1908:

> Across Jones Avenue was the Burch Place. Down toward [Hillsboro] Pike lived John Fleming, and up the other way was Edgar Jones. That was it. All between and beyond was woods and fields.[3]

In the first week of November, forest fires were burning in the hills south of the city. By Monday the ninth, the smoke was mingling with that from coalfires warming the homes in town and fueling the steam trains toiling to and from Union Station. Rain clouds were rolling up from the west, darkening the day still more.[4]

In late afternoon lamps flared in the parlors on Capitol Hill. Governor Patterson had recently occupied the state's first official residence, on Seventh Avenue between Union and Cedar, a short distance south of the statehouse. Although Nashvillians were segregating themselves along class and racial lines, rich and poor still lived in the vicinity. To the west lay the festering slum known as Hell's Half Acre. But along Fifth, Sixth, and Seventh avenues there stood imposing mansions in the Second Empire style, representing substance and influence in the affairs of the city and the state. The governor's neighbors included insurance broker Charles H. Eastman and

Duncan B. Cooper and Robin J. Cooper. Source: *Current Literature*, December 1908.

his wife, Kate, president of the board of the Women's Hospital. The editor of the *Nashville Tennessean*, former U.S. Senator Edward Ward Carmack, rented rooms from the Eastmans, whose house stood in the middle of the short block north of Cedar.[5]

Carmack had begun his journalistic career on the city's leading daily, the *American*, in 1886, just after a syndicate in which Duncan Cooper was an investor bought the paper. As an editorial writer Carmack put his vigorous prose in service of the dominant faction of Democrats, the Bourbon "regulars," and their platform of a revenue tariff, states' rights, white supremacy, and low-tax, low-debt approach to state government.[6]

In April 1890, Carmack married Elizabeth Cobey Dunnington, in St. Peter's Episcopal Church, across the street from the bride's home in Columbia, Tennessee. (Floy Cooper, daughter of Duncan Cooper, served as a bridesmaid.) On the happy occasion, the noblest Bourbon of them all, Isham G. Harris, sent his good wishes. "You possess splendid talents and all the elements of a chivalrous gentleman, and can make yourself anything you wish," wrote Tennessee's senior U.S. Senator.[7]

For six years Carmack cut a figure in Nashville journalism. He then resigned from the *American* to accept a position on the Memphis *Daily Commercial*, the beginning of a career that would take him to Congress, then to Harris's old seat in the U. S. Senate. In his leave-taking editorial, Carmack thanked his other mentor:

> I desire especially to acknowledge the debt I owe and the
> gratitude I feel toward Col. D. B. Cooper, under whose
> management I first became acquainted with the *American*
> and with journalism. . . . I cannot recall one word, act, or
> incident which has marred the harmony of our relations dur-
> ing the whole time of our intimate association.[8]

On November 9, 1908, Carmack's vest pocket still held a gold watch
inscribed "IGH to EWC." But his friendship with Duncan Cooper had
turned into vindictive hatred on both sides.

Fall came in November 1908 as it does still, with the shortening of the
days and the early fading of the light. About four o'clock Carmack finished
his work in the *Tennessean*'s offices, at Eighth Avenue and Church Street.

A candidate for governor the previous summer, former Senator Carmack had gone down to defeat at the hands of his ancient enemy, the incumbent Malcolm Patterson, and Patterson's chief strategist, Colonel
Cooper. Following that defeat, Carmack accepted the editor's post of the
Tennessean, a small, screaming, anti-liquor sheet founded the year before
by lawyer and entrepreneur Luke Lea.

On October 21 Carmack directed the attention of "the Honorable
Dunc Cooper . . . the Honorable Max Harlan, the Honorable Solomon
Cohn, and all the other honorables" to a certain political situation in West
Tennessee. Max Harlan and Sol Cohn operated the Hullabaloo, a dance
parlor in the notorious slum known as "Black Bottom," south of Broad
Street in Nashville. On Sunday, November 8, Carmack again insulted
Cooper on the editorial page, lampooning his alleged part in building Patterson's coalition for the coming struggle in the legislature over prohibition. In part he wrote, "All honor to that noble spirit, Major Duncan Brown
Cooper, who wrought this happy union of congenial and confluxible spirits,
separated by evil fates though born for each other."[9] Several friends, including Edward B. Craig and Alfred M. Shook, stood around the editorial
office about midnight Saturday, laughing as Carmack read his gibes. But
when they appeared in print the next morning, Cooper was not amused,
and he composed a note to Carmack. "You have no more right to say those
things in the newspaper than you do to my face," he wrote, "which so far
you have not had the temerity to do."[10]

That evening the colonel kept an appointment with Craig at the
Tulane Hotel regarding a private business matter. Cooper quickly dismissed that business and brought up the hateful editorials. "He was violent
in his denunciation of Senator Carmack," Craig recalled later. He offered
to go and see the editor, whom he had known for twenty years. Cooper did
not object. In his trial for his life, he depicted this acquiescence as an over-
ture for peace.

But Craig plainly saw that Cooper was "very much agitated, very angry, and very threatening." "'I am an old man, a private citizen,'" Craig quoted him, "'and it makes little difference whether I go or not.' He soon said that if his name appeared again in the *Tennessean*, he or Senator Carmack must die." Cooper insisted that his words had been "this town will not be big enough to hold us both."[11] Whatever the truth, it would not matter. As he walked from the Tulane Hotel across Eighth Avenue to the newspaper office, the gears meshed and the wheels began to turn.

Craig told Carmack that Cooper was incensed. He repeated the demand that his name not be printed again — and conveyed the colonel's threatening manner and demeanor. When he returned to the Tulane, he told Cooper, "I can accomplish nothing."

"Then, by God, this note goes!" Cooper fumed, striking his breast pocket that held it. Craig apparently tried to placate the colonel, offering the opinion that Carmack would not print Cooper's name again. "I believed that he knew what he was speaking of," Cooper said later.

As he would do up until the moment he looked into the face of his friend of old and enemy of late, Cooper acted with ambivalence. He did not have the note delivered to Carmack. But he borrowed a nickel-plated hammerless Smith and Wesson from Thomas Hutchison, a police commissioner of Nashville and ordnance officer on Governor Patterson's staff.[12]

Craig returned to the *Tennessean* and told Carmack that Cooper was going to send him a note that, in the colonel's words, "could not be misunderstood." When Craig left, Carmack sent word to Major William O. Vertrees that he wanted to see him. A loyal ally, the lawyer had been an attendant at Carmack's wedding. The editor told his friend that Cooper said that if his name appeared again, he or Carmack would have to go. "'There is nothing left for me to do,'" Vertrees quoted him, "'but put his name in the paper, and his name will go in in the morning.'" Carmack asked Vertrees to lend him a gun, and Vertrees gave him what he described as a "blue-steel pistol, a five-shooter loaded all around." Carmack remarked that he knew nothing about pistols, but the lawyer assured him that all that was necessary to shoot it was to pull the trigger. He unbreeched and unloaded it and pulled the trigger a number of times. Replacing the shells, he handed the gun to Carmack.[13]

Colonel Cooper opened the *Tennessean* the next morning at the Watauga Club and read Carmack's editorial, "The Diplomat of the Zweibund."

> To Major Duncan Brown Cooper, who wrought the great coalition; who achieved the harmonious confluence of incompatible elements; who wielded the pewter handle to the wooden spoon; who grafted the dead bough to the living tree and made it bloom and burgeon and bend with golden fruit;

who made playmates of the lamb and the leopard and boon companions of the spider and the fly; who made soda and water to dwell placidly in the same bottle, and who taught oil and water how they might agree—to Major Duncan Brown Cooper, the great diplomat of the political Zweibund, be all honor and glory forever.[14]

The title alluded to a sobriquet given Bismarck, the "diplomat of the Dreibund." But it was the "golden fruit" that enraged Cooper. These words accused him of corruption, and this after he understood from Craig that he would be left alone. He set out for Robin Cooper's office, in the Noel Block at Third and Church, where the young lawyer practiced with his uncle, James C. Bradford. Cursing Carmack, he showed his son the pistol he carried.[15]

Robin allowed the colonel to leave, then grew worried. He dialed the home of his sister, Mrs. Lucius Burch, and asked her to try to find their father by telephone and keep him off the streets. Then he hurried down the stairs and out into the town to search for the colonel himself. Not finding him at the Maxwell House, Robin crossed the street to Stumb's and telephoned William O. Vertrees at the Chancery Court. They had a case on the docket that morning, and Robin promised to join him as soon as he could.

Failing to locate his father at the Watauga Club or the Tulane Hotel, Robin returned to his office and called Governor Patterson. Then he resumed his anxious search up and down Church Street, through the lobbies and suites and gathering places that the colonel frequented. "I couldn't find him," Robin would testify, "and I believed I ought to get a pistol so that if I did find him, and it was necessary for him to be on the streets that I could be with him, and in case he were attacked, protect him." About eleven o'clock, he telephoned his uncle Robin Jones, who brought him a gun within the hour.[16]

Deeply upset by Robin's message, Sarah Burch also called Governor Patterson. Then she telephoned Dr. John A. Witherspoon, a colleague of her husband's and a warm friend of Edward Carmack. Hearing the anxiety in her voice, Witherspoon tried without success to reach Dr. Burch. Then he rang for Carmack, but the editor was not available. Unable to get word to him directly, Witherspoon sent a note to Frank D. Lander, managing editor at the *Tennessean*.[17]

Lander received Witherspoon's message between eleven o'clock and noon, went to his office, then returned to the newspaper and hurried in to see Carmack. Thus Duncan Cooper's blustering conversation with his son passed through its fourth paraphrasing. Lander recounted Dr. Witherspoon as saying that Mrs. Burch told him that her father was armed and very angry and intending to kill Carmack on sight.[18]

From Robin's law office, Colonel Cooper had gone to Sandy Brown's livery stable to see about a horse for his granddaughter. He rode the animal up and down the block, agreed to the purchase, and waited for a blacksmith to apply shoes. Then he hitched up a buggy and drove out Broadway to the Burch residence, accompanied by the liveryman's son. A servant hailed the colonel, and he dismounted, handing the reins to his companion, who wheeled and started back to town.[19]

By now nearly hysterical, Mrs. Burch met her father in the front hallway. Did she want him to lay down his manhood? he asked her when he saw her tears.

"He will kill you, Papa," Sarah Burch replied.

"He is as likely to get killed as I am," her father retorted.[20] But mindful of his daughter's fears, he decided to revise the note that he had composed the night before and changed the sharp sentence about Carmack's not having met him face to face. Seated at Dr. Burch's desk, he wrote

Nashville, Tenn., Nov. 9, 1908

E. W. Carmack
City
Sir:

I am a private citizen; I am neither an office holder nor an office seeker. I have violated no law, and consequently am not a legitimate subject of public attack or discussion. For many months, on the stump and through newspapers you have seen fit to offensively use my name and vent your malignity. You have no right in this manner to annoy, insult, or injure me than you would have to do so to my face. I notify you that the use of my name in your paper must cease.

Taking the streetcar back to town, Cooper went to the Maxwell House, where he hired a public stenographer to type the note.[21]

Governor Patterson, who had also gone searching for the colonel after the two telephone calls from his family, found him at the hotel. Patterson read the note, which was still unsigned, and urged his friend not to send it. James C. Bradford arrived and persuaded Colonel Cooper to give him the note. Bradford planned to ask Alfred M. Shook, a friend of both the colonel and the editor, to speak with Carmack. Bradford asked Cooper to come to his office at three o'clock, at which time he would report what he had been able to accomplish. Robin had at last caught up with his father, and Cooper promised him that he would not leave the hotel except to go to the conference with Bradford. The colonel spent the interval over lunch and in conversation with his dear friend Mrs. Katrina Williamson.[22]

Robin left the hotel with Patterson, walking with him as far as the Arcade. As they parted, the governor said, "Robin, if I was in your place, I would stay with my father as much as I could today." Patterson recalled that Robin had tears in his eyes. Young Cooper composed himself and returned to his case in Chancery Court. Following adjournment about two o'clock, he took lunch at the Utopia with his co-counsel, Major Vertrees. By three he was in James C. Bradford's office for the meeting.[23]

Bradford had gone to Alfred Shook's office, only to learn that he was out of the city. He decided to seek out John J. Vertrees, the major's brother, who sent word for Bradford to join him for lunch at the Utopia. Hoping that he could persuade Vertrees to go and talk with Carmack in the interest of a settlement, Bradford brought up Colonel Cooper's note. Vertrees misunderstood; he thought Bradford was asking him to deliver the note, and he refused to embroil himself in the trouble.[24]

Katrina Williamson believed from what the colonel told her that peace had been declared, "[that] mutual friends had adjusted the trouble." In time to keep his appointment, Cooper left her at the Maxwell House. Soon after he reached Bradford's office, Adjutant General Tully Brown came in.[25]

If Malcolm Patterson, Duncan Cooper and James C. Bradford conspired to murder Edward Carmack, this three o'clock conference must have been decisive in the plotting. Those who believed all of them guilty cited the recollection of a secretary there, Miss Daisy Lee. To her, Robin Cooper appeared "almost spotted over some big excitement." And later, when the telephone rang, Bradford had snatched the receiver from the hook; it was as though he knew it would be Colonel Cooper with word that Robin had killed Carmack. Miss Lee thought her employer oddly nonplussed by the news.[26]

What actually happened at the conference was that Colonel Cooper agreed to at least postpone the sending of a note. He apparently wanted Bradford himself to go directly to Carmack, believing the lawyer could adjust the difficulty.

As the meeting was breaking up, the telephone rang, Governor Patterson calling Colonel Cooper. Could he come to the mansion in twenty-five minutes? And would he bring Austin Peay if he saw him? Cooper started out the door of the law offices.

Robin realized that Carmack had no notice of Colonel Cooper's leaving the matter in Bradford's hands. The young lawyer hurried after his father and, over his protest, insisted on going with him. When they had gone a block, Robin proposed they turn north on Fourth Avenue.[27]

At the other end of Church Street, Carmack was just leaving his office. He stopped at a drugstore, where he drank a Coca-Cola and bought a cigar. He continued east, pausing to help a woman board a streetcar. At Seventh Avenue, he turned north. Jordan Stokes saw Carmack starting up the hill and pulled his car to the curb. The old friends shook hands and Stokes recalled that Carmack's manner had been pleasant and genial.[28]

John Sharp. Source: *Memphis News-Scimitar*, November 13, 1908.

The Coopers passed a lad selling the afternoon newspaper. At Stumb's Robin paused to drink a Coca-Cola. They walked on, the colonel greeting friends as they passed. Halfway down the block the Coopers crossed the street and turned into the Arcade, which connected Fourth and Fifth avenues. As they came to the post office within, Cooper hailed John Sharp. Once sheriff of Davidson County, Sharp had traveled with Malcolm Patterson in the recent campaign to gather political information and promote the governor's candidacy. Now the colonel invited him to walk with them toward the official residence, since he lived next door. Reaching Fifth the trio bore right. At Union they turned west and began to climb the gentle rise.

Beneath and away from the corner of Sixth and Union, workers were laying the foundation for the Hermitage Hotel. Sharp and the Coopers paused and peered into the pit. As Colonel Cooper lingered, Robin and Sharp moved on.[29]

At the crest of the hill, they waited for him. Wary, anxious, wanting

The scene of the killing, which took place by the utility poles at lower right, where the two men are standing. **Courtesy Tennessee State Library and Archives.**

to get his father off the streets, Robin Cooper looked about; and down Seventh Avenue, he saw the sight he most dreaded. Carmack was walking up the other side of the street toward them.

To Sharp, Robin said, "Don't let Papa see him." Then he turned and called out to his father to hurry. The colonel answered his son and shuffled on, at last reaching the corner.[30]

Robin seized his father's left elbow and turned him sharply to the right, stepping out into Union Street. The old man knew he was being rushed. He turned and he saw why. "Is that Carmack?" he asked, and without waiting for a reply broke away from Robin's clutch.

In his trial Colonel Cooper told the jury that he decided at that moment to approach Carmack and warn him that if the editorials did not stop, he, Cooper, would expose the editor's private life. The colonel crossed the street diagonally, reached the sidewalk on the other side, and bore down the hill.[31]

Ambling down Seventh in Carmack's direction was Mrs. Charles Eastman, arm in arm with an elderly and infirm male cousin. As they drew within speaking distance, just south of the Polk Flats, Carmack was about to pass between the pair and the street. He raised his right hand to tip his hat. "How do you do, Mrs. Eastman?" he asked.

Then from behind her, Duncan Cooper called out to Carmack, his right arm outstretched, his forefinger pointed toward the editor. His landlady remembered that over Carmack's face there passed a look of "surprised inquiry." His right hand fell from the brim of his hat. He raised his

The view down Seventh Avenue from the corner of Union Street. Source: *Commercial Appeal* (Memphis), November 13, 1908.

overcoat and reached to the hip pocket holding his gun. His left hand followed as he grappled for the weapon. In the same instant, he stepped to his left, which put Mrs. Eastman between himself and Cooper.

"Damned cowardly to get behind a woman with a pistol in your hand!" Cooper boomed.

Mrs. Eastman bolted to her right, dragging her relation with her through the gate of the Shanklin property adjacent to the Polk Flats. She mistook Colonel Cooper for a physician of the town whom he resembled. "Don't shoot, Dr. White!" she screamed. "Don't! Don't!" She did not see Robin, hurrying after his father and leaping onto the sidewalk in front of him.

As Colonel Cooper shouted and Mrs. Eastman jumped, Carmack dashed to his right into the street. He flung himself behind two utility poles that stood there side by side, and he raised his gun and pointed it toward Colonel Cooper. His first shot exploded in Robin's face. The bullet knocked the stone from the stickpin in his tie and struck him in the shoulder near his right collarbone. As Robin's momentum caused him to turn slightly, the second shot ripped through the left sleeve of his coat without touching him. He drew his gun and pivoted to the curb south and slightly below the poles.

Carmack stood in profile, his right arm raised to his chest, his pistol now pointed toward Robin. And Robin shot him three times as fast as he could pull the trigger.[32]

The first bullet tore through the fifth and sixth ribs on Carmack's left side, penetrated his heart, and lodged just under the skin on the right side of his body. The second shot entered Carmack's left shoulder, then his heart. The third bullet struck him in the back of the neck and exited near the tongue, shattering his front teeth. Blood spread from the mouth, pooling around this last shell that lay on the pavement.[33]

Robin Cooper leaned against one of the poles and looked down at the body. The right side of Carmack's face rested on his arm, the hand flung out toward the west. The dead man's left elbow lay against his body, the left hand in the street, holding a smoldering cigar.[34]

Duncan Cooper walked over to his son and put an arm around him. They shuffled down Seventh Avenue to Dr. Rufus Fort's infirmary. Night was coming. About half past six the rain began, washing Carmack's blood in rivulets down the street.[35]

CHAPTER TWO

The Senator

POLICE LIEUTENANT WINSTON PILCHER was relaxing at the Watauga, at the corner of Seventh and Church, when the shots rang out. "Somebody must be doing a little shooting out there," he remarked. A fellow clubman thought the noise was an automobile tire exploding. When they reached the street, they found a crowd gathering. Pilcher elbowed his way to the two utility poles where Carmack lay sprawled. Carmack's pistol lay beyond his outstretched hand. Pilcher picked it up, broke it open, and noted two empty cartridges in the cylinder.[1]

Hearing the gunfire, Dr. Richard Dake hurried from his infirmary, on the west side of Seventh. Kneeling on the pavement, Dake examined Carmack and saw that he was dead. He had been killed instantly, the doctor concluded, dying even before his body struck the street.[2]

Dake recognized the Coopers. "Robin was leaning against a telephone pole and was as pale as a sheet," the doctor told a reporter, apparently not realizing that one of Carmack's bullets had struck him. Duncan Cooper walked over to his son and put an arm around him.

At the clinic of Dr. Rufus Fort, Robin was helped to a sofa. Fort immediately sent for Dr. Lucius Burch, Robin's brother-in-law. Duncan Cooper telephoned Mrs. Burch. When she came on the line, he said, "Daughter, it is all over. Robin has killed Carmack."

The crowd pressing against the infirmary door worried the colonel. He asked that it be barred, and was heard to say, "I don't want to have to kill another man." Did he hope in the confusion to take the blame on himself for Carmack's death? It cannot be known. But he observed that Carmack's shots had been meant for him.[3]

Near Eighth and Church, Sergeant Robert Vaughn heard about the shooting from a passerby. Hurrying toward the scene he met Pilcher, who handed him Carmack's gun. Vaughn retraced his steps down Seventh Avenue to Fort's infirmary. There he arrested the Coopers. Robin asked his father to look in his coat pocket and give the policeman his gun. Vaughn broke open the weapon and a single spent shell popped out. Colonel Cooper's pistol was taken from him by patrolman Lee Sanders, who told a reporter it had not been fired.

Dr. Burch agreed to meet the wounded man at Baptist Hospital. Vaughn pushed the crowd back from the steps and drove away with the young attorney. A closed carriage transported Duncan Cooper to the police station.[4]

Dake had sent a runner to Dorris, Karsch, and Co., undertakers, which dispatched two porters. They lifted Carmack's body out of the gutter onto a horse-drawn ambulance and drove it to the funeral parlor. As darkness fell, the curious came to Seventh Avenue, striking matches to peer at the bloodstains on the pavement before the rain came. Attorney General Jeff McCarn was among those drawn to the scene.

The arresting officers charged Duncan Cooper with being an accessory to murder and carrying a pistol. His son was listed on the police blotter as "Robin Jones Cooper, murderer." The colonel was placed in the officers' room, where James C. Bradford soon joined him. Other men prominent in the Patterson organization also hurried to the private conference including political lieutenants Henry D. Morrow, Austin Peay, Michael Savage, the chairman of the state Democratic Executive Committee, and Adjutant General Tully Brown.[5]

After a night in custody, Colonel Cooper faced arraignment on Tuesday morning. Instead of being brought into court with the rest of the prisoners, he walked up the front steps of the courthouse accompanied by a detective. Listening attentively to the cases called before his, he smiled when an eccentric defendant rose to plead.

When Cooper's turn came, a deputy sheriff brought forward two state warrants charging him with murder and with carrying a pistol. His lawyers, James C. Bradford, Charles N. Burch, and William H. Washington, were not present, but the court granted their written request that formal appearance before the magistrate who signed the warrants be held in the office of the chief of police. There Cooper learned that Attorney General McCarn had asked postponement of the hearing until he could attend. Cooper's counselors, now at his side, waived examination, and the prisoner was returned to jail, accompanied by Burch, who was his son-in-law and a lawyer for the Yazoo and Mississippi Valley Railroad.

Friends offered to post bond for Cooper immediately, but he declined their help, saying he wanted to be seen as deserving his freedom once Carmack's death was investigated. He knew about jail, he added, and recalled his experience in a Union prison camp at the end of the war.[6]

Robin Cooper remained at Baptist Hospital under guard, suffering an inflammation of his wound, powder burns on his face, and the danger of blood poisoning. Two weeks after the killing, Dr. Burch allowed him to go.

Edward W. Carmack. Source: *Harper's Weekly* (June 29, 1907).

Deputies took the young attorney to jail and placed him in the cell with his father.[7]

The *Tennessean* called the Coopers "assassins" in its news stories. Twenty-four hours after the shooting, it reported, tables, chairs, and a carpet arrived at the jail for the prisoners' use, paid for by Colonel Cooper. Other parties alleged that the accused enjoyed special treatment. Former sheriff Charles D. Johns charged that his successor, Sam Borum, drove the colonel home every night and spirited him back to jail before daybreak. More reliable evidence suggests that the Coopers had a comfortable cell, one resembling a room except for the bars at the window.[8]

The state quickly tightened the manacle around the Coopers by charging the witness in the best position to help them with complicity in their deed. At noon on Thursday the twelfth, as the grand jury was hearing the case, Attorney General McCarn rushed out of the courthouse to the office of a justice of the peace. Shortly he returned, at the same brisk pace, and delivered to Sheriff Borum a warrant for the arrest of John Sharp on the charge of murder and aiding and abetting the Coopers.[9]

Borum and Sharp had been lifelong friends. During Sharp's years as sheriff, between 1894 and 1897, Borum served as a deputy. "Why, I would just as soon have arrested my own brother," Borum told a reporter, "but there was nothing else to do." He found Sharp at the office of his attorney, M. Henry Meeks, in the Chamber of Commerce Building. After some pleasantries, Meeks asked what the news was. "Mighty bad news," Borum replied and handed the warrant to the lawyer. As he was taken into custody, Sharp reminded his protégé that a new prisoner must be searched. That done, he walked with the sheriff to jail, where he was lodged in the cell with Duncan Cooper. McCarn objected to the confinement of the two men together, and in a few days, Sharp was moved downstairs.[10]

With Sharp's arrest McCarn came one step closer to Governor Patterson. The former sheriff had traveled with the chief executive throughout the campaign of 1908, as Patterson and Carmack rekindled their old feud. A loyal, influential lieutenant in the state administration, Sharp was also Patterson's neighbor. Oculist James Wittenberg, with offices in the Arcade, saw Sharp talking with the Coopers there a few minutes before Carmack was killed.[11] Could this have been a chance meeting? McCarn knew it was not. But if Sharp as defendant, rather than as defense witness, swore that his being in the Coopers' company at the time of the encounter was sheer chance, jurors would dismiss the testimony as self-serving.

On Friday, just four days after Carmack's death, the grand jury indicted the Coopers and Sharp for murder. In splendid redundancy, the indictment charged that the trio "did unlawfully, feloniously, willfully, deliberately, and of their malice aforethought, kill and murder, against the peace and dignity of the state." This last clause, drawn from the Tennessee Constitution, was in 1908 an absurd abstraction. The state was not at peace, but embroiled in a protracted war over prohibition. It had just endured a vicious gubernatorial campaign between Patterson and Carmack. Because they had long hated one another, each was seeking to vanquish his opponent and drive him from public life.[12]

The news of Carmack's death had come by telegraph to the Columbia *Daily Herald* on Monday afternoon. Members of the staff hurried to relatives of Mrs. Carmack to have the horrible news conveyed to her before it spread. Later in his life, Edward Ward Carmack, Jr., recalled looking up from his play to see a large, shadowy figure turn into the yard. At once, he said, he knew his father was dead. Then and there, he always insisted, he swore revenge against whoever was responsible.[13] He and his mother, accompanied by friends, left immediately for Nashville.

Carmack's body reposed overnight at the home of Frank Lander, managing editor of the *Tennessean*, in a coffin covered with black broadcloth. A pair of white horses drew the wagon bearing the body to Union Station that afternoon. Several hundred women, many from the Women's Christian Temperance Union, formed a double line from the entrance,

Malcolm R. Patterson. Courtesy Tennessee State Library and Archives.

across the waiting room beneath the great barrel vault ceiling, to the doorway leading down to the platform. They wore white ribbons, emblems of their cause, and gripped a long white streamer running the length of the floor and encircling their lines. As Edward Craig, Luke Lea, and others carried the casket past them, they threw white carnations on it. Following the body came Mrs. Carmack, borne on the arms of other mourners.

The coffin was taken down to the platform where the train stood waiting, the temperance women forming lines leading to the funeral car. As the remains were put on board, they sang, "Nearer, My God, to Thee." On schedule at 2:35 P.M., the conductor called out, "All aboard," and the train eased forward. As it gathered speed, Mrs. Carmack, her face drawn, looked back and waved to her weeping friends, receding from sight.[14]

Businesses closed in Columbia, and at 4:30 P.M., a thousand people met the train. They walked before and behind the hearse bearing Carmack's body to his residence on West Seventh Street. Many among them blamed Governor Patterson for the tragedy. When the *American*'s Tuesday morning edition was put on the curb for sale, some citizens kicked the newspapers into the street and set them on fire.

Each train to Columbia brought more flowers, until they covered the altar of the First Methodist Church, the city's largest auditorium. The dead man's friends spread them over the floor of the chancel beneath a portrait of him draped in black. Finally, there was no more room.

Wearing a red carnation, Carmack's campaign emblem, the Reverend R. Lin Cave of Nashville officiated at Wednesday morning's services. Two years earlier, with Carmack sitting on the same platform, Cave had eulogized the late temperance crusader Sam Jones. Now, standing before the mourners for Carmack, he read the lines that expressed for many the meaning of both men's lives:

> I said, Let me live in the fields; He said, No, live in the town;
> I said, The sky is black, There is nothing but dust and din;
> He wept as he led me back and answered, There is more,
> there is sin. I cast one look at the fields, Then turned my face
> to the town. . . .

Hundreds were turned away because there was not room for them in the church. The press of the crowd hindered the start of the procession to Rose Hill Cemetery, south of town. Three cadet companies from the Columbia Military Institute and members of local lodges of Elks and Masons preceded the hearse.

A cold wind was blowing, and the ground was wet from rain the night before. Mrs. Carmack, through the officiating clergymen, requested gentlemen to put their hats on and not to stand in the damp with their heads bared. The military escort halted in formation near the grave, and the Masons formed a semicircle around it. The pallbearers drew the casket from the hearse, carried it forward, and lowered it into the cedar box already placed in the ground.

The Masons cast sprigs of evergreen onto the black coffin. While the choir sang, the grave was filled with dirt. Then the mourners returned to their carriages, and the gravediggers heaped the muddy mound with flowers.[15]

His fellow citizens who hated liquor or its baneful effects in politics made Carmack an icon from the hour of his death. "[He was] a man sans peur and sans reproche," an admirer wrote to the stricken widow:

> a plumed knight, fearing no odds, ever battling for the Right,
> and going down at last in the forefront, he died like Nelson,
> with the paeans of victory ringing in his ears.[16]

Carmack's days as a moral crusader dated from his arrival at the offices of the Memphis *Commercial* in 1892. There he threw its editorial weight behind a "Law and Order League" that called for suppression of gambling, cleaning up a vice district, and prohibition. He also set out to reverse the *Commercial*'s financial difficulties by making circulation war on its competitor, the *Appeal-Avalanche*, and engaging in jibes against the latter's editor, William A. Collier. Collier, in turn, called "a common blackguard from the hill country . . . imported to put a little life into the moribund carcass" of the *Commercial*. When it was Carmack's turn again, he likened the *Appeal* to "a night-strolling trollop."

Which man challenged the other to settle their differences on the field of honor is not known. But to evade the penalties in Tennessee law for duelling, Carmack and Collier agreed to meet across the Mississippi border, at Holly Springs. An unknown party alerted the police. Bench warrants were hurriedly sworn out for the two men. Collier kidnapped and restrained the arresting officer and reached the rendezvous on schedule. Taken into custody, Carmack arrived late. Collier declared himself vindicated. Later in life, the two men became warm friends.[17]

As depression gripped the country, voters everywhere turned out sitting Democrats in the elections of 1894. The following May, Carmack stood before two thousand Memphians to introduce William Jennings Bryan, who declared the free coinage of silver as the solution to the nation's ills. Two weeks later delegates from every Southern and Western state flocked to a free-silver assembly in the city. By this time a true believer, Carmack concluded, "A convention more notable for its significance was never held on the soil of free America."[18]

Himself once a crusader after the silver grail, Memphis Congressman Josiah Patterson had recently recanted. Speaking at a rally in April 1896, Carmack attacked Patterson for his apostasy. As the editor stepped down from the platform, the congressman's son, Malcolm, accosted him. Words passed between them, and Carmack swung his fist at the young man who was defending his father. Police had to break up the fight. Two days later Josiah Patterson won renomination by the gold Democrats. On that same day, Carmack resigned from his editorial post, and in August he captured the Congressional nomination of a rival silver convention. In November Carmack apparently won the election with a four hundred vote plurality, and he took the oath of office.[19]

The incumbent disputed the election, and the contest reached the floor of the House of Representatives on April 21, 1898, the day after the nation went to war with Spain. In the debate Congressman Carmack defended his election on the grounds that the ballots had been fairly cast, and by Tennesseeans whose forefathers had fought at King's Mountain and New Orleans. He concluded with a tribute to the place of his birth, in words forever after known as Carmack's "Pledge to the South":

"The Corkscrew Democracy": A prohibitionist view of the Patterson administration. Source: *Nashville Tennessean* (August 3, 1910).

I speak, sir, for my native State, my native South. It is a land that has known sorrows; a land that has broken the ashen crust and moistened it with her tears; a land scarred and riven by the plowshare and billowed with the graves of her dead; but a land of legend, a land of song, a land of hallowed and heroic memories. To that land, every drop of my blood,

every fiber of my being, every pulsation of my heart is con-
secrated forever. I was born of her womb, I was nurtured at
her breast, and when my last hour shall come, I pray God
that I may be pillowed upon her bosom and rocked to sleep
within her gentle and encircling arms.

The house broke into wild applause and voted to seat Carmack. He owed
his triumph more to factional infighting among the Republicans than to his
magnificent words. But none who heard him that day ever forgot. "All happy
over your success," telegraphed a Tennessee friend. "Capture Cuba next!"[20]
That fall Carmack won reelection without opposition. To his political
success was soon added the joy of parenthood. In time Cobey Carmack
dressed Ned, Jr., in pantaloons and allowed his blond hair to grow in curls.
Sitting on his father's lap, he looked out onto the world with wide dreamy
eyes.

In the summer of 1899 U.S. Senator Thomas B. Turley announced he
would not seek reelection. Congressman Carmack lay seriously ill with
typhoid fever, but as he recovered he began exploring the prospects for
winning the seat once held by the late Isham Harris. "No more auspicious
time is ever likely to come," advised his lifelong friend, Memphis lawyer
Guston Fitzhugh. Prospective competitors soon left Carmack the field, and
in January 1901 the Democratic majority in the legislature elected him to
the Senate. In Memphis, Malcolm Patterson won the House seat that Carmack vacated.[21]

Senator Carmack of Tennessee came owing no one, a confirming experience for a man whose conviction of his own righteousness was without
irony. An opponent of the war against the Filipino rebels and a scourge of
President Theodore Roosevelt, Carmack's courtesy and bearing, quick in-
tellect, and skill in debate soon won him admirers in both parties and the
attention of the national press. "In [his] first senatorial year," the *New York
Times* observed, "he became one of the four regents who ruled the minority
in default of a real leader." To many at home he seemed a bulwark against
powerful and mysterious threats: the rise of cities, the power of the corporations, and the impersonal forces of mass, speed, and production that
were transforming the nation. [22]

Faithful to Democratic polity, Senator Carmack opposed increasing
the tariff rates on the grounds that the boost would increase taxes on working people. Deploring what he saw as a concentration of wealth in the
United States, he called for creation of an income tax. He supported the
Hepburn Act of 1906, giving the Interstate Commerce Commission addi-
tional authority over setting railroads' shipping rates, a measure vigorously

opposed by President Milton H. Smith of the Louisville and Nashville Railroad. Carmack's views on the race question he had maintained all his life: Black people were innately inferior, and the United States was a white man's country. He urged black Americans to return to Africa.[23]

People of other races or even other cultures could not be assimilated, Carmack believed. While he supported the war against Spain, he opposed annexing Hawaii and making Cuba a quasi-protectorate, both of which the war achieved. He also denounced his country's keeping the Philippine Islands, which Spain ceded to the United States with the peace. In some of the most eloquent passages ever uttered in an American legislative body, he argued for an end to the military campaign against the Filipino rebels who were seeking independence. While still in the House, he replied to those who said that once the flag was put up it could not be taken down.

> Would I take it down? I answer that when I find the flag of my country an exile from its native land, languishing in an uncongenial clime, drooping above timid serfs and crouching slaves, 7,000 miles from the nearest freeman, I would take it down and bring it home to wave over free men in a free country.

Imperialism departed from the principles and traditions of the United States, Carmack thundered. As England and Germany learned to their sorrow, colonies required vast expenses to administer and to protect with armies and navies. He pointedly reminded his colleagues from the north that the United States had proved an inept conqueror. "If the government we are about to establish in the Philippines is not ten thousand times better than the government you established and maintained with the bayonet here in your own country over your own people, may the Lord God have mercy upon the people of the Philippine Islands."

Carmack and several colleagues on his side of the aisle garnered enough votes to create a committee to investigate military misconduct in the war zone. Partisan bickering characterized the hearings with Carmack and Henry Cabot Lodge openly disdaining one another. Lodge imagined a "vast future trade and wealth and power" in the Philippines for American business. Protestant clergymen put forward plans to convert the heathen.[24]

Witnesses recounted stories of rape, torture, and wanton killing by Americans, and Carmack's hatred of the war grew. He would not blame the soldiers, since "every army on earth contains enough wicked, vicious, and lawless men to make its presence a hell on earth, if those men are not restrained." He condemned military authorities for failing to court-martial men who committed the war crimes he reviled. On many other issues in the life of his times, Carmack looked toward the past; in these views, he anticipated the commonplace barbarism of warfare in the years soon to come.

Many Southern Democrats feared the exuberant young president, Theodore Roosevelt, might be planning to pursue old designs of the Republican Party in the South. His constituents generally applauded Carmack for denouncing Roosevelt when he entertained Booker T. Washington over lunch at the White House. The senator also defended the people of Indianola, Mississippi, and their boycott of the black postmaster whom Roosevelt appointed there.

In November 1903, the president ordered the U.S.S. *Nashville* to interdict Colombian forces sent by Bogata in relief of troops resisting an uprising in the colony of Panama. The rebels took power, and Roosevelt immediately recognized the new government. He promptly sent the Senate a message urging ratification of a treaty for construction of a canal across the isthmanian nation. Many Southerners looked with dismay on Roosevelt's highhandedness. Carmack, who favored a Nicaraguan route for any interoceanic canal, was livid. He called Roosevelt's action a "pigheaded performance" and the president's message "the most flimsy and dishonest piece of reasoning ever issued from the White House."

So it was ironic that Carmack's most popular speech during his Senate years was one supporting Roosevelt. The Tennesseean's speech followed the president's dismissal of 159 black soldiers stationed at Brownsville, Texas, after a few of them fired into some houses in the town. When Republican Senator Joseph B. Foraker attacked Roosevelt's action, Carmack argued that his colleague was wrong about the completeness of the evidence that the president had examined before he dismissed the men. Carmack believed the soldiers were guilty, but Roosevelt's action was not punishment, he told the Senate. It was nothing more than "the President's exercising the legal and constitutional power to discharge a man from the army whenever he thinks for any reason on earth that the good of the service and the discipline of the Army would be promoted. . . ." Grateful for the Tennesseean's help, Roosevelt was quoted as saying of Carmack's speech, "It was fine. Oh, it was magnificent. It was grand."[25] Looking back from the age of Martin Luther King to the age of Theodore Roosevelt, it is easy to condemn the president's act as another mean manifestation of white supremacy. But most assuredly, Carmack's fellow Tennesseeans approved of it.

At home, Carmack called upon his popularity in his old base of Memphis to help his colleague, Senator William B. Bate, shore up a faltering campaign and retain his seat. But this political success quickly slipped through his grasp. By the time of the Brownsville speech, Malcolm Patterson was governor, and Carmack had failed to win reelection to the Senate.

A long period of peace for the state's Democrats ended—and Carmack's political troubles began—in March 1905 when Senator Bate died a few days after commencing his new term. Immediately the state Democratic Executive Committee, comprising allies of Governor James B. Frazier, caucused to nominate a successor. A week later the legislature ratified the panel's choice: Governor Frazier himself.

The haste in filling the seat angered former Governor Robert B. Taylor. He had missed election to the Senate in 1881 by a handful of votes in the legislature. Five years later, with Governor William B. Bate stepping down, the Bourbons meant to retain their factional hegemony in the Democratic Party. To do so, they needed allies among both farmers disgruntled by hard times and industrialists eager to build a New South.

Those times had summoned the man. Put Bob Taylor in a room, said a young lawyer from Jonesborough, "and just one grin on his face, with a fiddle in his hand, would send a crowd wild. It wasn't that Bob was a wonderful fiddler, but the way he looked when he was playing. Bob's whole person fiddled."

Just thirty-six years old in 1886, Taylor appealed to the young voters who had never followed a general; his fiddle delighted the farmers who needed a diversion from falling prices; he could win votes away from the Republicans in his native East Tennessee; and though he advocated industrial expansion, he ingratiated himself with the traditionalist leaders of the party.

To win his party's gubernatorial nod, Bob Taylor had to turn back several other prominent party men who felt they deserved the place. As the convention stumbled through ballot after ballot, he dispatched a telegram to the delegates: "A seedy individual once appeared at my mother's back door and said, 'Emmaline, if you don't believe I can carry a ham home, just try me.'" On the fifteenth ballot, the Democrats handed Taylor the ham.

The Republicans knew a united Democratic Party would beat them. Their strategy was to nominate for governor another politician and accomplished bowstring player from the uplands, Robert Taylor's brother, Alfred.

In the legendary contest that followed, each brother's supporters chose genteel symbols. Supporters of Bob Taylor wore the white rose of York, while backers of Alf Taylor pinned in their lapels the red rose of Lancaster. The two candidates traveled together, took meals together, shared the same lodgings and the same platform. But their debates seldom approached any serious discussion of state issues. Instead they spun sentimental stories, engaged in raillery against each other, and set listeners to tapping their feet to rustic classics like "Tramp the Devil's Eyes Out" and "Chicken in the Dough Tray." When the campaign set an appearance in Memphis on the same day as a traveling circus, there was considerable

Robert L. Taylor. Courtesy Robert L. Taylor.

speculation about which entertainment would attract the larger audience. One editor expressed relief when the candidates for governor changed their appointment, "so that Barnum might get a crowd."[26]

Bob Taylor won that election. Ten years later, a number of small-town newspapers insisted that that elusive entity "the people" wanted Taylor for governor again. The call, if it was a call or merely bewilderment at the party's lack of a leader of stature, came at an inconvenient time for Taylor. He was making money, traveling the lecture circuit billed as "the Apostle of Sunshine," entertaining with fiddle and word pictures whoever had a lonely evening to pass and the price of the gate. Some cerebral Democrats derided his "vision dreams." But no false modesty led him to decline what "the people" wanted him to have, and the party convention nominated him by acclamation.

"Nobody seems to ask or care what Bob Taylor thinks on public questions," a West Tennessee editor observed. "But he is good bait to catch the other fellow." The "other fellow," Republican nominee George N. Tillman, headed a unified Republican Party bent on vengeance for the legislature's denial of the governorship to industrialist H. Clay Evans, the apparent popular choice in 1894. They hoped to combine with disaffected Democrats and Populists on the common ground of honest elections, then attract enough New South Democrats to take revenge. And indeed on the morning after the election Taylor appeared to have lost. But when the last rural counties reported they gave him the election by seven thousand votes. Tillman took all but two counties east of the Cumberland Mountains, overwhelmingly lost Middle Tennessee to Taylor, and held onto five riverine counties that had exhibited Republican tendencies since the Civil War.[27]

Believing himself entitled to go to the Senate for having assured the governor's office, Taylor had contemplated a race against Carmack even before Bate's death. Now he accused the senator of aiding Frazier in a "snap caucus" and announced his candidacy for Carmack's seat. In an early exchange he commented upon Carmack's "proverbial bad humor and usual sulphurous method of personal assault upon all who have had the audacity to stand in the way of your ambition."[28]

Carmack appealed to the unwritten canon, which granted a faithful public official the reward of reelection. Taylor had traded Tennessee's honors to him for lecture fees, Carmack charged, and held no claim upon a seat in the Senate, despite his past services to the party. When the former governor challenged the senator to debate, then withdrew, Carmack asked archly if the "knight of the white rose" had become the "knight of the white feather." Taylor took up the symbol and pinned a chicken feather in his lapel. His campaign appearances included a sprinkling of jokes, Negro dialect stories, and fiddle playing.

Carmack took note of Taylor's charge that the senator's vigorous partisanship led the Republican majority to ignore Tennessee's interests. By way of an answer, Carmack's managers obtained letters from Senators Aldrich, Beveridge, Gorman, and Dolliver attesting to the esteem in which they held their colleague from the other side of the aisle. Carmack believed that President Roosevelt would respect the South less if a senator from

Tennessee met the issues with a joke and a song. Under no circumstances, he pledged, would he beg at the kitchen door of the White House for crumbs of patronage at the expense of his right to resist any attempt to force racial equality on the South.

Taylor and Carmack both claimed the temperance mantle. Each supported the Hepburn-Dolliver bill, making transportation of liquor from one state to another subject to the laws of the state through which the shipment passed. Quoting Taylor as saying that with recent legislation in Tennessee temperance measures had gone far enough, Carmack implied that intoxicating beverages should be further restricted. "If they defeat me for the Senate," he told a cheering Nashville audience, "it shall be my next ambition to be handed down in history as the last man ever defeated for office by the saloon power of Tennessee." The prohibition issue, the Nashville *American* observed, cast a "dim religious light" over the campaign. The denouement, the paper predicted, "will be the slaughter of one [candidate] by the other to slow music from the sacred organ."[29]

With Nashville lawyer and entrepreneur Luke Lea leading his forces, U.S. Representative Malcolm Patterson wrested the gubernatorial nomination from Senator Frazier's constitutional successor, Governor John I. Cox. Patterson stood on a platform of substantive, progressive reform, including the removal from the governor's hands of the power to appoint election commissioners.

While he detested Patterson, Carmack did not trust Cox. He urged supporters to "keep hands off and let the situation work itself out as it will." But Senator Frazier and many of Carmack's allies openly supported Cox for a full term in his own right, while partisans of Bob Taylor generally favored Patterson.[30]

Carmack later recounted a meeting during that spring's primary contest among Patterson, Patterson's "manager in Nashville" (by whom he may have meant Duncan Cooper), and Carmack's chief strategist, George Armistead. According to Carmack, Patterson and his aide sought out Armistead and "gave him earnest assurances that they would not lift a hand against us." Another correspondent quoted Cooper as saying, "I have tried to be Carmack's friend" and added that if Carmack did "the right thing," Patterson would join hands with him and Carmack would be renominated for senator. His listener asked what "the right thing" might be. Patterson's man replied that the Senator must come out boldly for the reforms that Patterson advocated.[31]

The popular primary, on May 12, 1906, was the first time that Tennesseans instructed a Democratic majority of the General Assembly in the election of a United States Senator. Carmack lost, receiving fifty-eight thousand votes to sixty-five thousand for Taylor. The winner took his native East Tennessee, including urban Knox and Hamilton counties, by a substantial margin. Taylor also won Davidson County and most of the rest of Middle Tennessee, although Carmack defeated him in the populous rural counties of Maury, Montgomery, Robertson, Rutherford, and Wilson. The incumbent overwhelmed Taylor in Shelby and the rest of his old Congressional district. But Taylor carried half the counties of West Tennessee, demonstrating his powerful statewide popularity.[32]

Friends wrote Carmack to console, to explain, to proffer the only soothing balm any defeated politician knows: that there will be another race, another time. Perhaps the best-known man in the state, Taylor had spoken at every crossroads, wrote banker R. N. Hutton. "The amiability of Tennessee has proved greater than the strength of her character and virtue," J. S. Cooper told Carmack. "After repeated solicitations, she has consented at last to go to bed with Bob Taylor."[33]

To casual friends Carmack replied that his was a "serene and cheerful spirit": His conscience approved both his record in the Senate and his course in the campaign, "and that is better than a victory won with dishonor." In truth he was filled with rage. His letters to confidants revealed how he really understood his defeat. "Of course I know that Patterson stuck the knife in me up to the hilt and that he did it gratuitously and without provocation." To Armistead, Carmack wrote, "I remember how [Patterson], Henry Morrow, and Dunc Cooper all expressed their appreciation of the straightforward fight we made without mixing in the governor's race, and yet I am convinced beyond question that [Patterson] . . . exerted himself in Taylor's behalf." Patterson's assurances had been the "acme of duplicity and bad faith," he charged. "[His] organization in the latter part of the campaign threw themselves bodily into the Taylor column in middle and west Tennessee."

Carmack resumed his duties in the Senate for the last year of his term. In the fall he made speeches for the Democratic ticket that Patterson headed, but it chafed his soul. He wrote a friend that he was "helping my most vindictive personal and political enemies who have conspired to destroy and disgrace me."[34]

Everywhere over the state he seemed to grow in stature as his service in Washington drew to a close. When the legislature convened in January 1907 and duly confirmed the people's choice of Taylor, a friend in the galleries recounted the scene to Carmack:

> The resolution commending your action in the Brownsville matter brought very much more applause from the members and spectators than did Taylor's acceptance speech and presence. . . . The people of the state now have their eyes open and realize your worth and greatness, and only await an opportunity to thrust honors on you.[35]

The senator divided his time that winter between Washington and Nashville. The allies of former Memphis mayor John Joseph Williams had in 1906 elected a legislative delegation pledged to oust the incumbent reformer, James H. Malone, by instituting a commission form of government. The Patterson administration vigorously supported the measure.

Carmack came home to work against the plan, convinced that it would strengthen the influence of liquor distributors and retailers in his adopted home and political base. He believed the governor had given doubtful legislators the privilege of naming local election officials and a certain number of pardons. Patterson refrained from replying to Carmack's charges, but he told friends that the proposed charter amendment would be a "fight to the death" between the senator and himself. The administration achieved the votes, passed the bill, and won the battle.[36]

When his term expired in March, Carmack announced that he would retire with good grace to private life. William Randolph Hearst offered him fifteen thousand dollars a year to edit the New York *American*, but Carmack declined. He considered returning to the editorship of the Nashville paper of the same name. According to one source, the struggling paper was up for sale but the owner, the Louisville and Nashville Railroad, refused to sell to the prospective buyer who wanted to employ Carmack, and the Patterson administration threatened to press regulatory legislation against the line if it struck the deal.[37]

In June 1907 the former senator traveled to Richmond for the dedication of a monument to Jefferson Davis. Recounting abolitionists' talk in the early 1840s of taking their states out of the Union, he compared it with the South's actual secession. The difference between Massachusetts and Virginia, Carmack declared, was "a question of nerve." A listener commented, "He'll never be President after that remark." Others thought he might. *Harper's Weekly* named him among the possible Democratic candidates in 1908 and printed his picture on its cover.[38]

"You are young," a friend told him, "and history is made fast." Many assured him that they sensed the direction of history's quick pace. To George Armistead one wrote: "The people of Tennessee are determined to prosecute a vigorous crusade against railroad domination and opposition and in favor of total prohibition. Carmack is the only man to whom they look for deliverance." He must lead or be left behind, Memphis lawyer B. L. Cockroft told him. Wrote another friend, "Circumstances over which you have no control will force you to run [for governor]. It will be necessary, in my judgment, to break up the present regime in order that your political salvation may be worked out successfully in the future."

Carmack's political goal surely was to return to the Senate in the election of 1910, dislodging Frazier. To do that he evidently believed that he would have to bring down Patterson. Once the governor was reelected, his organization would stand with a cudgel astride Carmack's path. But if he denied Patterson a second term, as Patterson in his mind had denied him one in the Senate, he would end the rule of what he regarded as a thoroughly corrupt political machine.[39]

Patterson, professing that he dreaded the confrontation, could barely restrain himself. "Well, Mary," he wrote to his fiancée that summer, "we are going to run into a storm. Carmack is to be a candidate. . . . I will not get out under fire and much prefer to be beaten but before I am there will be a hard struggle, and I surely believe I can win over him."[40]

In October 1907 Carmack announced his candidacy. He eventually published a platform proposing revisions in the criminal code, reform in the granting of franchises for utilities, restrictions on child labor, the creation of election machinery genuinely independent of the governor, and other reformist measures. He condemned the railroads for unduly influencing public policy and proposed to abolish free passes, a gratuity to legislators that made them friends. As his main issue, Carmack called for statewide prohibition in Tennessee.[41]

Most of the state was already dry. The Adams Law of 1903 allowed towns with fewer than five thousand people to reincorporate and come under the terms of the Four-Mile Law, an 1877 statute prohibiting the retail sale of liquor within four miles of any school. Every country town did so, except tiny LaFollette, founded by and home of Governor Patterson's ardent supporter, Harvey M. LaFollette. In 1907 Patterson signed the Pendleton Act (after opposing its passage), which allowed towns of up to one hundred and fifty thousand people to surrender their charters to the state and receive new ones that brought them under the jurisdiction of the Four Mile Law. Among the big cities, only Knoxville took the pledge. Chattanooga, Memphis, and Nashville did not.[42]

Carmack had in times past opposed some of the prohibitionists' goals. In the General Assembly in 1885 he voted against submitting to the voters an amendment to the state constitution to effect prohibition. As a newspaper editor he had ridiculed candidates of the Prohibitionist Party for their single-issue platform, without taking a position on liquor itself. But in Congress he voted for bills to prohibit liquor sales in Alaska, to require constitutions of new states to outlaw sales to Indians, and to restrict shipment of liquor into areas where prohibition prevailed.[43]

His biographer makes out a weak case that Carmack was an opportunist on the liquor question, but he is better understood as a man whose views underwent a gradual change over time, from regulation to prohibition. His path to teetotalism inscribes the same arc followed by the temperance movement itself. After the Prohibition Party faded, the Anti-Saloon League assumed leadership of the movement in alliance with the Women's Christian Temperance Union and Protestant evangelical churches. These temperance groups called for the most stringent legislation that the public would support at any given time. From the late 1890s until prohibition triumphed in Tennessee about 1915, they accepted and worked for expedient measures, gradually persuading a decisive minority of voters to support candidates pledged to restricting liquor. By 1905 the League's growing influence among congregations led it to foresee that Tennesseeans would in a coming biennial election send a prohibitionist majority to the General Assembly. The day of settling for partial measures was passing.

At the same time, progressive reformers from all walks of life, urban and rural dwellers, were calling for the reform of business, city and country life, schools, penal institutions, and state government. The saloon was seen by many of them as a major contributor to disorder, abuse, and injustice, wherever these were found, and drunkenness a threat to widely shared, middle-class values, notably family life. Norman H. Clark describes Carmack's stance precisely when he observes: "By removing a key link in the corrupt alliance between business, vice, and politics, prohibitionists would help free government from the control of other predatory interests and thus open the way to reform in general."[44]

By 1906 Edward Carmack was declaring that the liquor interests, along with railroads and other corporations, exercised an undue, malign influence in Tennessee politics and government. Consequently, the association of brewers, distillers, their distributors, and many retailers contributed to Bob Taylor in the Senate race.[45]

Four days after his defeat, Carmack wrote to a supporter:

> I have never been among the extreme or fanatical advocates of temperance but have always opposed the political domination of the whisky power. The trouble with them is that they are not content with pursuing a lawful business in a lawful way but insist on pronouncing sentence of death upon every man who demands they obey the law. This condition of things is intolerable, and a self-respecting people will not long submit to it.

Liquor might not be evil in and of itself, Carmack believed, but it had corrupted the public life of the state. In March 1908, after a convention of liquor dealers met in Nashville to propose that retailers regulate themselves, he told reporters, "The saloon has sinned away its day of grace in Tennessee." A short time later, he released his platform. Its first plank called for "the entire abolition of the liquor traffic" from the state.[46]

Carmack also called for a direct primary, so that Democrats could vote on the candidates, rather than for delegates to a nominating convention. In the 1906 campaign, gubernatorial candidate Malcolm Patterson favored this method of selecting the nominee by popular majority. Two years later, occupying the office, he was less sure. His strength against Carmack lay in the cities. Counties with the largest urban populations — Shelby, Davidson, Hamilton, and Knox — would be allocated the largest bloc of votes in a convention. And he calculated that a majority of city dwellers would vote for him.

Primary or convention? The decision rested with the state Democratic Executive Committee, which managed the internal affairs of the party. Most Democrats may have favored a direct primary. The *Nashville Banner* thought so, while noting, "It is well known that the Governor can control the action of the committee should he so choose."[47]

A "delegated primary" was the plan the committee adopted in February 1908. Each county would conduct a primary election on June 27, and the candidate who received the most votes in the county would win all its delegates to the state convention. The state committee appointed a subcommittee of three to receive the returns, while it left the naming of the actual delegates to the county executive committee. Wherever he spoke, Carmack reviled the plan, pointing out that under these rules, the people could not instruct the delegates who would write the platform. "But the people have the right to elect and instruct their members of the legislature," he thundered. "If they send the Democratic members there instructed to pass a statewide prohibition bill, I will sign the bill."[48]

The two candidates agreed to fifty joint debates around the state. Saturday night, April 16, was fixed as the date for the first one, and Chattanooga as the place. By six o'clock a restless audience packed the meeting hall. Following his introduction, Senator Carmack laid aside an overcoat he had thrown about his shoulders and strode to the speaker's table. He wore a bandage over one eye, affected by a cold. His partisans stood and cheered him, cutting swaths through the air with their swirling white ribbons.

The challenger accused the governor of appointing loyalists as local election judges, clerks, and receivers of returns, then permitting them to deny ballots to opponents. Patterson had also pardoned felons who robbed, and raped, and killed again, Carmack charged. He reminded his listeners that "we are the most homicidal nation on the face of the earth. There are more men killed by other men in the city of Memphis and the city of Nashville than in the great city of London."

As to Patterson's plea that he be given the party's traditional reward for creditable service, reelection, Carmack hurled down the gauntlet. "This revelation of the virtues of the second term precedent comes late in life to my honorable competitor," he thundered. "Not only did he defeat the claim of his competitor for endorsement of a second term, but he and all the leading spirits of his administration were united in a powerful combination to reject my appeal."

Carmack saved the liquor question to the close of his speeches. "The saloon is an unmitigated curse to the state," he told his audiences, "a great source of crime and corruption, a burden upon its industries, a blight upon its homes. I am not willing for Mr. LaFollette to bind his pestilence all over the mountains of East Tennessee, nor am I willing for the saloons of Nashville, Memphis, and Chattanooga to decide whether they shall carry on a campaign to promote drunkenness and debauchery throughout the state." Then he brought his supporters to their feet, shouting his name, and throwing roses and carnations toward the platform.

> When we see that the liquor element is concentrating its forces throughout the whole country in the three big cities of the state, I believe we should summon to our standard every enemy of the saloon from the mountains to the Mississippi, meet the enemy at the border, and end this war in one great pitched battle, and then we will write the victory in a law that will cover every corner of the state like a blessing from heaven.[49]

The two contenders traveled east to west, and the campaign wore on into the hot summer. Patterson everywhere asked, did his administration not deserve endorsement? "What I have done, and not what Mr. Carmack may say, is the issue before the people of Tennessee." Patterson pointed to the creation of agricultural institutes and an experimental station, the passage of protective forestry and game laws, and the law establishing county boards of education. If his administration spent freely, as Carmack charged, the expenses "were in the right direction—for schools and increased pensions for Confederate soldiers." As for the Memphis charter bill, which Carmack continued to attack, it was a local matter, supported by the Shelby County delegation in the General Assembly.

The big cities had at last held clean elections during his administration, Patterson claimed. He pointed to his signing a reform law that took away the governor's power to name local election officials directly and required Senate confirmation of his appointments to the state election commission. The delegated primary plan would preserve an honest ballot and an honest count, Patterson assured audiences: It provided for a direct vote of the people, as Carmack demanded, and it allowed the challenger to name his own election officials in the gubernatorial race.

Reminding voters that he had signed the Pendleton Act into law, Patterson placed before them his own credentials as a temperance man. Thus he depicted Carmack's challenge as both pointless and personal, disrupting party unity for no purpose. Would Carmack enter into an alliance with Republicans if he lost the race? Patterson asked. Some Democrats were unsure. The Republican platform called for extension of the Four-Mile Law to the cities — in effect, statewide prohibition — and Carmack seemed to have made a commitment to such a course, no matter what the Democrats' plank might say.[50]

Patterson asserted that if the people of Memphis, Chattanooga, and Nashville did not want to drive the saloons from their cities, statewide prohibition would violate their right of "local self-government." Still, he pledged, he would sign a statewide prohibition bill if the Democratic convention wrote such a plank into the platform. He taunted Carmack as "the great moral reformer" who, during his race against Taylor, had opposed the outlawing of liquor, only to "go to the head of the prohibition column" in this contest. "What is he doing it for?" Patterson thundered. "Is he doing it because he thinks it is necessary to do it in order to become governor?"

The race became an ugly contest between two gifted, proud, temperamental men who hated each other. In the debate at Fayetteville on May 1, Patterson charged fraud in Shelby County when Carmack had carried it in his 1906 senatorial campaign. Carmack answered that fraud had probably occurred but everything possible had been done to prevent it. Turning toward his audience, Patterson cried, "What do you think of an ex-senator, a candidate for governor, a man who calls himself a reformer, having to admit that he tried to be elected by fraud? Think of it!"

Carmack interrupted, "Did you say I admitted that I tried to be elected by fraud?"

"I said as much," Patterson answered.

"Well, it is false," retorted Carmack.

The governor started toward him, but the presiding officer stepped between them. Carmack quietly left the stage, and Patterson continued.

> I have told him that in his head was a bitter, viperish, vindictive tongue . . . I need now only tell [you] that he is a coward as well. . . . He knows we cannot fight, he knows there is no chance for a personal encounter. No man would before an audience of this character, where his hands are tied, and where he knows my hands are tied, take advantage of the circumstances. . . . A man who would do this is unfit to be governor of a great people because he is not game enough to stand.

A country editor remembered that rumor was rife that heelers were present at every speaking, ready to shoot Carmack down "if trouble had been precipitated, and everybody was expecting that trouble would be precipitated."

The personal struggle between the two men pervaded the lives of Tennesseeans. Carmack partisans trumpeted their cause from the pulpit or spoke of it earnestly over the mercantilist's counter. The campaign sowed deep division, not all of it the challenger's doing. A friend of Colonel Cooper's observed that in his county "there are so many who are afraid to go against what their preachers tell them. There are only 5 or 6 in our Club who have the nerve to resist the encroachments on personal liberty. I know a number who will vote for Carmack who are afraid they will lose some customers if they say they will vote against him."

In Franklin on April 30, Carmack spoke Cooper's name from the podium for the first time. He and James C. Bradford had tried to teach the governor to smile, Carmack told the crowd, but all Patterson could do was snarl. At Centerville on May 18, Carmack again named Cooper, calling him "a little, fat, bald-headed angel." On June 16, speaking at Ashland City, Carmack questioned the party loyalty of several Patterson associates, including Cooper. The last, he said, "surrounds the Governor as thoroughly as water surrounds an island."

Cooper was the puppetmaster, Carmack implied, who called the tune in the administration. The colonel dominated party machinery and said who received the state's appointed posts. He protected the privileges of the L & N Railroad. And, Carmack believed, he had persuaded Patterson to sign the Pendleton Act, which left the big-city saloons free to hold high carnival with their rinky-dink pianos, clattering wheels of chance, and clinking shot glasses.[51]

Carmack lost the race. Patterson won 52 percent of the 164,000 votes cast and 55 percent of the 1,319 county delegates to the state convention. The Governor's strength lay in Memphis, Nashville, and Chattanooga. He won more than 60 percent of the votes cast in those cities, achieving a majority over Carmack of some five thousand ballots. Since his statewide margin was 6,500 votes, his mandate was delivered by the last places where liquor could be lawfully bought and sold. Outside these cities the race was close. Carmack carried East Tennessee with 52.4 percent of the votes and fought to a draw in West Tennessee, winning 50.3 percent. Patterson's majority in the most populous grand division, Middle Tennessee, was 54.8 percent.

The leaders of the Anti-Saloon League and others leading the prohibition crusade could not deliver the voters for whom they claimed to speak, nor did all temperance people support Carmack. Patterson succeeded in depicting the anti-liquor forces as threatening the fragile harmony of the Democrats and ready to make common cause with dry Republicans. The two-term tradition held strong in Patterson's favor, especially in the Democratic heartland of the midstate. The declining electorate, nomination by primary, the rise of city bosses, the spreading power of circulation by newspapers all tended to favor a well-financed incumbent with an urban base.[52]

A week after the primary, the state Democratic Executive Committee changed the plan for the convention. It directed the county executive committees to choose delegates only from the lists provided by the state party's subcommittee of three that had originally been appointed to receive returns. The member or members of that panel representing the candidate victorious in the county prepared the list.

The move quashed any influence by Carmack over the platform. The county executive committees might have sent Carmack delegates instructed to vote for Patterson but free to endorse statewide prohibition. On the stump the governor had said he would sign an act outlawing liquor in Tennessee if the party called for it. Now the modified rules assured Patterson the delegates—and the local option plank—that *he* wanted.

In the convention Carmack supporters put forward a minority report on the platform. It called for a direct primary with public disclosure of expenses and contributions, removing election commission appointments from the governor's influence, a primary to elect the state Democratic Executive Committee, and the prohibition of alcoholic beverages in Tennessee. The convention rejected the report.

Carmack was entitled to the votes of delegates from the counties he had carried, but he allowed Patterson to receive the nomination by acclamation. The governor was magnanimous toward his old foe, while subtly bidding him farewell from the state's public life. "As the years stretch forth," Patterson told the convention, "it is my sincere wish that they may bring forth to him peace of mind which is not always to be found in the dust and heat of political strife, and those full rewards which belong to a man of his splendid gifts."[53]

Perhaps Carmack felt most alive in opposition. He had new work to do; still, he knew no peace, and would have none. In the editorial columns of the *Tennessean*, he promised "its support to all the nominees of the Democratic party, both national and state." But in September he inveigled Patterson into an exchange of letters in the *Tennessean* columns. The editor charged that the governor had lured prohibitionists with his promise that he would be bound by the platform, and as the people would select convention delegates through the county committees, they could write the plank on liquor. When the party's executive committee changed the plan, said Carmack, it thwarted the people's will, which was clearly to abolish alcoholic beverages from Tennessee.

Patterson replied that the vote for the gubernatorial nominee settled the prohibition question, and he accused Carmack of sowing discord by abandoning the party platform. Still, the editor kept up his charges, to the dismay of some loyalists. A friend confided to Colonel Cooper, "Just between you and me, Dunc, he has lost all hope of political preferment and wishes to destroy the Democratic party for defeating him. He is acting to my mind as if he would destroy the Democrats if he had to pull the temple down on his own head, which I candidly believe he has already done."

On October 21, he printed the editorial linking Duncan Cooper by name with the saloon keepers of Nashville's lower Broadway. That same day he had delivered to James C. Bradford a letter that read: "Some friends of ours in Maury County have quoted you as making the charge that I had been drunk since the late contest for the gubernatorial nomination. . . . The purpose of this note is to inquire whether you were correctly quoted." Bradford replied with aplomb that he had no personal knowledge that Carmack ever drank liquor to the point of intoxication. The editor pronounced the statement as entirely satisfactory and the matter as closed.[54]

For two weeks Carmack campaigned throughout the Midwest for William Jennings Bryan, making his third race for the White House. Shortly after the former senator returned to the state, Governor Patterson and Governor Cox met and talked.

Now Carmack was sure that Patterson had never meant what he said. Cox once again sat as a member of the state Senate. When he was its speaker before his elevation to the governorship, he had fought the extension of prohibition to the cities. It now appeared to Carmack that Cox and Patterson meant to work together in the next General Assembly to stop the anti-liquor momentum.

Voters sent to the legislature that November a majority, drawn from both parties, pledged to enact a bone-dry law. When they examined the returns in the *Tennessean* office, Mrs. Silena M. Holman, state president of the Women's Christian Temperance Union, saw that the crusade was won. Turning to the editor she said, "Mr. Carmack, if we do get prohibition in the next legislature, it will be more through your work than any one influence."

"If we do get prohibition, I will feel recompensed for all I have lost, all I have been through with," he replied.[55]

The victory was not yet theirs. The Cox-Patterson coalition blocked the way. Duncan Cooper, Carmack assumed, had reconciled the two men, who had fought each other so bitterly in 1906. On the Saturday after the election, he wrote the editorial that concluded:

> All honor to Major Dunc, and may the blessings of the Peacemaker be upon him. May he be heir to all the beatitudes and especially for the blessing reserved to those who do hunger and thirst after righteousness.[56]

When he read it on Sunday, Colonel Cooper cursed the author and declared he would take Carmack's abuse no more.

As the years passed Carmack seemed more and more a one-dimensional man, the hero of an epic or a folktale. His friends insisted that his name would endure "to the last page of Tennessee history . . . whose annals are crowded with the splendid deeds of splendid men and gemmed by the names of Jackson, Polk, and Carmack." Often those who loved him recalled him in abstract or sentimental terms. N. W. Baptist remembered Carmack as "modest, sympathetic, brave, truthful, loyal, frank, faithful, and unselfish."

Edward Carmack, Jr., on the other hand, summed up his father in perceptive detail. "He had a battle-face," Ned wrote, recalling an incident from the last campaign.

> I met it once, and I have not quite forgotten those swift onrushing brows that met like surcharged clouds. From a back seat in one of his great audiences, I saw his lips upcurl in a cold wave, while the upper face was overcast and stern, like an iron sky, and that was not a pleasing face. It was thus he looked when he rose to reply to an opponent's charge . . . that at a certain time in 1888 my father had been assisted to his hotel room insanely drunk. "The Governor," he replied, "is greatly excited to find I was no better a man twenty years ago than he is today."[57]

People called Carmack brilliant because of his gift of words. He turned it to power, but like other legendary men given a great talent, he struggled to be its master rather than its subject. He could no more resist a sarcastic rejoinder than the drunk whom he condemned could resist another drink. He was learning self-control, friends insisted, when he was cut down at the hands of one who had started him on his way, provoking his own death with words, which had carried him so high. Old soldiers who had worn the Confederate gray bared their head to the "Pledge to the South," declaimed by one who was an infant at the time of secession. Upon Carmack's death many of them had damned Duncan Cooper, a guerrilla and prisoner of war whose earned colonelcy Carmack ridiculed in his last editorials. Majors held horses for colonels, as Carmack had once stood holding editorial copy outside publisher Cooper's door.

Loyal friends told the world that Carmack concealed his private convictions, including his conversion to Christianity, from public view.[58] His opponents objected that he was a latecomer to the cause of prohibition, that he used the anti-liquor movement as a stepping stone to political restoration. Those same skeptics said that he drank and whored and that he advanced his ambitions by pandering to superficial popular sentiment and to people who clung to the past. Like him, his enemies were proud, brave men, and they, too, memorialized the passions he could inspire: Tennessee Congressman Wirt Courtney named a son for Robin Cooper.

Some defended the Coopers by insisting that the dead man had courted his own demise. "I have expected such an ending for the brilliant and gifted Carmack," a friend wrote Colonel Cooper. "He has taken such liberties with people who honestly differed with him and often assailed prominent citizens who were defenseless and his hatred of anyone who dared stand in the way of his ambition was without limit. How kind the Lord was to him in many respects and how irrational he was to himself."[59]

Carmack had seemed at first to take his loss to Patterson with equanimity and poise, much as he had when Taylor defeated him for the Senate. But neither for him nor for the righteous brigade whom he led was there any substitute for victory in the moral war of 1908. Soon his rapier pen and scathing tongue were telling the world how he had been martyred for his cause, until he brought about that fate, in accidental collaboration or chance collision with men as arrogant and careless as he. When he lost his life, his followers proclaimed this his ultimate victory, and they stripped the man they claimed to love of human definition.

On the Sunday after his funeral, several thousand people filled Nashville's Ryman Gospel Tabernacle, not far from the spot where Robin Cooper shot Carmack to death. They sat subdued until George Armistead quoted the late senator's declaration of the spring before: "'The saloon has sinned away its day of grace in Tennessee. It refuses to be reformed; it must therefore be destroyed.'" Then applause shook the house, rolling like a wave.[60]

The Gospel Tabernacle had been built in 1892 by Thomas Ryman, a two-fisted roustabout who made a fortune in the steamboat trade and the saloon business. His boats stocked liquor for their hard-working crews, until the day Ryman heard the Reverend Sam Jones preach beneath the tent where he customarily held his Nashville revivals. Jones's message touched Ryman, and he pledged himself to Jesus and teetotalism. Legend holds that he personally upended the liquor bottles aboard his boats and poured the contents into the Cumberland River. He also turned his wharfside saloon into a chapel, then built the great church of brick and stained glass windows for the preacher whom he had once ridiculed.

The Reverend Jones's crusades sent streams of reform purling through the city, which teemed with refugees from the country, black and white, seeking opportunity in the factories and business houses of the New South. Some prospered. Others, observed young James E. Caldwell, "meandered through the immoral shoals" of saloons, brothels, and cheap showplaces to disappear from view.[61]

Those who heard Jones and went away to organize charities or found schools for workingmen longed to cleanse the city's life, to make it orderly and rational, to make it gentler. They sought to repossess an actual or remembered time, when neighbor knew and cared for neighbor, before the growing city split along class and racial lines and before ruinous, soul-destroying business competition pitted a man against his fellows. By 1908 Jones and Ryman were dead. But the preacher's crusade against whiskey and the infidel's redemption from it were strong in the memory of many who sang and wept for Carmack.

The family—sitting beside a blazing coal fire in the hearth or quaking in the hovel and tenement with the approach of winter—was the concern of many reformers. Against this cornerstone of society, the saloon seemed to chip away. In popular understanding and sometimes in fact, it was a place with a spit-drenched floor, whores with painted cheeks, "free" or cheap lunches laden with thirst-inducing salt, and games of chance played around the clock. These, and the glass of spirits before him, robbed a man of his rest and efficiency for the work of a city and of a nation hurtling toward commercial empire.

In the prohibitionists' view, there was a world to gain from the destruction of such vile places. Abolish the saloon and the laborer would not squander the wages that clothed his children. Take away the stimulus of liquor and Negroes would remember their place, and the Irish politician his humble origin. With the tills empty, the owners and brewers and distillers would have no money to purchase officeholders. When all the saloons were made into halls of worship, ward heelers would have no place to swap a drink for a vote and men restored to sobriety would elect the honest government that they by nature preferred. Having led the crusade to victory, women would prove themselves worthy of the ballot. When the barrooms were gone, none need fear disintegration of her marriage into an alcoholic hell, nor an encounter in the street with a reeling drunk. Padlock the doors of the saloons, and crime would decrease, while life expectancy among former drinkers rose.[62]

Because they believed that the manufacture and sale of alcoholic beverages stood between them and the coming of God's kingdom on earth and because Carmack had demanded an end to the business, the prohibitionists of Tennessee proclaimed him a martyr in their crusade. "The Chief is fallen! But the Flag / In rippling roll / Waves proudly," wrote a young reporter named Grantland Rice in the columns of the *Tennessean*. With Carmack's spirit leading the way, they prepared to take their cause to the General Assembly, and Rice made clear that war was at hand:

> Up! Boot and saddle! To the Fray!
> And in the mad wild charge today
> God pity him who blocks the way
> Or bars the goal![63]

Criminal Court Judge William M. Hart had been elected to the bench in 1902, defeating a candidate endorsed by the Reverend Jones. Now as emotions ran high over the killing of Carmack and suspicions of conspiracy wove through many theories of it, some feared that Judge Hart would sympathize with the men charged with the murder.

By custom defendants were allowed to plead without coming to court, but on motion of Attorney General Jeff McCarn, Hart required the Coopers and Sharp to appear in person and present their pleas. On November 25 the accused men stood before the bench and heard the charge of murder read against them. Duncan Cooper appeared calm and self-possessed. "Not guilty," he answered in a firm voice. Robin seemed to a reporter nervous and withdrawn. "Not guilty," he murmured. John Sharp was defiant. He stared at his brother, the clerk of the court, through the reading. Then he boomed, "Not guilty, sir!"

Three weeks later, the defendants applied for bail. The court heard the leading witnesses — and so did the rest of the world as their testimony appeared in the daily newspapers. Hart took the matter under advisement while the accused men spent Christmas in jail. Then he denied their application. Perhaps he thought they might flee, since the colonel had spent considerable time in Honduras, a haven for fugitives from North American law. The judge may have wished to demonstrate his impartiality. Whatever his reasons Hart did not divulge them. As lawyers for the Coopers sat in stunned silence, he adjourned court and deputies marched the trio back to jail.[64]

Rumor flew that Governor Patterson would grant clemency to the defendants if they were convicted of murdering Carmack. In case the governor had not read Rice's doggerel verse, others made its message plain. At the memorial service for the dead man, applause had thundered through the Ryman Tabernacle when Bishop E. E. Hoss declared, "It is for us to create a public sentiment that will not tolerate lax use of the pardoning power."[65]

CHAPTER THREE

The Colonel

IN THE SPRING OF 1907, Dr. and Mrs. G. B. West of Oliver Springs
in East Tennessee had called at the Capitol to beg from Governor Patterson a pardon for their son, a convicted murderer incarcerated in the state
penitentiary. They did not get to talk with the governor. "You can never
realize our disappointment," Mrs. West wrote to Duncan Cooper. "Had it
not been for your pleasant face and words of comfort, we would have
returned to our lonely home almost ready to give up."[1]

William West, according to his own attorney an habitual drunkard,
killed H. C. (Pony) Cash, marshal of Oliver Springs, on September 28,
1904. That night the two men met, apparently by chance, and according
to the defense, Cash said something hateful to West and reached for his
gun. West then drew his pistol and fired. The state stipulated that Cash
spoke to West but then without provocation, West shot him. Cash's weapon
was found firmly fastened in its holster.[2]

After his meeting with the Wests in the executive chambers, Duncan
Cooper called on their son in prison. Later that summer he visited them
in Oliver Springs to tell them that the boy was well. In letter after letter
Mrs. West importuned him about the pardon. As Edward Carmack
brought his gubernatorial campaign to his East Tennessee stronghold in
October 1907, Mrs. West promised Cooper that her family, "Democrats of
some influence," would do whatever they could to help Governor Patterson. But Thanksgiving came and went, then Christmas, and no word about
the pardon arrived from Nashville. In the spring the Wests circulated a
petition for their son's release. The mayor and all the aldermen of Oliver
Springs signed it. Should she send this document to the governor? Mrs.
West asked Colonel Cooper, and she added, "The one who penned these
lines is bowed down with a sorrowing heart."

A crowd of citizens met the train bringing Will West home in July
1908. "Some of them cheered for Patterson when they seen him," his
mother recalled for the colonel. She regretted not seeing their "noblest

49

Matthew D. Cooper. Source: *Tennesseans, Nineteen Hundred and One and Two* (1902).

friend" before they left Nashville and hoped no misfortune would ever befall him. "I will teach the little ones to love the name Colonel Duncan B. Cooper," she wrote.

Mrs. West wanted Cooper to share her faith. "Come to the Savior now," she implored, after he told her he knew no religion but to do good to someone. His friend Katrina Williamson, who was jealous of the attentions he paid other women, accused Cooper of being a rationalist and agnostic. A fervent convert to Catholicism, she prayed for him against his wishes.[3]

At his birth on April 21, 1843, Cooper was named for his grandfather, the Reverend Duncan Brown, and when the colonel died he was buried in a Presbyterian churchyard. In between he fought for the Confederacy, mined for silver, managed extensive business interests in Central America for the Astors, and became during the Patterson administration the most influential man in Tennessee. He charmed many who met him, leaving them avid for his friendship. Yet he was convicted for murdering his protégé after the two had provoked each other into unreasoning rage. And his son Robin lived with a lien upon his life for doing the actual deed.

Duncan Cooper's paternal great-grandfather, Hugh, born in Ireland and a weaver by trade, died in South Carolina. One of his offspring, Captain Robert Cooper, a blacksmith, fought in the Revolution and parlayed his noted handsomeness into a runaway marriage with a Miss Jane Hamilton. She raised twelve children, of whom Matthew Delamere, Duncan Cooper's father, was the youngest, being born in the Chester district of South Carolina in 1792. About 1804, following her husband's death, Mrs. Cooper took her family to Middle Tennessee and settled near the old town of Haysborough, not far from Nashville.[4] Citizens of this western country were nationalists and expansionists, eager for war against Britain and Spain. General Jackson told them they could take the harbors of western Florida, including Mobile, from the Spanish while crushing the Creeks, who many believed were incited by the European enemies to attack white settlers. Young Matthew Cooper went to war as member of a regiment under Thomas Hart Benton. Cooper eventually loaned Jackson money to pay his soldiers, a loan that seems not to have been repaid.[5]

Cooper's later life's work was bound up with finance and the mercantile business. By 1822 he was engaged in the latter at Columbia, the county seat of Maury County. From 1840 to 1862 he served as president of the local branch of the Union Bank.[6]

In three marriages Matthew Cooper fathered fourteen children, who when they wed the sons and daughters of his peers produced a remarkable tangle of cousins. "The relations of one are the relations of all," observed one chronicler of local history. To Cooper's third wife, Mary Ann Witherspoon Brown, whom he married in 1841 when he was forty-eight and she eighteen, seven children were born. Duncan Brown was the second child, the first son.[7]

By then Matthew Cooper was an influential man and becoming a wealthy one. He was present when the Masons of Tennessee, with former Grand Master Andrew Jackson presiding, welcomed the Marquis de Lafayette to Nashville. Cooper's eulogy to Ralph E. W. Earl, Jackson's resident portraitist, suggests that he was a guest at the Hermitage.

Cooper himself became Grand Master in 1826, and the following year opened a commission house, Cooper, Caruthers, and Company, in New Orleans. By the time the war came, his merchandise, land, and slaves were valued at $100,000. But he would watch a Confederate general order the burning of his place of business so the Yankees could not take it, and it was the end of his fortune.[8]

The catalog of Jefferson College, where his parents sent young Duncan Cooper, admonished them to provide fully as much support as the student needed but no more, "extravagance and running into debt" being the two great evils of college life. The small Presbyterian institution at Canonsburg, Pennsylvania, near Pittsburgh, had been founded by ministers like

Duncan Cooper's grandfather, who were taking their doctrine and polity into the raw western country.

Perhaps the Reverend Brown influenced Cooper's choice of schools. In any event he enrolled in Jefferson's freshman class of 1859. Some two hundred young men were studying there, very few of them from the South. Cooper read Ovid, Herodotus, and Horace and received at least a smattering of geometry, trigonometry, and surveying. "My studies are few," he blandly wrote Matthew Cooper, "as they [the faculty] believe in taking a few things and doing them well rather than to take a great many things and not half doing any (a pretty good motto it is)." In a postscript to his mother, he added, "Give my love to old aunt Charity and tell the rest of the darkies howdy."[9]

A few weeks before the firing on Fort Sumter, Mary Ann Cooper died. That tumultuous summer many of the young rallied to the cause of the Southern revolution. Sources differ on the date of Duncan's enlistment in the service of the Confederacy, but in the spring of 1862 Corporal Cooper was riding with John Hunt Morgan against federal lines in Kentucky. That fall he was elected lieutenant of Company G, Ninth Tennessee Cavalry, at its organization on the Columbia fairgrounds. There was no drill, one of his comrades recalled, and very few guns, almost no pistols, and no sabres.[10]

The unit crossed the Tennessee River to join Nathan Bedford Forrest's forces in December 1862. Cooper's precise whereabouts during the following year are unclear, but he raised several companies under his command, first with the rank of captain, then by mid–1863, of colonel.

The river valleys of Middle Tennessee were rich with corn, hogs, cattle, mules, horses, and cropland. Yankee and Rebel armies contended for these and for control of the roads and rail lines to Chattanooga and Atlanta. Cooper's guerrillas hindered federal forces from pacifying whatever countryside they held and caused them to have to fortify towns they captured. One who saw Cooper work observed that "they were the angriest set of soldiers I ever saw during the whole war. They exhibited so much temper and made so many threats."[11]

The Union press rejoiced in the autumn of 1863 that the Fourteenth Michigan Mounted Rifles, newly arrived in the field, would allow Colonel Cooper little rest. He replied by setting fire to a hundred and fifty bales of cotton in Lawrence County, furthering the South's campaign to deny England raw materials and compel her recognition of the Confederacy.[12]

One cavalryman of the Fourteenth Michigan recalled an encounter with the marauders, in a letter to Cooper himself. "I was at Lawrenceburg when my horse got his bridle rein over his head and ran away with me among you boys and you were good to me." A Mount Pleasant neighbor, a child at the time of the war, remembered her alarm at the fate of some Yankee prisoners under Cooper's guard. "The gentle kindness of manner and the pains you took to soothe a little girl's fears impressed me at once that you were brave and good to everybody."[13]

Here were the grace and charm that were bound up in Duncan Cooper with a ferocious sense of honor. He hated the Union invaders en masse but would not shoot an enemy at the mercy of a bolting horse. Members of his band might seize and drown an informer, as they once did, but he stopped, rifle in hand, before a little girl to assure her that he was only taking the Yankees to jail.

In the gray dawn of February 16, 1864, a Union detail patrolling near Columbia came upon three mounted Confederates. Seeing they were outnumbered, two of the Southern soldiers put spurs to their horses and sped away. The third turned, aimed his pistol, and fired, grazing the left wrist of Francis C. Ward of Company C, Fiftieth Illinois Volunteers. Then the Southerner raced in the direction of his fleeing comrades. Quickly he overtook and rode past one of them.

The Yankees, including the wounded Ward, pursued. The trail led up a creek, whose limestone bed was worn slick and smooth. After almost a mile, the Confederate who shot Ward tried to break out of the streambed, but the hooves of his mount slipped and horse and rider tumbled and fell. As the comrade he had passed caught up, he turned to leap on behind him but the loose saddle slipped, dropping both men in the water. And the enemy was upon them.

One of the Union soldiers waved a pistol in the face of the Southern shooter and yelled, "Surrender!" "Hell," his prisoner replied. "Would you shoot a man when he is down?" He was dressed in a new gray uniform, now splattered, and high-top boots. On his coat collar was an officer's insignia. "Who are you?" Francis Ward asked him. "Colonel Duncan B. Cooper," the soldier answered.

The federals searched the two captives and found among the papers Cooper carried the likeness of a young woman. After they had passed it among themselves, Cooper casually asked to see it again. When they handed it to him, he dropped it on the ground, grinding it under his heel. One of the Yankees archly observed that Cooper's gesture was a gallant one. Cooper answered that it would at least protect the woman. When the Union men related the incident to their superior officer, he was appalled. The lady was undoubtedly a spy, he fumed, and Colonel Cooper had outwitted his captors.

Flashing a roll of greenback dollars, a major bought Cooper from the men who had taken him and later claimed that he had captured "the Francis Marion of the Confederacy." The brave major placed his charge in the stockade at Columbia. Was "the original of the broken picture" among the young women who had brought Cooper food? Francis Ward wondered. Perhaps, although no one could say. A local Union newspaper taunted "the foolish girls and brainless boys" who openly admired the prisoner, while the editor printed a sarcastic note of thanks from the jailer for the ham, eggs, pound cake, and wine that had been meant for "the boy Cooper."[14]

Soon Cooper was transferred to confines at Nashville, then to Fort Delaware. There he studied the moat surrounding the prison and decided he could walk across it by strapping canteens under his feet to buoy him. The attempt failed, the guards had to pull him from the water, and he remained in his cell for the last months of war. In the spring, as he was being taken south for exchange, General Lee surrendered.[15]

In Colonel Cooper's trial for the murder of Edward Carmack, his lawyers traded powerfully upon his service to the Confederacy. In his time of trouble his former comrades gathered around him. Even as their own footsteps were faltering, they offered to come to his aid. "I am 75 years old," Lebanon, Tennessee, merchant J. A. Woollard told the colonel, "and love all my old Confederate soldiers and always will. I am good for 10 or 15 thousand dollars and at anytime you have to make bond if you need me wire me at once."[16]

W. R. H. Matthews of Columbia wrote that his son had gotten into a fistfight after defending Cooper and Governor Patterson. The colonel sent a silver cup to his correspondent's grandson, and the little boy's father replied, "You have a Host of good Honest brave old Soldier friends here . . . I am a Reble boy and love all the old boys in Grey." His son, he added, was often complimented on his name, Duncan Brown Cooper Matthews. [17]

So it was ironic that by the time he was tried for his life, Cooper was a man of the New South and of the new century, seeking the fortune that ever eluded him in automobiles, mechanical patents, and insurance. He traveled to New York and Philadelphia and Detroit, staying at the grand hotels where the local Democrats had their headquarters. Like his father before him, Cooper made his way among influential men — financiers, wholesalers, brokers, developers, prospectors — men at ease in the world. They quested for money, recognition, advantage, and they openly enjoyed their worldly gains and pleasures, which often came about through personal acquaintances. "Your religion is mine," a friend observed to Cooper. "Fidelity to friends and damn your enemies." Cooper apparently believed that the things he wanted everyone wanted — he remarked once that it was human nature to love and want power — and that to deny such desires was hypocrisy.[18]

Cooper's strong, unqualified love of personal freedom impressed those who knew him. The colonel was steeped in the Southern antebellum tradition that regarded with skepticism the idea of progress insofar as it meant the perfectibility of man. As Alexis de Tocqueville observed, that tradition did not hold "man's faculty of self-improvement . . . to be indefinite." Society might become "better, but not essentially different."

Reformers could not create virtue. The state could be merciful to a man whom liquor had ruined, like Will West. But it could not make a drinking man virtuous. Government could not make the world even, or just, or fair. It could not even give satisfaction for defamation of character.

Friends of his youth, friends of his later years had powerful, enduring memories of Duncan Cooper's sense of personal honor. Edward Carmack spoke of "character," the lonely practice of virtue. There is no community, only private duty in Carmack's luminous, austere, and inspiring essay of that title. But Duncan Cooper claimed his honor before his blood kin, his friends, his state. He looked to those in that circle to grant him his place and his standing. In turn, by his generosity of spirit, he bound men and women to him for life. Thirty years after the incident, Francis Ward recalled the young colonel who had shot him in the arm and wrote to ask if he "might" be permitted to renew an acquaintance of only a day in '64."[19]

Cooper married Florence Fleming following the end of the war. During their marriage that ended with her death in 1870, three children were born to them. The making of his family proved easier than finding a vocation. He read law under a practicing attorney and was admitted to the bar. For a time he tried farming near Helena, Arkansas. As he looked on, several of his brothers rose in the world. Henry, who had served as a Whig member of the General Assembly and been appointed to the bench by Governor Andrew Johnson, returned to the legislature in 1869, a senator from Davidson County. Edmund sat in the state House of Representatives after serving as assistant secretary of the treasury during Johnson's presidency. William Cooper had been elected to the Tennessee Supreme Court in 1861, but when the courts resumed operation after the war the radical Governor William G. Brownlow prevented Cooper from taking the seat because of his Southern sympathies.[20]

Two years after Florence Cooper died, her father, Chancellor Fleming, named Duncan Cooper the clerk and master of his court. It was an esteemed office if a minor one, and the duties allowed Cooper time to advance brother Henry's fortunes at the expense of Andrew Johnson. The former president's ambitions were undiminished, despite his impeachment and brush with conviction, and his hatred of the Southern aristocrats spurred him to return to politics in Tennessee. In 1870 he plunged into the race for U.S. Senator. The legislature was divided evenly between Johnson partisans and Johnson foes, and the contest heated to a boil. In the House, Edmund Cooper numbered himself among the former president's friends. He would vote for Johnson, he proudly declared, over any man save his own brother. When they heard that remark, the anti-Johnson men nominated Henry Cooper, who received his brother's vote and was elected to the U.S. Senate.[21]

Johnson flew into a rage. His erstwhile secretary, he fumed, was a base

Henry Cooper. Source: Kenneth D. McKellar, *Tennessee Senators as Seen by One of Their Successors* (1942).

William F. Cooper. Source: Robert F. Ewing, *William Frierson Cooper* (1909).

ingrate. Duncan Cooper announced that the former president would not be allowed to make the charge in Maury County. Johnson set out at once for Columbia and mounted a speaking platform in the courthouse square. According to one account, Johnson's words were "Jesus had his Judas, Caesar his Brutus, Washington his Benedict Arnold, and I, Andrew Johnson, had my Edmund and Henry." He then looked up at the young clerk and master sitting in the window and thundered, "These eyes have not beheld the man this heart fears." Cooper made no demonstration, and the incident closed.[22]

Duncan Cooper may have accompanied his brother to Washington. An unconfirmed source says the colonel worked as a contractor for the Corps of Engineers on the completion of the Washington Monument, built public works for the city, and made a wide acquaintance in the Grant and Hayes administrations.

The contracting firm of Duncan B. Cooper and J. W. S. Frierson appeared in the Washington city directory only once, in 1880. That year the army engineers completed the strengthening of the foundation so they could build a structure six hundred feet tall. They placed hoisting equipment atop the shaft, left unfinished since before the war, and raised the first new stone into place. None of their reports to Congress mention Cooper and Frierson. Yet the colonel never denied the story, circulated widely at the time of his arrest in 1908, that he had undertaken the "arduous work of . . . twist[ing] the whole structure about to 'square with the compass.'"[23]

Cooper was only thirty-three when, in 1877, he married his second wife, Mary Polk Jones, age twenty-two. On her mother's side her family tree traced back to Colonel William Polk, soldier of the Revolution, legislator, and president of the North Carolina State Bank. The United States paid for his war service in western lands, some fifty-six hundred acres along the turnpike between Columbia and Mount Pleasant, Tennessee. When the Civil War came, the mansions built by Colonel Polk's kin lined the road.

Mary Polk Jones grew up among the ghosts and legends. She knew Duncan Cooper's reputation for gallantry, and one day in the spring of 1873 she witnessed an instance of it. The two were in a party that made an excursion from Ashwood Hall, one of the Polk mansions, to Rattlesnake Falls, on the headwaters of the Big Bigby River. "This is the wildest and most romantic scenery in Maury County," noted a contemporary account. "The water is carried splashing and foaming over a bluff nearly a hundred feet high." The picnickers clambered up and down the basin. The only casualty was "Old Rye, the friend of all the party," lost over the falls; it had been taken along to cure snake bites.

That day Duncan Cooper had his eye not on Mary Jones but on another female member of their set. At his suggestion, the merry band

resolved to change the name of the place from Rattlesnake Falls to Antoinette Falls in honor of Antoinette Polk. Perhaps he was recalling the day
in wartime, when, on a visit to relatives in Columbia, she saw a Confederate major dash by the house pursued by Union cavalry. With gauntlets in
one hand and her hat with its long ostrich plume in the other, Antoinette
ran for her horse and made a wild dash through the woods to warn Southern
troops camped in the vicinity of Ashwood Hall in time for them to escape.

In November 1864 the army of John Bell Hood passed through Maury
County heading north toward a vainglorious disaster. In the company was
a French military attaché, the Comte de Charette. We do not know how
the young nobleman and Antoinette Polk met. We have none of the words
that passed between them as they walked beneath the bare trees of the old
town nor the repartee they exchanged before the fireplace at Ashwood
Hall. Nor is it known what they said as the count mounted his horse with
the jangle of spurs and the creaking of leather and rode off with the
homicidal Hood toward the slaughter at Franklin. But their words led them
to love. On December 1, 1877, Antoinette Polk became the Baroness de
Charette. Young princes of Europe's royal houses spent their holidays at
her residence on the Riviera.

Wed that same year, Mary Jones Cooper gave birth in 1878 to her first
child, Sarah Polk. The Coopers' eldest son, Robin, was born in 1879.[24]

Duncan Cooper's quest for fortune and power dated from these days
of his youth, and from the time of his first political success, he used his influence to see that government fostered the business interests of men like
himself. Elected in 1880 to represent Maury and Williamson counties in
the Tennessee House of Representatives, Cooper vigorously supported a
plan favored by the bondholders for the repayment of the state debt.

Tennessee incurred the debt when the war-weakened railroads to
whom it had loaned its credit proved unable to retire bonds they had sold
for expansion. The dominant issue in Tennessee politics for a decade, the
$43 million obligation was the principal and accruing interest for which the
state was now liable. But Tennessee's economy, itself not yet recovered
and floundering in the national depression, would not permit settlement
on a dollar-for-dollar basis.

Should there be a negotiated compromise with the bondholders,
thereby upholding the state's credit? Or should Tennessee repudiate the
debt and decrease taxes? The Democrats split over the issue in the 1880s,
and their perplexity led to the election of Republican Alvin Hawkins to the
governorship.

Two years later, when the state Democratic convention approved a
plank calling for funding only part of the obligation at one hundred cents
on the dollar, Duncan Cooper gained the floor. After denouncing the action,
he withdrew from the hall, leading bank presidents, railroad executives,

and prominent public figures with him. They held their own convention, affirmed Tennessee's obligation to pay what it owed, and selected John H. Fussell as their standard-bearer for governor. But the regulars' nominee, William B. Bate, managed to unify the party. He went on to become governor, and his administration settled the divisive debt question.[25] From that achievement, Bate rose to the U.S. Senate, and his death in that office ironically led to the sundering of the Democratic Party, the defeat of Edward Carmack, and all that followed.

In his private life Cooper pursued wealth as partner with his remarkable friend Van Leer Polk. In the early 1880s they placed their hopes and their cash in a silver mine in Mexico. Instead of fortune, tragedy stalked them. On February 4, 1884, robbers set upon Cooper, Polk, and Henry Cooper near Culican and left the former U.S. Senator dead in the road.[26]

Grand nephew of the former president, Polk was educated in Europe, related by marriage of his sister Antoinette to French nobility, and served diplomatic appointments in India and South America. Growing up on the baroness' estate, Polk became acquainted with boys his age who happened also to be the crown princes of Europe. Among his friends he counted Edward Prince of Wales, Leopold of Belgium, Humberto of Italy, and Germany's Wilhelm.

After Polk reached manhood, he occasionally returned to Tennessee to run for the legislature, take some other part in politics, or work on a newspaper. In 1901 Jere Baxter brought him home as editor-in-chief of the Nashville *News*. Polk preferred doing his work from a stuffed chair at the Hermitage Club; meanwhile Baxter was finding it difficult to meet the payroll. It might be best, he told Polk, if he were to resign. Polk cheerfully agreed and accepted a week's salary and a railroad pass to New York as severance pay. Three weeks later, the telegraph brought to the office of the *News* a dispatch datelined Kiel, Germany. The news item read in its entirety: "The Emperor William II embarked today on the imperial yacht 'Hohenzollern' for a six weeks' cruise in the North Sea. His only guest was Mr. Van Leer Polk of Tennessee."[27]

Duncan Cooper gambled at cards as well as horses and speculative business. Games of chance were his one indulgence, his friend Henry Doak acknowledged, categorically denying that the colonel drank inordinately or pursued women. The Cooper story that delighted the New York papers after his arrest — that he had won the Nashville *American* from W. I. Cherry in a poker game — Cherry himself denounced.[28] As with the apocryphal story of his work on the Washington Monument, Cooper took no trouble to establish the facts. Was he happy to keep the legends about his exploits alive, especially since neither his business ventures nor his record at the track suggests that he could with any regularity pick a winner?

Van Leer Polk. Source: Tennessee General Assembly.

By whatever means, Cooper on January 9, 1886, became president of the *American*. Less than a month later Edward Carmack first appeared on the payroll. Ousted in the spring of 1887, when a rival syndicate acquired a majority of the stock, Cooper was back at the helm when the board of directors purchased the *Democrat* and brought Carmack back to the *American* staff. Once again, Cooper left the business. The following May he returned as president, his last and longest tenure.[29]

One of the leading newspapers of the South, the *American* was created in 1875 with the merger of two morning journals. Like those predecessors, it supported the New South movement of industrial growth and carried the torch for the Democratic Party. But the nineties saw the beginning of the venerable journal's long decline as its ownership passed back and forth among business syndicates and party factions. An evening rival, the *Nashville Banner*, outstripped it in circulation, and newspapers of Louisville, Atlanta, and New Orleans surpassed it in quality. It would live on its reputation, under effective control of the L & N Railroad, until Luke Lea acquired it and merged it into his *Tennessean*. Lea kept the name *American* on his masthead for a time, setting it in small type above the headlines that mocked the Coopers in their trial.

The irony was bitter because the *American* made Duncan Cooper a powerful man. In much of the South after Reconstruction, the Democrats returned to office and remained securely in control. But in Tennessee the party was perpetually rent by feuds, and the Republicans wherever they made alliance with bolters or blacks achieved notable success. In Nashville Thomas Kercheval, the "Red Fox," captured the mayor's office for the Republicans in 1872 and was reelected eleven times. In 1894 H. Clay Evans, twice mayor of Chattanooga, won the governor's race in the campaign conducted by Edward Carmack for the ailing Democratic nominee Peter Turney. When the Democrats contested the election in the legislature, Evans was counted out, and with that the Republican threat was turned back until the death of Senator Bate tore the Democrats asunder.[30]

Cooper himself returned to public life in 1894, as one of Davidson County's two members in the Tennessee Senate. Senator Cooper's legislative interests were varied, if parochial, and he served more conspicuously as a party leader than as a lawmaker. When it appeared that H. Clay Evans had defeated Governor Peter Turney for reelection, Cooper presented the incumbent's petition to his colleagues. "This result," Turney's brief intoned, "is due to gross and fraudulent disregard and violation of law."[31] Bourbon Democrats held a solid majority in the General Assembly, and, after rigorous investigation made with all solemnity and formal due process, they discovered a majority in the disputed ballot boxes for Turney. The Republicans vowed to avenge the deed in 1896.

Long resenting the Republicans' alleged theft of the White House from Samuel Tilden in 1876 — he was ever afterward referred to as "President Tilden" in its news columns — the *American* eventually found another New Yorker to champion, Grover Cleveland. Under Cooper's management it held fast for him in 1888. Four years later, the endorsement of Cleveland from Cooper's editorial page was even more valuable, as more blacks were disfranchised and the Republicans were thus losing part of their coalition. After Cleveland's victory in 1892, Tennesseeans wrote to beg Cooper's help for appointments as postmasters, foreign ministers, and assistant Cabinet secretaries.

Many men in Cooper's orbit knew Nashville and New York City and traveled between them. Seth Low and Sawney Webb, the former to be mayor of Gotham, the latter to be a U.S. Senator from Tennessee, belonged to the Open Letter Club of Nashville and New York. New York City resident E. Bright Wilson, originally of Gallatin and former speaker of the Tennessee House of Representatives, joined Cooper for an afternoon at Belmont whenever he came to town. Chauncey DePew spoke at Vanderbilt University's commencement in 1895. The dapper New York senator lent his name to the letterhead of a company building railroads in Honduras, and whether through him, or at the racetrack, or in the parlor of the

Chauncey M. Depew. Source: *Nashville American* (June 18, 1895).

E. Bright Wilson. Source: *Nashville American* (Jan. 8, 1901).

Hoffman House, Cooper met the management of that swashbuckling enterprise.

The Honduras syndicate, made up of northeastern capitalists, Colonel Cooper, and other investors, announced plans to build a railroad ocean to ocean across the isthmus, continuing the fifty miles of track already laid. The firm further proposed to liquidate the national debt, which was mainly bonds held by French and English banks; collect all the customs revenue due the country and pay it a specified sum instead; run a line of steamships; and establish the national bank to hold the government's money. In exchange for these services, Honduras agreed to grant the syndicate a half million acres of land and the privilege of mining and colonizing it. John Jacob Astor sat on the board of directors, as did financiers George Scott, William Valentine, and Minor Keith.[32]

On a visit to Honduras about 1895, Richard Harding Davis rode by train "through jungles where palms grew in the most wonderful riot and disorder so that their branches swept in through the car windows and brushed the cinders from the roof. The jungle spread out within a few feet of the track on either side. . . ." Whatever entered Tegulcigalpa, the capital, he observed "must be brought on the back of a mule or the shoulders of a man."[33] So the railroad had to come first, if the syndicate's grand plans were to make its members wealthy men. As General Manager Cooper traveled to Honduras in the summer of 1898, when with some twelve hundred men at work and five miles of track completed, the Spanish-American War halted the digging. Despite the delay, in June 1900 the Hondurans renewed the agreement. Cooper and John E. Bleekman, managing director of the syndicate, personally brought home the papers signed by the president of Honduras.

But for nought. In the summer of 1903, a revolutionary regime declared the Americans in default of their contract and seized the railroad, provoking an angry protest from Secretary of State John Hay. "There were only two passenger cars on the road," the Honduran emissary retorted, and they were "little better than cattle cars." The mileage of the track remained unchanged from where it had been five years before.[34]

The only potentially paying proposition the syndicate ever held was the mines. "There is not much in Honduras except mountains," Davis observed, but some thought the mother lode of all time lay beneath them. "California will be outdone," a commercial agent of the French government told the New York papers. "Out of every cubic yard of soil from sixty to seventy five cents of gold can be extracted." A prospector at home, Colonel Cooper was evidently pursuing gold in Central America.[35]

Besides his fellow investors in the Honduras venture, Cooper formed many friendships in New York. Journalist Frank Marshall White, who crusaded against the Black Hand and for child welfare, wrote the colonel as he was awaiting trial: "I do not remember ever to have been more impressed by courtesy and gentleness in all relations with others as well as myself or have been more desirous of being able to call an acquaintance a friend." Henry Proctor Waugh, an editor at the New York *Herald* and member of the Southern Society and the Tennessee Society in the city, telegraphed his support to the prisoner.[36]

The banker J. Coleman Drayton, who claimed Southern roots and who had divorced Augusta Astor after challenging her admirer to a duel, corresponded with Cooper. In the financial houses of Broadway and Wall Street, the colonel had still other friends. Bruce L. Rice of Daniel, O'Dell and Company, banking and brokerage firm, took the prisoner's part: "I know zealously you have always guarded your personal honor, and I know what your feelings must be when you believe that your honor and good name have been assailed." Edwin Taliaferro, advisory counsel in the Harry K. Thaw murder case, talked of Cooper's being employed by the family. Upon Cooper's arrest after the shooting of Carmack, Taliaferro wired, "I am with you for everything in my power."

The prosecution in the Cooper case offered employment to a former president of the borough of Brooklyn, Martin Littleton, originally from Tennessee. His uncle Jesse Littleton of Winchester vigorously dissuaded him. "Colonel Cooper is our kind of people," wrote the former Republican nominee for governor. "He is a red-blooded American, a hard-boned Tennessean with a brave and kind heart and noble, generous impulses." Littleton continued:

> If you were to go into this case, you would go in leading the
> d---dest set of unreasonable fools and cranks and preachers
> and W.C.T.U.s that ever headed a crusade against the liber-
> ties of the people. If the crowd back of the prosecution could
> try Col. Cooper and his son without a witness, deny them
> counsel, and crucify them without so much as allowing them
> to say "Lord, have mercy," they would do it, and then go
> about their foolish ways declaring to themselves that they
> were preserving the right of trial by jury, the bulwark of
> American liberty.

At the Hoffman House, Colonel John Peacock acknowledged Cooper's letter from jail, in which the prisoner reported his good spirits. Recounting a conversation with another party about Cooper and Carmack, Peacock declined to defer to the dead man's memory: ". . . I told him there was as much difference in the two men in New York City as to their vices and their goings-on as there is between a tallow candle in Tennessee and the bright sun. . . . Carmack has been trying to get somebody to kill him for the last

Riverwood. Courtesy Metropolitan Historical Commission of Nashville/Davidson County.

twelve years, commencing with the Presidents of the United States, and it falls on my poor friend, who never gave any man offense in his life."[37]

In October 1903, the syndicate collapsing and his investment with it, Cooper received a proposition from a New York speculator for shares he owned in certain Honduran mining properties. Then the colonel returned to Riverwood. Mary Jones Cooper had died there in December 1893, and their son Flavel lived on the place, breeding stock. Rental of part of the eight hundred acres, along with investments in real estate and phosphate mines, provided Colonel Cooper the leisure to pursue his only vocation, politics.

Cooper and Carmack were allies in the presidential campaign of New York Appeals Court Judge Alton B. Parker. Southern conservatives like the colonel welcomed the repudiation of William Jennings Bryan, and a revival of the New York–New South axis. Carmack had to wrench in reversing course; eight years before he had stood by Bryan as the crowds cheered for the Commoner, Carmack, and free coinage. Nonetheless, from the podium of the Democratic convention in 1904, he seconded Parker's nomination and reproved Bryan's criticism of the judge as the candidate of Wall Street. Parker was certainly Cleveland's man, and the colonel and the former president met and talked over the Democrats' dismal prospects in the face of Theodore Roosevelt's tumultuous popularity.[38]

Colonel Cooper sought to do business with the administration. He lent his support to Van Leer Polk's effort to get a profitable part of the contract for digging the Panama Canal with coolie labor. Cooper, Polk, E. Bright Wilson, and writer Alfred Henry Lewis were the president's luncheon guests at the White House in March 1906, undoubtedly to discuss Polk's proposition. Secretary of War William Howard Taft scrawled across the proposal that the "great difficulty is to avoid peonage in these Chinese labor contracts," and that seems to have ended the matter. After the killing of Edward Carmack the Knoxville *Sentinel* reported over lunch that Roosevelt had suggested Cooper help defeat the senator. In a letter for the colonel's eyes only, Wilson could not recall Carmack's name even being mentioned during the conference.[39]

Whatever the truth, by then Cooper had broken politically with Carmack, was supporting his opponent Robert L. Taylor, and was managing the gubernatorial campaign of Malcolm Patterson. While Cooper's reasons for his political stance in 1906 are not entirely clear, the most likely explanation can be found in the volatile political situation in Tennessee. After Taylor narrowly beat Republican George Tillman in 1896, each Democratic nominee in successive biennial elections won substantial pluralities over his opponent. But these comfortable margins concealed the Democrats' peril, apparent by the election of 1904. That November Jesse Littleton came within three percent or exceeded Tillman's percentage of the vote in sixty of the state's ninety-six counties. In three-fourths of East Tennessee counties, he did as well or better than Tillman. Such was the case in nearly two-thirds of Middle Tennessee counties. The Republican ran less well in West Tennessee, where somewhat fewer than half the counties awarded him Tillman's percentage or better.[40]

The Democrats had other reasons to worry about their prospects for 1906. While the Republicans were holding their loyal voters, fewer Democrats were going to the polls. Robert Taylor's administrations of 1887–91 accomplished a so-called "purifying" of the election process that disfranchised large numbers of voters, white and black. After these reforms, voters had to register. They had to mark separate ballots for state and federal offices. Most discouraging of all they had to pay a poll tax, required by the constitution of 1870 but unenforced until the 1890s.[41]

As their numbers declined on election day, the fragile unity of Democrats made their fortunes still more tenuous. Since redemption, the party had split over the state debt, the agrarian revolt, the free silver question, and, to a lesser extent, the counterrevolution of 1904. A period of peace reigned when Benton McMillin, then James Frazier governed. But both of them, along with Bob Taylor, longed to go to the Senate, and each pressed friends to ally with his cause and abjure the interests of rivals.

Perhaps to Duncan Cooper, studying the situation after the death of Senator Bate, the portents appeared ominous. Once again in 1906 the Democrats faced H. Clay Evans, the most formidable opponent the Republicans could field. The new governor, John I. Cox, wanted election in his own right, but he was generally known as Frazier's lieutenant and shared in the resentment against the self-appointed senator. If Cox were nominated, Cooper may have reasoned, he would fail to recoup the decline in Democratic voters.

As Edward Carmack's last editorial suggested, Cooper and Cox held little in common by temperament. On at least one public occasion, they differed profoundly. With Cox voting in the majority, the Frazier administration supported legislation that ratified the city of Nashville's million-dollar subscription to the Tennessee Central Railroad, Jere Baxter's defiant challenge to the wealth and power of the L & N. Duncan Cooper was a friend of the giant corporation, and it of him. In the special legislative session of 1898, the line employed him to assure that its tax privileges were continued.[42]

Some Democratic leaders may have supported Cox, a native of East Tennessee, to reduce the Republican plurality there. But a Cox-Taylor coalition was unthinkable: Taylor could not attack Frazier on the "snap caucus" issue and support Cox. Neither was any combination possible between Carmack and Malcolm Patterson, who had despised each other since they exchanged blows a decade before.

So the fateful alliances, more accidental than created, fell into place. Taylor, an East Tennesseean, could boost the west-state native Patterson in the upcountry. With no Middle Tennessee candidate in either race, Taylor's ready fiddle and humor appeared to give him advantage there. If Evans came over the mountains with a substantial plurality and held Tillman's percentage in the midstate, the voters of West Tennessee could decide who would be governor. And they knew whom they wanted. "People in that section will have no one but Patterson," Trenton lawyer Sparrell Hill wrote Duncan Cooper.

"The only salvation," Hill continued, was the alignment of Patterson and Taylor. "If Carmack should happen to be [re]nominated, the Patterson forces would go to pieces and the Carmack crowd might nominate somebody—I hardly think Cox, but I don't know, it might be." Hill implored Cooper to go to work for closer relations between Taylor and Patterson. "You can do it better than anyone if you will put your head to it."[43]

For the three principal figures, the campaign of 1906 harked back to old friendships and rivalries. Carmack not only had to win reelection; he had to thwart Patterson from becoming governor and head of the party. Robert Taylor relished the role of harmonizer and saw himself playing it once more, as he had in 1886 and again a decade later. Duncan Cooper had helped defeat H. Clay Evans in the legislature in 1895; now he refused to see the Republicans have their revenge. When he went to work whole-heartedly for Patterson, it meant supporting Taylor tactically — and at last breaking with Carmack politically.

But when and why did they become mortal enemies? As late as December 1904 Cooper received a bluff and cheerful letter from Carmack, expressing his admiration for T.R.'s "aggressive fight against monopoly and corporate power." He wanted, said the senator, to talk with Cooper "along those lines."[44]

But in less than a year their relations began to sour. The years of 1904 and 1905 saw sharply renewed tensions between the old enemies, Congressman Patterson and Senator Carmack, as the two struggled to dominate the politics of the day. In the winter of 1905 Carmack provided crucial help to Senator Bate with members of the legislative delegation from Shelby County, where the rivalry had its roots. A contemporary account held that Duncan Cooper had always opposed Bate since the compromise over the state debt and that he pleaded with Carmack not to assist his colleague's reelection bid in 1905. This uncorroborated source says that Carmack brusquely rebuffed him and that began their trouble.[45]

Carmack and Patterson also clashed in a Memphis courtroom, with the senator serving as prosecutor of a gambler accused of shooting a police deputy during a raid, and Patterson defending the man. Out of the sensational incident arose a coalition of progressives who persuaded voters to send a reform delegation to the General Assembly. An ensuing legislative battle over a charter amendment explicitly making it the duty of city officials to suppress vice was widely seen as a Patterson-Carmack struggle.[46]

Although the colonel and the senator met and talked during the campaign of 1906, there were no more personal relations. When Carmack announced for governor in the fall of 1907, Cooper began bending every effort to defeat him and thus subjected himself to the same brutal attacks that Carmack was liable to hurl at any political opponent.

In the gubernatorial campaign, Patterson labeled Governor Cox a "machine candidate" — a hoary charge even in 1906 — and accused him of personally profiting from back tax assessments when he was a state revenue agent. The machine charge linked Cox's campaign with Carmack's, as Taylor attacked the senator for being a party to the "snap caucus." Cox failed to put the corruption charge behind him (although no surviving evidence suggests he committed any unlawful acts as a tax collector).

But doggedly the governor battled Patterson for delegates county by county.

In Davidson County Cox won the popular vote and so claimed that under the unit rule he was entitled to the whole local delegation in the state convention. Patterson carried Davidson districts electing a total of eighty-five delegates, compared to Cox's seventy-two. Davidson's entire vote was his, he insisted. In a tumultuous meeting, the Patterson men, organized by young Luke Lea, stood their ground and won the entire delegation for their candidate. Cox could not regain the momentum, yet he continued to maintain that Patterson could not be nominated. "It might be that neither of us should be," he confided to a supporter. Wary that a Republican victory was in the offing, others talked of a compromise candidate. The name mentioned most often was Edward Carmack. But the lame-duck senator declined, saying that his candidacy would give new life to the charge of machine politics.

The state convention met on May 29, 1906. From the opening gavel Cox and Patterson fought to elect their allies as officers. Cox controlled the party executive committee, but Luke Lea's corps forced it to select a candidate other than the governor's for convention chairman. When the Patterson men then turned back a Cox challenge to certain of their local delegations, the governor abandoned the fight. The convention nominated Patterson by acclamation.[47]

Once elected Patterson proceeded in the mild delusion of righteousness and exemplary purpose. To pass his legislative program, to elect allies to the General Assembly and to party posts, the governor built his own machine, and Colonel Cooper kept it running. He put before Patterson the names of loyal administration men for appointment to patronage jobs—physicians in the prisons, livestock inspectors, interim judges.

In moments of political crisis, Patterson drew on Cooper's energy and resourcefulness, fairly begging his help. "Hope . . . after picking a winner, you feel like coming home," he wrote the colonel in New Orleans in February 1908. "The [state Democratic Executive] Committee meets on the twentieth. I am needing you badly." Probably they were "Governor" and "Colonel" to one another, not "Ham" and "Dunc." But Katrina Williamson was jealous of their bond. "Your love and care of Governor Patterson is the ruling thought of your life," she observed archly to Cooper that fall, shortly before the election. "Success is very lovely, and when I see you, you will be drunk on this loveliness."[48]

Industrialist Harvey and his wife, Katherine, LaFollette, whom the colonel loved as friends and upon whom the governor counted for support, contrived to bring Cooper and the widow Williamson together for long evenings on the pagoda at Glen Oaks, their home in the corporate hamlet they had founded. Cooper first visited there in the summer of 1907, possibly

Harvey M. LaFollette. Courtesy *LaFollette Press* (June 19, 1986).

when Patterson's interests—and the matter of Will West's pardon—took him to East Tennessee. From that time forward they implored him again and again to return. Robin Cooper and Sarah Cooper Burch regularly received and accepted invitations to Glen Oaks, too.

Mrs. Williamson was also a friend of Senator Taylor and by courtesy a relation through the marriage of her nephew Hillsman Taylor—subsequently a speaker of the Tennessee House of Representatives—to the senator's daughter. On her visits to Washington she stayed at the Taylors' apartment in Stoneleigh Court and from there traveled in the city, sometimes in the company of the LaFollettes and their relation, the senator from Wisconsin, Robert LaFollette. "Mrs. Williamson went with us to the Willard," Katherine LaFollette wrote Cooper in the winter of 1908. "The peacock row brought you to our minds." Doors in Washington society opened to Katrina Williamson because of her connections or her pugnacious charm. During the colonel's trial for murder, she wrote him, "At the

Japanese legation yesterday, the 'Cooper-Carmack' case came up, and I rose to my feet to let them know my position so no one would be seriously hurt."[49]

At the time Harvey LaFollette met Duncan Cooper, his company boasted that it dug two hundred and fifty tons of anthracite coal out of the Cumberland Mountains every day. Many of the miners who worked in the pitch-black tunnels came from Italy, Ireland, Germany, and France. Because East Tennessee natives declined to abandon their hillside farms to work underground, LaFollette brought immigrant labor from the Catholic countries of Europe.

As the company prospered, producing iron ore, coke, and coal, LaFollette opened a bank with himself as president and his brother as cashier. He employed engineers to build a water, light, and telephone system. In 1908 the town of twenty-eight hundred people was, along with Nashville, Chattanooga, and Memphis, one of the places in Tennessee where a toiling man could legally buy a drink.[50]

If he would only come visit, teased the two K's, Glen Oaks would be "wine, widows, colonels, and cards." Katrina Williamson warned him that if he married, he could not bring his wife; and Katherine LaFollette implored him to be on the train east by hurling back his own words: "You say what better religion can one have than giving happiness."[51] He often failed to appear when they counted on him.

His thoughts, nonetheless, were in East Tennessee and on the politics there. Patterson and Cooper planned to defeat prohibition in the state Senate by securing a majority of members pledged to local option. (In essence, their plan was no different from the prohibitionists' grand and ultimately successful scheme of combining Democratic bolters and dry Republicans.) Harvey LaFollette urged Cooper to concentrate the fight in twenty districts across the state. In the east they should seek to elect seven favorable Republicans, "including one at Bristol in lieu of John I. Cox." The wet cities like Chattanooga afforded "wondrous opportunities," LaFollette observed. "There have never been over 4,000 votes cast in the Democratic primary in Hamilton County," he continued.

> All agree that the 64 white bars are good for ten times that many votes. The distillers, wholesalers, brewery, and "mailing houses" actually employ over 300 people, all Democrats. The police and fire departments (including street laborers and other employees controlled absolutely by that power) are . . . worth from five to six hundred votes. The county vote . . . including teachers, school directors, etc. will yield at least 500 voters in the primary. If to these special elements . . . there is added the influence of a thorough organization with an expenditure of at least $15 thousand back of

> it, it does look like the result of the primary there should not
> be in doubt.

The brewers were meeting in Nashville on April 10, and LaFollette predicted they would raise fifty thousand dollars from Nashville, Memphis, Chattanooga, and their national organization.[52]

On November 3, Patterson defeated Tillman by the comfortable margin of twenty thousand votes. But from Glen Oaks the next day, Harvey LaFollette anxiously inquired of Duncan Cooper: "Do you believe there will be sixteen Democratic members of the Senate who will stand upon the Patterson platform in favor of local option?"[53] When the colonel studied the returns, he knew there would not. They had lost, Edward Carmack and Luke Lea had won, and the Democratic Party was split in two over liquor.

"Old Tennessee is going dry!" proclaimed the Nashville *Tennessean* on January 15, 1909. A week after the paper's gloating headline, a bill extending the Four-Mile Law over the whole state — including the cities and LaFollette — passed the Senate twenty to thirteen.

Disorderly debate and demonstrations from the gallery disrupted the House the next day, but the measure passed there, sixty-two votes to thirty-six. Later that afternoon the WCTU held a joyful thanksgiving service at the place on Seventh Avenue where the dead Carmack fell in the gutter. Katrina Williamson sniffed at the spectacle. "We have fallen upon evil days when a lot of creatures in petticoats, calling themselves women, fanatics for the most part with a sprinking of various varieties even less admirable, dictate to the voters of the state."[54]

To friends Governor Patterson accused those same voters of intellectual dishonesty in choosing both him and this legislature. On January 11, he returned the prohibition act with an eloquent veto message. Neither his grumbling nor his reasoning made the slightest difference. The Senate overrode his veto on January 19 and on the twentieth, the day the Cooper-Sharp trial opened, the House outlawed liquor in the state of Tennessee.[55]

CHAPTER FOUR

The Trial

WITHIN MINUTES AFTER the courtroom doors were opened, not one of the five hundred seats reserved for spectators remained. Filling out the crowd to the very walls were witnesses, reporters from around the nation, and prospective jurymen. Judge William Hart gaveled the vast chattering crowd to quiet and looked down to the tables where the accused, their lawyers, and the prosecutors sat. "Gentlemen, are you ready?" When they announced they were, the trial of the most noted criminal case in the history of the South began.[1]

Attorney General Jeff McCarn and co-counselors obtained a recess to study the jury list, intent upon their right to challenge men with a bias in favor of the defendants. In 1903, while special prosecutor for a group of citizens who wanted laws against gambling and Sunday tippling enforced, McCarn had been indicted for carrying a gun. Unhappy when a succession of mayors failed to pursue saloon keepers and gaming operators as rigorously as they wished, members of the group took matters into their own hands. They themselves purchased whiskey on Sunday or took a seat at the faro or poker tables, then instigated a police raid upon the establishment and arrest the violator. McCarn appeared before the city judge on the reformers' behalf and argued strenuously that the full force and effect of the law be applied.[2]

The chief prosecutor had loved Edward Carmack and followed his crusading campaign of 1908 with close attention. Two weeks after McCarn's election as attorney general in May, he wrote his hero, expressing admiration for his restraint under the charges being hurled at him. "Your conduct," McCarn assured Carmack, "draws to you thousands of indifferent Tennesseeans and binds your friends to you with hooks of steel."[3]

Like Carmack, McCarn came from Scots forebears. Born in Arkansas in 1867, the son of a teacher, merchant, and Confederate veteran, McCarn moved with his family to Texas when he was nine. Upon his father's death when McCarn was sixteen, he went to work on a ranch until he reached twenty. Providing the greatest part of his earnings to his mother, young McCarn arrived at Vanderbilt University with less than a hundred dollars. Soon he had established a bookstore catering to other students and with the profits met his expenses for four years as an undergraduate and two years in the law school. He received the LL.B. degree in 1894, later claiming that he had "got through on less work and lowest grades in the history of the institution."

Judge A. B. Neil recalled McCarn as "an able and dominant figure, a crusader against lawlessness of every kind, a young man of ability and unblemished character." But he added, "I could easily sum up McCarn's personality simply by saying that if he wanted to crack a peanut he would insist on using a sledgehammer to do it." No one in all the world "holds the name of your 'lost love' and our 'great chieftain' in more tender and sacred memory than he," Mrs. McCarn wrote Mrs. Carmack. "How often have I heard him as shaken by sobs and with faltering voice, he has turned to the pictured face on the wall and said 'Old man, come what may, I will stick by you—yes, even if it costs me my life!'"[4]

Reporters "can hear the name of almost every lawyer of prominence in the state discussed in connection with the Cooper trial when it reaches court," a Chattanooga newspaper reported within a few days of Carmack's death. One who stepped forward was Guston T. Fitzhugh, who assured the widow that he had "put agencies to work which will develop the whole truth. I am absolutely unfit for any other work save that of bringing to justice all who are involved in the awful crime."

A native of Mississippi, Fitzhugh had been born in 1866 to a professor at the state university. At that institution, young Fitzhugh became the valedictorian of the class of 1886 and three years later won his law degree. Entering practice in Memphis, he maintained an interest in politics. Fitzhugh had actively supported Carmack for Congress in 1896, and in 1900 he worked for the congressman's election to the U.S. Senate. By the time of the Cooper trial, Fitzhugh was a prominent lawyer of Memphis, enjoying mainly a chancery court practice and representing the Nashville, Chattanooga, and St. Louis Railroad and the Mutual Life Insurance Company of New York among others. He would long be remembered for prosecuting the lawsuit that ousted Memphis Mayor Edward H. Crump from office in 1916 for laxity in enforcing the prohibition statutes.[5] Assisting McCarn and Fitzhugh were Attorney General Matthew N. Whitaker of Winchester and Job B. Garner of Lawrenceburg, a former district attorney.

In the afternoon of the trial's first day, jury selection began. Both sides could strike jurors for cause. And both could refuse jurors for reasons they need not disclose. These preemptory challenges weighed in favor of the defense. The state held a total of eighteen, while the three defendants had seventy-two altogether.

Criminal Court Judge William M. Hart. Source: *Nashville American* (Sept. 5, 1910).

Jeff McCarn. Source: *A History of Tennessee and Tennesseans, The Leaders and Representative Men in Commerce Industry and Modern Activities* (1913).

For the next four weeks, the clerk of the court asked each man summoned if he owned property, if he had formed or expressed an opinion as to the guilt of the defendants, and if he was related to them or to Sam Carmack, the prosecutor and the dead man's brother. Both sides had investigators in the field and from their intelligence could probe deeper on the same points.

The first ten who answered to their names had formed an opinion about the case from what they had read of the evidence during the hearing for bail. Hart ordered them and many more who made the same admission to stand aside. Other prospective jurors claimed that business, illness, or some other cause ought to excuse them from serving.

On and on it went, hundreds called, then disqualified or challenged, and sent on their way. Before a jury could be secured, more than three thousand names would be drawn from the box, six venires summoned, and twenty-four panels exhausted. By the end of the second day, five men filled seats in the jury box. Then in the first sensation of the trial, two were challenged, one by each side, on the grounds that they had already formed an opinion. Hart dismissed them both.

While the protracted debate about these biased jurors went on, a blizzard struck the South. Nashville suffered from gale-force winds and temperatures as low as twelve degrees. Judge Hart, in good humor despite the delay in the trial, reminded the deputies delivering the subpoenas that there were warm cabins to drop into on their rides and gave them permission to take along any "necessary appliances" for the weather. "But get the jurors!" he ordered. One reporter observed that the summons bearers met with better success during the cold, finding those sought "hugging a big wood fire at home. The officers didn't have to go 'way back yonder just t'other side of the woodslot' to find the juryman."

Rural men qualified more readily than city men; the newspapers circulated more widely in Nashville than among the separated and scattered homes in the nearby countryside. A writer for one of the daily journals observed that nine out of ten men from the city "have very fixed opinions" as to the guilt or innocence of the defendants. So when the twelfth juror was finally seated, the Coopers and Sharp faced a panel comprising a businessman, a carpenter, and ten farmers.[6]

Only a few saw in these last the Jeffersonian ideal, the stalwart yeomen who owned land and lived independently by the fruits of their labor. Even in Nashville, reporters and editors called attention to the jurymen's rustic appearance and inability to read and write and assumed that this meant lack of sophistication, even impaired understanding. "Study their faces and trousers," read the caption below the photograph of the panel that appeared in the magazine published by Senator Robert Taylor and sentimentalist poet John Trotwood Moore. One expected to see such insults in the

Guston T. Fitzhugh. Source: *Tennesseans, Nineteen Hundred and One and Two* (1902).

Job Garner. Courtesy *Nashville Banner* (Dec. 11, 1936).

New York press, and Gotham did not fail to betray its provinciality. The *Herald* printed a cartoon with caricatures of the jurors, each holding up a card saying he didn't read, couldn't read, or never tried to read. On the jury box was affixed a sign, "Selected by the law for their mental qualifications, Nashville, 1909."[7]

Northeastern editors, and those who aped them, did not understand how much it mattered whether or not potential jurors read the local press. The *Banner* gave the killing a balanced coverage; but Luke Lea's *Tennessean*, making circulation war on the afternoon paper, held Carmack as the apotheosis of human virtue and Malcolm Patterson the embodiment of evil. It was not necessarily better if one steeped himself in such a source than if he remained innocent of it. A lack of reading might mean that a man was ignorant of crime as defined by statute or exploited for political ends. It did not prove that he had no sense of justice or aptitude for reasoning on the facts of the case.

Jurors Will A. Adcock, Jacob Frutiger, Shiloh Hyde, Gus Knipfer, and Caspar Schnupp all farmed land on Paradise Ridge, in northwest Davidson County. Of Hyde, little is known, nor of Adcock, save that he died mysteriously in 1939, shot in the back while hunting alone.

Jacob Frutiger proudly told the attorneys examining him that his father had brought the family to the United States from Switzerland and voted for Grant for president. Frutiger insisted that he would have to hear evidence before he could return a verdict to hang, adding that if a man is guilty he ought to be "hung," but "if he ain't quite guilty all over, he ought not to be."

Like Frutiger, Gus Knipfer was a Methodist and an immigrant, coming to the United States from Germany. He betrayed a little accent when he mentioned his native country in his testimony as a prospect for the jury. Caspar Schnupp married into the immigrant family of Antonio Molinaro. Among the possessions he brought from Italy when he arrived in 1877 were cuttings from his vines. They burgeoned and bloomed under the hot sun of Tennessee summers bearing bushels of Concord grapes.

The arrival of the families from Germany, Italy, and the Netherlands transformed Paradise Ridge into a fertile region of orchards, vineyards, and gardens. Its historian also credits the foreigners with bringing civil order to bear upon a formerly wild and bloody district. Before and just after the Civil War, the Ridge had harbored many who ran afoul of the law in the city. "Matters were regulated there without a call to court and men knew it," observed a reporter. But by the time of the Coopers' trial, police authority had been established as superior to local and vernacular justice.[8]

Of the other farmer jurors, G. A. Lane, who could read, and Robert McPherson, who could not, worked land near Donelson and Nolensville,

Nashville's new criminal courthouse. Source: *Nashville Banner* (Jan. 21, 1909).

respectively. The tenth juror selected, J. A. Woodruff, was like McPherson a friend of Sharp's. But both men testified that their oath would supersede that bond. J. H. Vaughn told the court that he had not studied any of the accounts as he could not read, nor had he discussed the case with anybody. The twelfth man chosen, William Hows of Bellevue, had served as the jury foreman in the trial of Tom Çox, Hon. William M. Hart presiding, wherein Cox was convicted of killing a policeman. Eating poison smuggled into his cell, Cox died the day before he was to hang.

Only two members of the jury pursued an occupation other than farming. E. M. Burke lived at Flat Rock, on the Nolensville Turnpike, practicing his trade as a carpenter; and even though he had read about the case and had conscientious scruples against the death penalty, he was accepted and became foreman of the jury. Frank O. Beerman, an accountant, was the only city dweller, but like many successful businessmen, he had a place in the country.[9]

Nothing indicates that any of the jurors, except Hows and Beerman, had entered a courtroom before. But the caution that Jacob Frutiger set before himself, that there might be degrees of guilt and innocence, revealed more sophistication than displayed by the lusty partisans calling for the Coopers' vindication or the ferocious supporters of Carmack who wanted them to hang.

The Jury in the case. Left to right, front row: foreman E. M. Burke, William Hows, Shiloh M. Hyde, Jacob Frutiger, Gus Knipfer, Frank O. Beerman. Back row: J. Newsom, deputy sheriff; J. A. Woodruff; A. P. Kirk, deputy sheriff; G. A. Lane, Casper Schnupp; J. M. Omohoundro, deputy sheriff; J. H. Vaughn, Will A. Adcock, Robert McPherson; T. J. Patton, deputy sheriff. Source: *Nashville Tennessean* (Feb. 14, 1909).

At twenty-five minutes after nine on February 16, the day testimony began, a heavily veiled Cobey Dunnington Carmack entered the courtroom, supported on the arms of relatives and friends. Alongside them walked a bright-faced little boy, nine year old Edward Carmack, Jr. Mrs. Carmack made her labored progress to the deep chair behind the defense table and collapsed into the cushions. Now and then she sobbed convulsively and cried out loud as Jeff McCarn read the indictment. For a time she leaned on the shoulder of her small son.

McCarn naturally called the poor woman as the state's first witness, and she was helped to the witness chair. If they did not comprehend the arguments that lay ahead, the jurymen would remember the prostrate widow, wringing her hands, and little Ned on her right, his fist clenched as he tried to keep back his tears. Hardly able to respond to the lawyers' questions, Mrs. Carmack added nothing to what was already known about her husband's death.

The state's chief witness, Mrs. Charles Eastman, followed on the stand. A prominent clubwoman, she was Senator Carmack's friend and landlady, and one of the people who saw him die.

Kate Eastman recounted important details of the terrible event. She recognized the editor as he approached her, raised his hat, and started to pass to her left after a word of friendly greeting. Then from behind she heard a voice, an "old voice," which called out, "Well, here you are all right, I have the drop on you now." And she watched as a look of surprised inquiry passed over Carmack's face. Within seconds Carmack fired, Robin Cooper returned fire, and the dead man's corpse slammed against the pavement and lay still.

None there could comprehend all that took place in those few moments, and Mrs. Eastman had shared in the confusion. She testified that Carmack's weapon seemed to hitch in his pocket and believed he could not have loosened it in time to shoot before he was shot. She did not see Robin Cooper leap onto the sidewalk but only observed him at the south utility pole after Carmack's corpse lay bleeding in the street.[10]

And that was of almighty importance. The prosecutors argued that young Cooper had crossed Seventh Avenue, not on a straight line to reach his beleaguered father, but to the south, down and below the utility poles. Then, claimed the state, he walked up behind Carmack and shot him in the back of the head.

Befuddled jurors, expectant audience, and all the world met the defense's flamboyant associate counsel on the first day of the trial. So handsome he might have been in theater, William Henry Washington often held the stage in the trial and dramatically so in its closing days.

Washington traced his line from the progenitor of George Washington's

Kate Eastman. Source: *The* [Nashville] *Democrat* (Feb. 2, 1913).

John M. Anderson. Source: *Nashville Banner* (Jan. 21, 1909).

family in the New World and possessed the most impressive formal credentials among lawyers on both sides. Washington was elected attorney general for Nashville in 1878 and convicted the treasurer of the state, Marsh Polk, for stealing $366,000 of public money. In 1907 in the court of Judge Hart he presented the state's case against Dr. Herman Feist on the charge of killing Mrs. Rosa Mangrum, opposite John Anderson for the defense.[11]

Now, cross-examining for the defense, Washington won from Mrs. Eastman the admission that Colonel Cooper's outstretched hand held nothing, that she saw no shots fired by anyone, and that she was "laboring under great emotion, great excitement," and so could not give Cooper's words to Carmack exactly. Still, she boldly clung to her interpretation of what happened. When she heard the voice from behind her and saw Carmack draw his pistol, Washington asked, "Who did you expect to do the fighting?"

Answered Mrs. Eastman, "I expected the man who called him a coward in my rear and told him to get from behind a woman was going to do it on the one hand, and I presumed Mr. Carmack was going to defend himself. . . . I thought Colonel Cooper did [the shooting]." Thus Washington failed to undo the basic damage the witness had done: putting Robin

William H. Washington. Source: *Tennesseans, Nineteen Hundred and One and Two* (1902).

Cooper south of the poles and depicting Carmack as in a pleasant frame
of mind when set upon. "He wasn't in a fighting mood," she testified. "The
voice attracted his attention and was in a way an assault . . . he was not
the aggressor."[12]

The state followed with a drumfire of corroboration. John Tindall, a
twelve year old newsboy, claimed that he overheard Colonel Cooper say
to Robin, "We'll get him," or "We'll catch him," as the two men walked past
him on the corner of Fourth and Church in the direction of the Arcade.
Carey Folk, a civil servant, had been walking along the north side of Union
Street when he saw Colonel Cooper laboring up the hill toward the corner
where Robin Cooper and John Sharp stood in conversation. "'Are you going up this way?'" Folk heard Robin ask his father, nodding toward Seventh
Avenue, North. "Colonel Cooper replied exactly or in substance, 'No, I will
wait awhile yet.'"[13]

And John Sharp knew what was about to happen, according to Miss
Skeffington, the state's next witness. When she asked Sharp what the shooting was, he answered, "'It's Dunc Cooper shooting Senator Carmack.'"

Mary Skeffington. Source: Tennessee House of Representatives.

No fewer than six men subsequently testified that Sharp had in their hearing cursed Carmack and damned him to hell.[14]

McCarn proceeded to preempt the defense's argument that Carmack prepared himself to meet Cooper. The state called Finley Dorris, the undertaker, who received the corpse and searched through the pockets. He had kept the clothing at his establishment in his private wardrobe. When attorneys Washington and M. Henry Meeks of the defense asked to examine them, he gave his permission. According to a member of the funeral parlor's staff, Washington had tried on Carmack's coat, reached his hand into the right pocket, then drawn it out, exclaiming, "What is this?" He grasped a pistol scabbard, a rubber shield that fitted over the muzzle and along the barrel of a pistol and kept it from rending the cloth.

In his questions of the witness, Washington got onto the record and into the jury's hearing the possibility that Carmack was stripping the scabbard from his gun when he swept his left hand to his right side. McCarn for his part elicited from Dorris the statement that he had twice searched the clothing without finding the scabbard, leaving the jury to infer that someone planted it there.[15] Then, after only four days of testimony, McCarn and his associates rested their case. The jury retired to their quarters

M. Henry Meeks. Source: *Nashville Banner* (Aug. 6, 1910).

upstairs for two days' respite, as lawyers for the defense prepared to call Robin Cooper.[16]

The trend of public sentiment seemed against the Coopers during the weeks following their arrest. James D. Anderson, an editor at the *Tennessean*, named several friends of the colonel who thought he deserved conviction. Railed Anderson, "I believe Duncan Cooper ought to be hanged by the neck until he is dead, dead, dead."[17]

Anderson's vituperative letter was addressed to his brother, former Judge John McFerrin Anderson of Nashville, resting from chronic respiratory trouble at a Colorado sanitarium. His sibling's opinion notwithstanding, John Anderson became head of the brace of lawyers for the defendants. To the task he brought experience as chancellor and, before that, judge of the criminal court and city attorney.

Born in 1862 in Nashville, Anderson chose the law as his work while a boy, or through his temperament or parental suggestion, it chose him. Besides reading the standard texts under a lawyer's tutelage, he rode into Gallatin from his parents' Sumner County farm to attend the circuit court and "better learn how the thing was done." The practitioners he admired combined analysis and oratory, arguing their cases for hours without notes.

Fewer volumes in Anderson's library related to criminal law than to any other subject. Nonetheless his brother recalled his many victories for defendants, even when those victories were compromises like jail and penitentiary sentences. "To one client Judge Anderson was peculiarly indebted for a record as an attorney who never had a client hanged by law," James Anderson wrote, since Tom Cox had taken his own life in his prison cell.

In 1900 Anderson left the bench of the Criminal Court to become attorney for the corporation that operated the city's electric light and street car systems. J. C. Bradford, president of the Nashville Railway and Light Company, put the opportunity in Anderson's way. The young attorney won a major victory for the line that consolidated under its control three companies formerly operating streetcars in the city. Anderson defended the turfmen who deliberately broke the state's anti-betting law for a test case, and won his clients' acquittal when Judge William Hart voided the measure on constitutional grounds.

In cases that lay in the future, Anderson would represent Vanderbilt University in its struggle for independence against the bishops of the Methodist Church. Other clients included the Tennessee Central Railroad, the Standard Oil Company, and the giant private utility, the Tennessee Electric Power Company.[18] Also sitting at the defense table, representing John Sharp, was M. Henry Meeks, fifty-seven, a native of McNairy County, Tennessee, an alumnus of the law school of Cumberland University, and a former attorney general.[19]

His Honor William M. Hart looked out on the raucous proceedings as few others in the courtroom did, with patience and a sense of irony. He never betrayed his sympathies, although he possessed some. He tolerated the protracted squabbles that filled page after page of the record. He used his gavel lightly, but ruled firmly, and he sent the case to the jury with utter fairness. Hart often recessed court on a jocular note or settled a point with mild repartee. He seemed glad to puncture any pretense and often chided the attorneys for making speeches rather than arguing the case. But it was his comic invention that would cause students of the case to smile, so many years after all those there and the world they lived in were long dead and the hatred they bore their opponents and the fierce loyalty they felt for friends had been reduced to slender accounts in neglected books.

"Your Honor," pleaded one of the reluctant veniremen, "I've been trying to get this woman to marry me for years. She has finally said she would, and I'm afraid if I have to serve, she'll change her mind. What must I do?"

Hart, no doubt appearing grave and sympathetic, said, "Serve on the jury." Immediately he relented and let the anxious groom go. To the packed courtroom, he said, "Six months from now, he'll be back in here, saying he wished like anything I had made him serve."

Robin Cooper on the stand. Source: *Nashville Banner* (Feb. 23, 1909).

Sixty-four when he presided over the Cooper trial, Hart had as an attorney made a specialty of criminal law. He served as assistant attorney general from 1886 to 1894 when he made an unsuccessful race for the chief prosecutor's post. Hart returned to his profession until 1900 when Governor Benton McMillin named him to an interim appointment as judge of the Criminal Court, succeeding John M. Anderson. In 1902, he defeated temperance champion I. L. Pendleton, whom the Reverend Sam Jones endorsed from the pulpit of the Gospel Tabernacle.[20]

How small a world it was, the bench and bar of this Southern capital at the beginning of the twentieth century. In 1909, Nashville had approximately two hundred lawyers serving a population of one hundred and ten thousand people, or one attorney for every five hundred citizens. And James Anderson remembered that his brother "was no exception to the general rule that lawyers render much service to friends and kindred and others free of charge." Seventy years later, the Nashville bar comprised seventeen hundred lawyers, and the population had grown to four hundred and fifty-five thousand, making a ratio of one to every two hundred and fifty. But legal advice and counsel was priced well above what persons having the median income of families in the city could afford. Only destitute people could obtain free help.[21]

The lawyers in the Cooper case lived and practiced their profession in a world of kinship, friendship, and knowledge carried to the heart. The newspapers could refer to players in the drama by name or title and surname, aware that their readers would know all the rest. Such cryptic information occasionally frustrates the historian, yet of itself reveals the compact setting in which the Coopers were tried.

On Saturday, February 20, the defense called Robin Cooper, the most important witness in the case.

Questioned by Anderson, Cooper testified with calm self-possession, in a quiet, polite, plain-spoken way. He portrayed Colonel Cooper as angry, but not homicidal, on the morning of Carmack's last editorial, and he told the jury that he remonstrated with his father for conveying to Carmack the words about the town not being big enough for both of them if the colonel's name appeared again in the *Tennessean*. The state objected when he added, "I warned him that Senator Carmack might resent the message which had been sent to him." Here at first blush was the defense's strategy to portray Carmack as seething with prideful rage, determined to have his way, armed and poised to meet his enemy.

Cooper related the circumstances of his anxious morning through his obtaining a pistol, finding his father, and helping obtain his promise to stay off the streets until the three o'clock conference in Bradford's office. Then from the time of the agreement made there, he testified, he had been satisfied about his father's acceding to peace, but still wary for his safety because Carmack knew nothing of that resolution.

Then Robin Cooper told how he killed Edward Carmack.

When his father started in Carmack's direction, he hesitated then gave way to his apprehension. "After he had gotten about half way across the street, I felt it was my duty, as he was my father, and that I believed he was unable to protect himself, if he should be attacked, to go with him and be there if Senator Carmack should attack him."

The sight of Carmack drawing his pistol "paralyzed me for a moment," Cooper said. But as Carmack made for the utility posts, "intuitively I jumped forward on to the sidewalk between my father and Senator Carmack.

"A shot exploded, it seems to me, almost in my face. I could see the pistol and Senator Carmack's arm. He was standing right in the gutter at the lower, or the south post. . . ." That bullet hit Cooper's tie, dislodged the jewel from the stickpin, and struck him in the shoulder. "Just as quick as I could, I started toward that south pole," Cooper recalled. "And as I started towards the south pole, a second shot came between the posts." This bullet tore through the left sleeve of his coat.

"Go on and state now," his counsel directed.

"As I stepped to the south pole, I put my hand on it, and stepped around to the curbing; and instantly when I stepped around, Senator Carmack had stepped back, it seemed to me, two or three steps, or four or five . . . his pistol pointed at me, looking towards me, and his side slightly to me, and I fired as quickly as I could."

"Why is it that you shot Senator Carmack?" Anderson asked.

"I believed that he would kill me if I didn't," Cooper answered.

"Did you believe that it was necessary to kill him at that time, or to shoot him at that time?"

Over McCarn's objection, the court let the defendant answer.

"I do. I think if I had waited an instant later he would have shot me again; I believed it then; I do now."

Thus, Robin Cooper put forward his case for self-defense. Anderson tried to impress upon the jurors' minds the force and effect of Carmack's firing. He made the defendant put on the coat with the bullet hole through the sleeve, and he passed Cooper's bloodstained shirt over to the panel.

Anderson boldly turned to the mysterious bullet Cooper had found in his hospital bed. Was the ball from the first shot still in his shoulder? Anderson asked. Cooper believed it was not, since on his first morning in convalescence, he had discovered a bullet under the covers, down about his knees. He produced the slug. Anderson had him match it to a shell case found near Carmack's body, and they fit.[22]

The defense finished its questions on Saturday evening. The trial resumed on Monday morning with a packed courtroom, audience come to hear McCarn cross-examine the witness. Robin Cooper remained cool, courteous, and respectful under the prosecutor's onslaught. His brow was wrinkled at times, but on occasion his face bore a smile.

After obtaining at length Cooper's account of his movements on the day he killed Carmack, McCarn turned to the most damaging testimony against the defendants. Did the witness know why the lad John Tindall should perjure himself? What about the two witnesses who had sworn that Cooper had broken into their conversation on the streetcar into town and cursed Carmack? And Carey Folk and Mrs. Eastman, did Cooper know what reason they would have to lie under oath? Over objection by his counsel, the court allowed Cooper to answer.

"Of my own knowledge, I do not, no sir," Robin replied each time. McCarn allowed him to state that these witnesses' statements were false and that each one misconstrued what they heard. But the defense's mild objection to the whole line of questions and Cooper's polite answers must have left the impression in the jury's mind that McCarn wished.

The prosecuting attorney brought Cooper down from the stand and had him demonstrate how the editor had stood in the gutter, north of him. "The pistol was about at his breast," Cooper said, ". . . pointing in my direction." McCarn asked Cooper where he had his pistol aimed.

"I didn't point it at any particular spot; I just shot at him. I didn't take any aim," Cooper answered. "He had backed back some, but we were very close together."

Did the witness know that a Colt automatic was the most deadly pocket pistol? Was he aware that the weapon could be fired three times within a half-second? Could it not shoot more rapidly than the Smith and Wesson .38 picked up from the street near Carmack's outstretched hand? Cooper claimed he had very little knowledge of the gun he had wielded in so deadly a fashion.

McCarn spent a great deal of time on the wound that Carmack inflicted in Cooper's right shoulder. Before the prosecutor cut him off, Cooper made the point that the wound had been probed only slightly and dressed but not packed. With a few more inconclusive questions, he allowed Cooper to step aside, having failed in any important particular to undermine his account of the killing of Carmack.[23] Throughout his days on the stand, Cooper's testimony remained consistent and constant. Except for statements by Mrs. Eastman that she never saw Robin until he was at the post, the state introduced no proof to support its theory that Cooper crossed Seventh, came up to Carmack from behind, and shot him in the back.

When the defense called John D. Sharp to the stand following Robin Cooper, a ripple of excitement passed over the courtroom. Many interpreted the move to mean that Colonel Cooper would not testify.

Meeks examining, Sharp told the jury that, except for greeting Colonel Cooper as he sat talking with Mrs. Williamson at the Maxwell House, he did not see or speak with the other defendants on Monday until they came up to him in the Arcade. "Colonel Cooper made a request of me to go up to the Governor's mansion with him," the former sheriff continued. No one mentioned Carmack's name during the walk of several minutes that brought them to the corner of Seventh and Union.

Sharp told the jury that after Colonel Cooper broke away from Robin's grip, he, Sharp, continued across Vine Street in the direction of his home. "Many things ran through my mind," Sharp testified. "It occurred to me that his son was very anxious to get his father to come on. Then with the Colonel's action in springing away, it occurred to me that the result of the meeting might be more serious than at first anticipated."

Sharp turned around to look. In that dramatic moment, others on the scene had their perceptions wrenched by fear and excitement, but not Sharp. He told the jury how Carmack drew his pistol and moved toward the poles; that Robin Cooper jumped on the sidewalk and "got somewhere near the opposite of the poles." Carmack fired twice. Then "Robin proceeded south and I saw a drawn pistol in Robin's hand, and he opened fire on Senator Carmack."

"How many times did he fire?" Meeks asked.

"Three times," said Sharp without hesitation.

"Then what?"

"I saw Senator Carmack fall."

Sharp was equally precise about his conversation with Miss Skeffington a few moments later.

"She asked me, 'Mr. Sharp, what was that?' I said, 'Shooting between Cooper and Carmack. . . . And I fear Mr. Carmack has been killed.'"

Job Garner cross-examined the witness, accusing Sharp at times of evading his questions. Finally he forced him to agree that if the Coopers "hadn't proceeded south, there would have been no killing at the telephone poles that time, would there?" If Carmack had wanted to kill Colonel Cooper, what prevented the editor from shooting him as he stood there on the sidewalk? Sharp was unable to say.

The witness testified that when Carmack first fired his face was toward Robin Cooper. Then "as Robin fired his first shot, Carmack turned his head away from Robin and kinder danced around that way."

Garner bore down on this crucial point. "Did he turn so that Robin might shoot him in the back of the neck so that the bullet might come straight out under his tongue?"

"I don't know," Sharp went on doggedly, "but he turned his head to the right."[24]

Did Sharp really recall in almost preternatural detail the events that he witnessed from at least fifty yards away? Or had he during the long hours in jail with his friends reconstructed those few seconds down by the utility poles? It cannot be known. But the state did not vigorously pursue the conviction of Sharp. They wanted him as defendant so he could not be a defense witness. He corroborated Robin Cooper's testimony, but did so as an indicted conspirator in Carmack's murder.

If the defense had stopped there, the outcome of the trial might have been different. Instead, their lawyers put Colonel Cooper on the stand, and he convicted himself and his son.

"Be temperate and restrained in this trial," Katrina Williamson warned the colonel. "Please do not give way to any reckless impulses of speech. Do guard well that unruly member the tongue and repress indignation or any emotion." She knew her friend, and she pleaded, "Can you, will you listen to me this one time?" Taking the stand, the colonel seated himself well back in the witness chair and crossed his right leg over his left. Throughout the two days of questioning, he punctuated his answers with gestures with first one hand, then the other, sometimes thrusting his glasses out before him. One reporter thought that Cooper's testimony revealed "his natural habit to command those about him." But the writer also observed what Mrs. Williamson dreaded: "If the old gentleman desired to say something, he said it invariably."[25]

Cooper maintained his composure under the gentle probing of his own counsel. William Washington led him through the history of the relations between himself and Carmack, from the days when the colonel brought the young editor to Nashville through their merely formal dealings during the campaign of 1906 to the time of the bitter primary two years later. At first Carmack "ceased to speak entirely on meeting," Cooper said. Then there came the first real note of discord between them, an editorial by Carmack in a Memphis newspaper in March 1908.

Over the state's objection that authorship had not been proved, Judge Hart ruled that since Colonel Cooper had relied upon information attributing the editorial to Carmack the jury could hear the part that offended him. Mr. Washington read the paragraph the judge marked.

> . . . We may mention Col. D. B. Cooper of Davidson, and Col. Robert M. Gates, of Madison, both of whom are gentlemen of many amiable qualities, who have been consistent bolters and have at last come together in the rivalry of enthusiastic devotion to the political interests of the first Governor the L & N Railroad in all its history of crime, political debauchery and general corruption and degradation ever actually owned.[26]

Then in the gubernatorial debates, "it was a daily occurrence for him to use my name," the colonel insisted, "first in a spirit of ridicule, then it began to carry veiled insinuations of corruption." After the primary, Carmack took up the cudgels against him in the *Tennessean*, Cooper recounted. Washington placed in evidence the editorials that linked the defendant with divekeepers of Black Bottom and that accused him and his allies in the governor's camp of buying votes for Patterson and Taft with "money of the gin dives, and the crap dives and the faro joints."

By that history the witness and his lawyer came to Sunday, the eighth of November. The colonel let Ed Craig go to Carmack that evening, then heard Craig out. "He stated to me that nothing could be done, that [Carmack] was in an ugly humor, or words to that effect, and that he was sorry to tell me that he could accomplish nothing. And he left me without at all indicating that Mr. Carmack had indicated to him, but he said to me, of his own motion, your name will not appear any more. . . . I believed he knew what he was speaking of, although I had no promise through him from Mr. Carmack."

In his account of his peregrinations around town the next day, Cooper depicted himself as amenable to his daughter's fears and to his friends' entreaties. Over vigorous objection from the state and long arguments based in Tennessee opinions, Cooper's counsel won him an opportunity to state whether the result of Bradford's peace conference was satisfactory "from a pacific or belligerent standpoint." Cooper sidestepped the chance; he insisted he "did not agree not to send the note."

Cooper managed to hold himself in peace as he recounted the walk to the corner where Carmack died. Then he described how he turned from his son's grip and saw the editor approaching in their direction.

> The impulse formed at that moment that I would go and remove all of this condition that was distressing my friends and worrying them to death, and worrying my children and me, and I would go over and have a direct, plain talk with Mr. Carmack. He had known me well, and I had known him well. I went over to have that talk directly with him, to protest against this constant attack upon me, and see if it couldn't be stopped.[27]

The elder Cooper's testimony revealed both his powerful wish to silence Carmack and his apparent passivity before his friends' and family members' influence. He wrote the editor two notes, but he held back from sending either. He had shown Robin Cooper the borrowed pistol and declared his readiness to meet Carmack, then casually went to buy a horse and wait while it was shod. He told his daughter that he was as likely to kill Carmack as Carmack was to kill him; then he left his intimate friend Mrs. Williamson to understand that peace was in the offing. He apparently gave little thought to the effect of his words, even as he charged Carmack to take full responsibility for his.

The colonel probably told the truth when he testified that he decided on the spur of the moment that he would talk forcefully with Carmack. But as Cooper crossed Union Street, the anger rose up again in him like bile. He started down Seventh Avenue through the gloom, heedless of the consequences.

Guston Fitzhugh for the state returned to that corner, after some hours of pitiless cross-examination. But first the Memphis attorney probed back, down, and deep into Cooper's past. ("There is bones from one end of his life to the other," Jeff McCarn once told the court, "there is nothing in his pathway but blood and bones.") Fitzhugh tried to introduce evidence that Cooper had failed to pay over certain moneys that he received for selling property under decree of the Chancery Court in Maury County, when he was its clerk and master almost forty years before.

Washington leaped to his feet, objecting that this matter was remote. But Fitzhugh responded, Weren't these charges "ten thousand times stronger than the trifling editorials which are claimed by him to be the cause of this wounded feeling of honor?"

Judge Anderson rose and faced the bench. "It has never been insisted, may it please the Court, that Mr. Cooper killed Senator Carmack on account of anything Mr. Carmack said about Colonel Cooper."

Mr. Fitzhugh asked Anderson, "Was it not your contention, and is it not now your contention, that the witness now on the stand was laboring under great distress on account of the alleged attacks on his honor?"

"Yes, sir," Anderson replied, "but it was not that that produced this killing. Our theory is that Robin Cooper killed Senator Carmack in self defense."

Hart allowed the state to introduce the matter about Cooper's conduct of his office, holding that the jury could decide whether it bore any significance when considered with the whole weight of the evidence. The colonel acknowledged that his brother Edmund, one of his sureties, had satisfied claims against him during his first term, totaling the full penalties of his official bond.[28]

Having struck deeply with the charge of malfeasance, Fitzhugh twisted the knife. Did not Marshall Polk, the former state treasurer who stole several hundred thousand dollars, invest that money in a walnut business in connection with Cooper?

Not one dollar, Cooper shot back.

Continued Fitzhugh, "Is it not also true that M. T. Polk, while Treasurer

of the State of Tennessee, invested ten thousand dollars . . . in the effort
of yours to purchase the *Daily American* of Nashville?" And didn't the witness know that due bills of his, amounting to tens of thousands of dollars,
had been found in Polk's rooms?

"No, sir, none on this earth. This is absolutely false. If there ever was
one there, it was a forgery and absolutely false." Cooper, like all his clan,
cherished his friends, and described Polk as "as loyal and big hearted a man
as I ever knew." Having pinned him to the mat, Fitzhugh asked Cooper if
he had been in earnest or was he bluffing when he sent word to Carmack
his name must not again be published or the town wasn't big enough to
hold them both?

"Well, I have always believed that a man who kept a fighting tongue
should keep a fighting body," Cooper answered.

The prosecutors had set out to make him angry, by the same deliberate method that Carmack had done: charging him with corruption and at-
tacking his friends. He responded in the same impulsive way.

Fitzhugh drove on. Did he see anything in the debate at Nashville in
reference to him? At Tullahoma? At Sparta?

Cooper said Carmack referred to him "practically every day."

"What do you mean by 'practically'?" Fitzhugh asked.

"Well, you define that meaning yourself," Cooper replied. "If you cannot understand it, possibly the jury can. . . . I heard of them practically
every time they came up." He evaded Fitzhugh's question, from whom?
"Gentlemen talked to me about it [in] the general connection of ridicule."

Didn't he swear that his name occurred in the debates every day after
a certain date? asked Fitzhugh. And he demanded, "Is it true or not?"
evidently lunging in the direction of the witness chair.

Anderson leaped up to object. "Counsel should keep his seat. There
is no use of violence." But Cooper joined in the row. "Let that go. I encourage that. I like to see it, that is pleasant."

Why had he not objected to any editorials except Carmack's critical
of himself or the Patterson administration? Fitzhugh wanted to know. "Did
you send any note expressing your resentment, and giving any threats to
the editors?"

"Nor did I for that article," answered the witness, referring to the editorial in the Memphis *News-Scimitar* in March 1908. "It went on months
and months afterwards before I did that, before patience ceased to be a virtue." As for other editors' attacks, there had been no personal malignancy
at the bottom of them, he told the court.

Returning to the Sunday night interview with Edward Craig, Fitzhugh
asked, "Now, Colonel Cooper, if you had received a message from a gentleman that if you did a certain thing again that the town wouldn't be big enough
to hold both of you, how would you have constructed that language?"

"We object to that as argumentative," Washington called out, but Cooper had started to anwer.

"I would—"

"Wait a minute, Colonel, when we object," his counsel begged.

"I want to answer that so bad." Hart ruled he could do so. Cooper's reply was the one Fitzhugh sought, having prepared his witness to make another outburst.

"I would have either quit offensively using it," the colonel growled, "or I would have prepared myself to meet him." By this time his lawyers must have put their elbows on the table and cupped their faces in their hands.

At midday, fatigued and perhaps sensing that he had hurt himself and his case, Cooper lapsed into an anecdote. He had the year before borrowed money against Riverwood, but just as he received the loan he heard of the needs and hardships of an old Confederate soldier, and he gave the money to him. "I have never mentioned it to this time, but you have asked about the black deeds, and I want to let it all come out, the good as well as the black."

They resumed that afternoon, for the end of the cross-examination. Fitzhugh led Cooper into admitting that he used profane language—"I am given to swearing pretty freely"—and may well have done so on the morning of Carmack's death, when he met with Craig on Sunday night and Robin Cooper on Monday morning. Hadn't he in fact said he would rather be in hell or go to the devil than to stand the attacks?

"I have no recollection of using that language. I may have said everything. I don't know."

"If you said it, you meant it, didn't you?" Fitzhugh goaded him.

"I might have done so, and I might not, I don't know what the context of that statement was. I would have to have it all." Denying, evading, weaving back and forth, Cooper once again allowed Fitzhugh's charges to stand.

The prosecutor led the witness to acknowledge that he had not been gainfully employed for ten years, that James C. Bradford ("the closest friend that I had on earth") had helped when he "needed a dollar in distress," and that Cooper was a betting man.

"Colonel, you have gambled a good deal, haven't you?"

"Gambled a good deal, yes, as you have."

"That was one reason you didn't have enough to pay your honest debts, wasn't it?" The court sustained the defense's objection to the question, but Fitzhugh had it before the jury of yeomen.

Having depicted the witness as a profane, dissolute, intemperate man, Fitzhugh suggested that he could have prevented the tragedy, "You didn't say, 'Mr. Carmack, we are here on a peaceful mission'? 'We want no difficulty,'? Didn't you say "'It is damned cowardly to get behind a woman with a pistol'?"

"I did," Cooper acknowledged. "I said that."

"Couldn't you have said the other in the same time that you said that?"

"I might have said anything."

And when Carmack made his way toward the poles, wasn't his pistol pointed in the witness's direction? The colonel conceded that it was.

"What prevented his firing at any time?"

"God in heaven knows; I don't."

"What did you expect to say to [Senator Carmack] when you got there?" the lawyer asked. Fitzhugh counted on Cooper to entrap himself, and throughout his brilliant cross-examination, he gave the defendant ample opportunities. Angry, hostile, arrogant, Cooper missed none of them. Now Cooper waded into another damaging statement.

"I had made up my mind, the method of thought. We had known each other a long time, was in my mind, and this was folly, the line it was going on, and that it should cease, and if not, if it didn't cease, that I would retaliate in kind."

Now the prosecutor moved in. "So you were going on a peaceful mission ... with the fixed purpose to say to him, if you don't stop, I am going to expose your personal life; that is the peaceful mission you were on, wasn't it?"

The colonel lashed back, "I was not on a peaceful mission. I was on a mission to stop this attack on me."

"And you were going to have peace if you had to kill somebody for it?" Fitzhugh charged. "Weren't you seized with a mad impulse to kill?"

Cooper denied it, saying, "I never had the impulse to kill anything in my life." But Fitzhugh closed the review of the events by asking Cooper to recall how Carmack's body lay in the street. "I don't know. It was an unpleasant thing, distressing in the extreme. . . . The tragedy was enacted and over, and I got my boy and started to his relief."

Fitzhugh was done, and he closed with simple grace. "That is all," he said. Court recessed for the day, and all of them left the courthouse, the jury, too, walking with sheriff's deputies for the exercise that these countrymen missed in their confinement.[29]

Cooper's calamitous testimony under cross-examination countered his own counsel's strategy, which was to prove that the case was not about the editorials but about Edward Carmack's shooting Robin Cooper and the young lawyer's returning fire before he was fired upon again. As the trial drew to an end, the defense displayed new power and authority for this interpretation and forced the state to try to refute it.

Governor Patterson took the stand on Saturday, the 27th. Judge Hart,

Opposite: **Governor Patterson testifies for the defense. Courtesy Tennessee State Library and Archives.**

James C. Bradford. Source: *Tennesseans, Nineteen Hundred and One and Two* (1902).

having previously ruled that a witness might give the results of a meeting or conference but not indirect quotations from it, dismissed the jury at the request of both sides. The move allowed the defense to place in the record the governor's account of what had passed between him, Colonel Cooper, and the others who met at the Maxwell House.

Mr. Anderson resumed. Patterson recounted arriving at the Maxwell House to find Cooper dictating a letter. (One of the few men who might keep the governor of Tennessee waiting, the colonel told him that he would be with him in a few minutes.) Patterson added the detail that when J. C. Bradford took this letter from the colonel, he said to the kin and friends gathered around that he would settle the matter with honor to both parties. Patterson recalled Robin Cooper's anxious state and tearful countenance. But when the jury was brought back, the account that the court allowed Patterson to give only corroborated that Cooper had turned over the note to Bradford and agreed to the three o'clock meeting.

Here before the world sat the man whom Mrs. Edward Carmack and many others accused of conspiring with the defendants to murder her husband. Here was the governor who his enemies said drove on a juggernaut a political machine built in the roundhouses of the L & N and stoked by illicit money from the saloons. Yet Patterson was allowed to step down with no questions from the state. The prosecution was aware that many of the jurors had supported the governor in the last election.[30]

McCarn and associates had bought the services of the physician who exhumed Carmack's body and conducted an autopsy. He was Dr. McPheeters Glasgow, and what he discovered would not hang the Coopers and John Sharp. Naturally, McCarn refused to call him as a witness. Now Anderson did. The prosecution was on its feet, objecting that Glasgow was theirs and if they did not want him to testify, that was that. Finally McCarn relented when the defense agreed to settle the state's bill for the doctor's services.

Anderson led Glasgow through Carmack's wounds in the order the defense believed they happened: side, shoulder, neck. But did death come instantly, as the first two bullets penetrated vital organs? Glasgow under questioning by Fitzhugh testified that medical literature recorded cases where victims had lived after receiving a gunshot wound through the heart. As to the severing of the spinal cord, it could have produced a spasm through the body followed by paralysis. If paralysis had been instantaneous, Carmack would not have been capable of any voluntary action and the cigar he held would have dropped from his hand. Since it had not, the jury was left to reason, perhaps he survived for a few moments, long enough to shoot Robin Cooper after Cooper had shot him in the back of the head.[31]

The gentlemen of the defense would not have it. They called one S. J. Benning, a pitiable, apparently eccentric man who swore that he had seen Carmack twirling the cylinder of his pistol. The state put on witnesses who overheard Benning to say that if he had been on the scene "five minutes earlier" he would have seen the killing. McCarn foolishly had Benning arrested for perjury.[32]

And so the testimony came to an end. Both sides agreed to three speeches each in the closing arguments.

Guston Fitzhugh opened on Monday morning, March 8. Once again, he distinguished himself to the damage of the defendants. He interpreted the testimony to show that Colonel Cooper had gambled, welshed on his debts, and embezzled money. The defendant could have found no offense in the editorials, unless he was searching them "with jaundiced eye and malicious heart," argued Fitzhugh. Craig knew what Cooper meant, and the senator's friend warned him. Yet Carmack returned no threat; so "the only effect in [Cooper's] not sending the note was to catch Carmack off his guard and shoot him down like a dog."

Fitzhugh put forward two principles to which the state adhered to the last in the prosecution of the Coopers. In crossing the street and hurling angry words at Carmack, the colonel committed an overt act to carry out the threats he had made against Carmack; thereby he could not argue that the killing was self-defense. And if the father was at fault the son must be equally guilty: Did not Robin Cooper admit he went over to help his father, and did not the colonel testify that he drew his gun to kill Carmack if he killed Robin? "Oh, gentlemen," he asked, "what chance did Senator Carmack have?" After nearly five hours on his feet, Fitzhugh finished, his voice nearly broken. Carmack's life inspired men like this to defend his memory, and Fitzhugh did so with fortitude and eloquence.

On Tuesday morning, Henry Meeks opened for the defense. He began with the abstract proposition that "when a man uses the freedom of the press for the purpose of persecution and insult, he's an enemy to the country and an enemy to society." But the Coopers' meeting with Carmack "was entirely accidental." Meeks' client John Sharp had only been indicted to throttle his evidence. All Sharp had done and said on the corner of Seventh and Union followed from his reasoning that trouble would ensue when Duncan Cooper pulled away from Robin Cooper and started over towards Carmack since the colonel and the editor were bitterly estranged.

For the state, Job Garner stood to reply. He asked the jury to remember that "whatever Carmack may have said in editorials or debates, the law says that does not justify the taking of human life." As for "the unwritten law" that Meeks alluded to, "is it not going too far to apply it to editorial writers?" Meeks had tried to make the jurymen feel the pain of Carmack's assaults in print. Garner, and the prosecution generally, made Carmack's peril and undoing more vivid and searing. Reviewing how certain witnesses had sacrificed to give their testimony—Miss Lee, for example, who had resigned her job—he arrived at the case of Mrs. Eastman.

> You know what an impression she made, with her white hair not indicative of years, but an adornment from God Almighty. I sat at her feet as she gave her testimony—it reminded me of my dear mother....

Yet, "they say she lied!" Garner stormed. "Hell never instigated a blacker calumny. They say you can't believe a woman because you can throw a dead lizard among them and they will scatter."

In this high dungeon, the young Lawrenceburg attorney closed over the issue of the scabbard. "The state didn't put that scabbard in the pocket, but somebody put it there. Why fabricate the evidence if you are innocent?"

Then began the great marathon argument, part of the lore of the trial, the closing speech of Washington that lasted nine and a half hours. For that herculean effort, what did he accomplish? He tried to plant the idea in his listeners' minds that Carmack's purpose in writing the editorials had been "hitting at Patterson." Here was the defense's portrait of Carmack the aggressor. He had wanted all along to provoke Cooper, Washington insisted. He penned "'The Diplomat of the Zweibund' for the purpose of making Colonel Cooper write him a note or oppose him on the street—he didn't care which." Washington went on to depict how Lander's message about the colonel's intent to kill the editor on sight had converted him into a "stick of dynamite, a powder keg."

Washington taunted and tweaked opposing counsel, not caring if he provoked an explosion himself. "Garner belongs to that class of lawyers that can't treat a witness fairly," he told the audience. "Did you ever see a bee-martin flying at a hawk? Now, I don't mean to call Garner a bee-martin for the bee-martin has good qualities and is a valuable bird. The simile came into my mind, however, when I saw that big, honest man John Sharp writhing under the attacks of this bee-martin." To general laughter, Washington promised that one of the things he was going to avoid in the future was going through the Arcade.

Washington set up a pair of spittoons and showed how Carmack could most certainly have fired between them. (Garner had staged the same demonstration using lawbooks and proved to his satisfaction the opposite.) As for Robin Cooper, he had a right to be there. Washington's voice rose, hurling his words at the jury, "He would have been a cur if he had not been there!"

The state had presented no theory about who shot whom and in what order, Washington accurately pointed out. But he believed that Carmack had seen his opportunity, to make the poles not a shelter but a breastwork, and taken advantage of it. Then the defense attorney overdrew his point, as both sides continually did. Robin Cooper had been only a "peaceful bystander," who had stood "in perfect amazement" until he was shot twice.

Like Garner, Washington fixated on the problem of the scabbard. If it had been in the overcoat pocket where he found it, that seemed to say that Carmack had pulled it out of the barrel when he swept his left hand across to his right as he reached for his gun. If the defense planted it in the pocket, as the state charged, then it might have been found in the street and that obscured the matter of when Carmack fired, as the state wished to do. Washington referred to pistol and scabbard as "Ruth and Naomi" and warned the prosecutors that they could not impugn his integrity without a fight.

In closing, Washington repaired to the law and applied it to the mental condition of the Coopers as the colonel set out across Seventh Avenue. Colonel Cooper had the right under the law to approach Carmack and speak to him. As for Robin, it was his duty to himself and to his father to draw when he saw that in the next minute his father might be a dead man. "Go back to your family and tell your good wife you have been trying a boy for defending his father and place a mark of honor instead of disgrace upon his brow," he pleaded and at last, took his seat.

Only two players remained on the stage, John Anderson and Jeff McCarn. Like his associates for the defense, Anderson tried to persuade the unlettered jury that Carmack's last editorials justified Cooper's wrath. Yet the colonel never sent the note he composed. And he committed no overt act in crossing Seventh Avenue and angrily confronting his enemy. "Colonel Cooper's action depends on its character and intent, and not upon the fact that he went across the street." Carefully, he put the defendants' claim: "Colonel Cooper had a right to seek Senator Carmack and demand that the use of his name be stopped, and if Senator Carmack made a deadly assault on Colonel Cooper or Robin they had the right of self-defense."[33]

For the last scene, McCarn took his place before the jury box and opened with a salvo of wit against opposing counsel. "They talk about birds," he noted. "If I were going to compare Washington to a bird, I'd say he was a peacock. I want to tell you he has the longest tail of any peacock I ever saw. It's nine hours and thirty minutes long." He recalled Washington's pledge to avoid the Arcade and supposed it would "be deserted by all the ladies."

Carmack wrote his editorials in "a vein of pleasantry," said the attorney general, and he called up the image of the widow and her son who suffered now for what had only been innocent gibes. "Oh, what memories it brings! Did you hear that wail when I asked her on what day her husband was murdered? It was the day that she put on those sombre colors. It was the day on which that beautiful boy was orphaned." Turning to the jury and looking into the eyes of one, he asked, "What are you going to tell that little girl, Mr. Frutiger, that told you about the killing? That little girl is going to believe Mrs. Eastman. Everybody is going to believe Mrs. Eastman, except defendants' counsel. You are going to have a hard time with your family if you don't punish these men."

Could not Colonel Cooper shoot a gun? Of course, he could, McCarn insisted. He picked up a pistol, doubled his third and fourth fingers into his palm, and snapped the trigger. The colonel had lost use of those two digits years before in a cider press accident.

As for the peace conference on the fatal afternoon, "you might as well turn Mount Vesuvius bottom upwards in hell to cool off as to take Colonel Cooper to [Bradford's] office." McCarn quoted Miss Lee as attributing to Bradford the words, "'I could have killed Carmack with as little regret as I could have killed a rattlesnake.'"

"I do say Colonel Cooper left that office with hell in his heart and thirsting for blood. I don't care if he did fool some people there. But subsequent events proved it!" McCarn cried.

Proving bathos kin to ferocity, McCarn depicted witnesses against the Coopers as heroines and heroes. Would Miss Lee lie and give up her job? Would young Tindall lie? "I know his mother now, Mrs. Kate Tindall, and I know she's a good woman. . . . But General Washington has a foot on your neck, Johnnie! And the foot has a silk stocking on it. Oh, Johnnie! probably that's the first time you ever had on a silk stocking."

To call a man a goddam son of a bitch, as witnesses said Sharp had done, was "usually considered the first lick in Tennessee." And hadn't he "been down there all the time in jail in the same cell, yes, apartment—I'll not say cell—with the others? They've had an opportunity to talk together, to think of these matters. . . . They haven't been locked up separately like you would be, Mr. Hows, or like I would be. No, these are different kinds of defendants. They've had free and unrestrained access to all their friends, contrary to the statutes of Tennessee." As for the now-famous scabbard, he and Fitzhugh had not found it in the overcoat when they searched the dead man's clothes.

Washington interrupted. "Did you tell Mr. Dorris you were looking for that scabbard?"

"I did not," McCarn answered. "I didn't care to open up my case to Mr. Dorris. I didn't know it was there. I knew of it and was trying to find it."

"Did *you* tell Mr. Dorris you were looking for it, Mr. Washington?" McCarn demanded. The audience erupted, and Judge Hart pounded his gavel. "Another such outburst, and I'll clear this courtroom!"

McCarn closed in anger, sentiment, and genuinely felt grief. "Make it the first shot or the last shot, [Senator Carmack] was shot in the back!"[34] Colonel Cooper had time and opportunity to say "'Senator, I would like to speak with you when you are at leisure.' It would have been in a measure a withdrawal of the threat. Oh, the tears and the blood he could have saved if only he had said that!"

Henry Meeks had referred to Colonel Cooper's lineage. Now McCarn ridiculed the claim. We may imagine him bowing toward the defendants, then rising to face the jury. "I don't believe in jerking the head off ancestry, but I do believe the tail ought to be yanked off! . . . Justice doesn't feel the hand to see if it is smooth or hard; justice doesn't feel the fibre of the cloth to see whether it is coarse or fine."

Drawing now toward the end, McCarn must have struggled for control over his feelings, as he recited Carmack's pledge to the South. "Those bullets haven't stopped yet . . . . Those bullets have gone on and on and will go on into the years," he predicted. And then he stood aside with a word to the "spirit that's gone— gentleman, orator, statesman, patriot, Christian— farewell."[35]

As court adjourned Sheriff Sam Borum accosted McCarn. Their exchange as reported in the press was formal, stilted, probably euphemistic.

"If you say I treated the three defendants differently from what I have treated any decent prisoner in my charge, you state a falsehood," Borum supposedly said.

"Go easy," McCarn answered. "You see my physical condition, but I said just what I believed and just what the Code will bear me out in saying. I felt what I said, and I believe it now, and if you want me to I'll show you the Code."

"If you show me any law to warrant your statements, I'll apologize," Borum offered. McCarn invited him into his office.

"I haven't got time to talk to you now," replied the sheriff, and he walked away.[36]

Two days later, to a packed house, Hart gave what was reportedly the longest set of instructions ever before delivered in a criminal case in Tennessee. He spent twenty minutes on the theory of the state, then forty minutes on the case that the defense made. But first he charged the jury on the law.

Murder in the first degree meant killing another person by any "willful, deliberate, malicious, and premeditated" act or in the course of other felonies. "The distinctive feature of first-degree murder is premeditation," the court explained, but the design or intent need not have existed in the murderer's mind for any definite period of time before he committed the act. Was the death of the slain party the object? That was the material point.

The principal ingredient of murder in the second degree was malice, the court continued. And malice need not be confined to the intent to kill the person, as in first-degree murder. It included an intention to do any unlawful act that "may probably result" in depriving the person of life. When the killing was done "under such cruel circumstances as are ordinarily indications of a wicked, depraved, and malignant spirit, outrageous in its nature and beyond all proportions to the offense, it is the presumption of the law that the killing was done maliciously." If the killing were done upon sudden heat and upon reasonable provocation, the killing would not be murder but voluntary manslaughter. However, if sufficient time had elapsed between the provocation and the killing for a reasonable person to gain control, the provocation would not mitigate murder to manslaughter. Involuntary manslaughter was a case of killing where it plainly appeared that death was not intended but was the result of some unlawful act or an act done in an unlawful manner and without due caution.

Judge Hart explained that the law allowed a defendant to plead self-defense when he could show that he had to kill the deceased or suffer death or great bodily harm. But the accused could not plead self-defense if he assaulted the dead person, menaced him by an overt act, or provoked the difficulty with the intent to kill him if he resisted the approach.

"If you convict the defendants of first degree murder," Hart told the jury, "you will have nothing to do with the penalty." By law they would suffer death by hanging, unless the jurors found mitigating circumstances and the court commuted the sentence to life in prison. If the panel returned a verdict of murder in the second degree, it could fix the punishment at time in the penitentiary from ten to twenty years. Voluntary manslaughter meant from two to ten years; involuntary manslaughter not less than one year nor more than five.

The jurymen must take the law as he had laid it down, Hart continued, and apply it and the facts to each other. If the twelve believed that Duncan Cooper had meant to take Carmack's life should he resent Cooper's approach or to give the editor a reason for shooting, and if Robin Cooper crossed the street behind his father to second and assist him, both were guilty of murder in the first degree. If the jury understood that Duncan Cooper had threatened Carmack's life, and that when he saw the editor approaching that intention revived and he crossed the street to carry out his threat, then it was up to the jury to decide if their approach caused Carmack to fear for his life. "In that event, he would have the right to defend himself from the threatened attack," and if he fired the first shots and the defendants returned fire, they could not plead self-defense. "Whether there was or was not an overt act," Hart stressed, "is a matter for you to determine." If they intended to kill Carmack should any difficulty ensue out of the conversation, they could not argue that they killed him because he opened fire. Only if they approached him on a mission of peace and there was no act or word to indicate any other purpose, but still the deceased attacked them, only then could they plead self-defense.

"You may take the case now, gentlemen, and retire to your room." As the jury filed out, a spectator reached down and picked up little Ned Carmack. Then from arm to arm, he was passed around the courtroom.[37]

Raised voices could be heard from the jury's chamber that first day. A deputy sheriff was stationed on the landing a short distance from the door, and no one got close enough to make out the words. Anticipating a verdict, crowds swelled the courtroom the following morning, only to hear Judge Hart take up cases postponed for the murder trial.

The next day the jury found John Sharp not guilty. As to the Coopers foreman E. M. Burke told the court that the panel was hopelessly tied. Judge Hart ordered the jurymen to return to their room for further deliberation.

"We understood the foreman to say they were 'hopelessly tied,'" Anderson said. The clerk of the court read his entry, and those had indeed been Burke's words.

"Is that not a complete verdict, then, Your Honor?" Washington asked.

"I have ordered the jury to retire to their room," Hart replied.

Friends crowded around Sharp, grasping his hand. The Coopers' supporters likewise came forward. As the colonel and his son left the courtroom, the former smiled in satisfaction.

The next morning, March 20, the jury found him and his son guilty of murder in the second degree and sentenced them to twenty years in prison.

Telegraph instruments had been placed around the bench, and the operators tapped out the words of foreman Burke as he spoke them at about nine-thirty. In a minute the news was in Chicago, St. Louis, San Francisco, Omaha, Washington, Brooklyn, and every other city where the wire services had offices. Fifteen minutes after the verdict, newsboys in many places were crying "Extra! Extra! Read all about the Carmack verdict!" The *Nashville Banner* sold ten thousand copies of its special edition that day. The calls handled through the city's telephone exchange jumped from an average of nine thousand an hour to thirty-six thousand an hour.

Defense lawyers perfunctorily moved a mistrial on account of the partial verdict of the day before, and Hart promptly overruled that motion. Anderson announced the defendants would seek a new trial. He then made application for bail, McCarn agreed, and the Coopers went free on bonds of $25,000 each after four months behind bars. It was an uncommonly high amount, even in a murder case, but before noon twelve sureties signed for a total of more than $270,000. James E. Caldwell qualified for the full amount of each bond himself. Others guaranteeing the Coopers' appearance were railroad magnate E. C. Lewis, the squire of Belle Meade plantation Walter O. Parmer, and Harvey M. LaFollette.[38]

An unconfirmed newspaper story presumed to give the proceedings of the jury. By this account, foreman Burke had immediately called for a vote on the most serious charge, first-degree murder. That received one vote. When he asked for a show of hands on second-degree murder, pandemonium broke out.

Burke announced a second ballot, on the charge of murder in the first degree with mitigating circumstances. This time four jurors voted "aye." Four cast their ballots for murder in the second degree and three others for manslaughter. One juror wanted to acquit the defendants altogether.

After the second ballot, was the question only the severity of the sentence and not guilt or innocence? In the end, the jurors reportedly voting for murder in the first degree were William Hows, W. A. Adcock, F. O. Beerman, Caspar Schnupp, G. A. Lane, and E. M. Burke. Robert McPherson, J. H. Vaughn, Gus Knipfer, J. A. Woodruff, and Jacob Frutiger supported a verdict of second-degree murder. Shiloh Hyde argued for acquitting the Coopers. "Those who favored murder in the first degree came down to twenty years," the uncorroborated account continued. "Those who were for a much lower sentence came up to twenty years."[39]

Why did the jury find the Coopers guilty? According to the leading student of homicide in rural Tennessee during this period, the community was inclined to forgive an offender if the motive for the crime was justifiable. Colonel Cooper believed that personal honor sustained him, and he expected the jury so to find. But McCarn and his associates portrayed Carmack's death as resulting from some trivial editorials, and the defense failed to impugn that interpretation. The men of the jury who attached little importance to the printed word heard nothing in Carmack's attacks on Cooper to exonerate him.[40]

Anderson and his defense team did not challenge the testimony of Johnny Tindall, Mary Skeffington, or Carey Folk. In acquitting Sharp the jury necessarily rejected Miss Skeffington's interpretation of his words to her as they met moments after the shooting. But taken together the other two statements made out a case of premeditation, which justified those jurors who favored a verdict of murder in the first degree.

John Tindall when he grew to manhood recanted his story and admitted that he perjured himself. About seven years after the trial, he appeared one day in Robin Cooper's law office and told the attorney he wanted to make amends. His mother had died recently, Tindall said, and on her deathbed she made him promise to lead an honest and God-fearing life. Now his false testimony lay on his conscience. He explained that he had bragged to his fellow newsboys about knowing Robin Cooper and that he had overheard Colonel Cooper make the remark, "We'll get him!" or "We'll catch him!" The district attorney heard of this, sent for him, and took his statement. After that he was afraid to admit that he had lied.[41]

The jury did not know of Tindall's perjury, of course. That testimony, along with Carey Folk's, was damning, and the defense's failure to refute these two witnesses helped lose its case.

But the state failed to convince a majority of the jury that the Coopers had conspired to murder Carmack. If Cooper meant to reach the corner of Seventh and Union on time to meet his enemy and shoot him down, he made the journey like a boulevardier. He paused with his anxious son at a soda fountain; he passed the pleasantries of the hour with acquaintances on the street; he halted to peer down into the excavation for the Hermitage Hotel. And he could scarcely have predicted Carmack's detouring to the drugstore and pausing to help a lady onto the streetcar. The story of these two proud, arrogant men is rich with ambiguity and studded with irony. But there is one fact in the Cooper case that seems incontrovertible, that the colonel and the editor met by accident. Carmack had goaded Cooper; Cooper demanded that he stop. Both took up guns and behaved like two adolescent schoolboys, daring each other to step over a line in the dust. Only their chance meeting led to terrible tragedy that engloomed the lives of many.

Did Fitzhugh's brilliant cross-examination of Colonel Cooper expose the witness's malice and therefore prove murder in the second degree? As a man justifying himself by honor, Cooper exhibited his contempt for anyone's opinion about the fatal encounter. Yet the jurymen saw his private defense of his honor as the justice of the frontier. In their remote rural place they had recently organized themselves to settle disputes by other means. They had taken honor's standard — that the esteem of one's fellow men determined one's worth — and placed its upholding in the hands of magistrates.

A minority on the jury believed that Cooper planned to murder Carmack. By press reports, the rest thought he meant to do him harm, that he crossed the street thinking Carmack might die, and that that result was out of proportion to any injury the editor had done Cooper. That view prevailed. Fixing the maximum punishment for murder in this second degree apparently satisfied the faction who wanted to see the defendants hang.

But the evidence did not justify this verdict. The state did not prove that Cooper crossed Seventh Avenue from a malignant spirit, believing his approach to Carmack would probably lead to his death. There is nothing in the thousand pages of testimony to show that Cooper accosted the editor except in the unreflecting, impulsive anger of the moment.

If Colonel Cooper was not guilty of murder, was he guilty of anything? He did not intend to kill Carmack, else he would have drawn his gun. He could not know and did not expect that Robin would run and leap and pivot and shoot the editor to death. But he ought to have known that his sudden appearance before Carmack would cause him to believe that his life was in danger. After that, anything could happen — and Cooper did not care. In crossing the street, he committed what Judge Hart called an "act done without due caution," and his imprudence led to the horror that followed.

Robin Cooper entered the fray with no intent to shoot, and he fired only after being fired upon. There cannot be two interpretations of the forensics evidence that went to the jury: Carmack fired twice, levelled his pistol at Robin, and then died as Robin's first shot struck him.

Did Robin Cooper shoot Edward Carmack in the back? The state described how one of Cooper's bullets entered Carmack's neck and exited his mouth, and for a long time the ghastly image remained seared on the minds of those who hated the killers. Carmack's collar — indeed all other physical evidence in the case — has long vanished, and a modern pathologist has little by which to judge.

This we know, by Dr. Glasgow's testimony: that Carmack was struck first in his torso, and with that, he was dying. Others, not all of them friendly to the Coopers, saw the body turn as it fell. The state insisted that that motion could not possibly have happened fast enough to cause Cooper's third shot to strike the corpse at the collar.

Something else must have happened, and here we speculate. Although most young Southerners of his time probably handled firearms at one time or another, the state produced no proof that Robin Cooper was proficient with them. Suddenly, on the corner of Seventh and Union, he drew and pointed this powerful pistol. An experienced shooter would have instinctively steadied his hand against the recoil. Young Cooper, in his words, "just shot," as fast as he could pull the trigger. And most probably with each shot, his arm drew back and up, the natural reaction, propelling the third shot on an upward trajectory, into the neck of the corpse as it rotated.

In their bid for a new trial, the Coopers' lawyers alleged that Judge Hart had excluded certain evidence that should have been admitted, such as part of Robin Cooper's testimony that shed light on his mental condition and his father's. Portions of Hart's charge relating to the theory of the state were also defective at law, they said. Finally, the court ought to have charged the jury according to a number of special requests that the defense made, including their grand theory: If Robin Cooper had crossed the corner believing just what his father told him — that he, the colonel, wanted only a peaceful talk with the editor — and then if Carmack began firing upon Robin, he had a right to shoot Carmack for self-protection, even if Colonel Cooper had meant to provoke a difficulty.[42]

Altogether the defense alleged forty-six errors, and arguments on their motion took place the third week of April, as spring burst into bloom on the public square and in the nearby countryside. Mr. Washington argued for separating the father's and the son's conditions of mind. Mr. Fitzhugh retorted that the record showed that Robin knew the motives actuating his father and had actually intervened, testifying that he crossed the street to help his father.

Judge Hart overruled the motion for a new trial. "They were all greatly relieved," wrote a cousin of the Coopers. "Now it will be taken to the Supreme Court, and if it is not then reversed, the governor will pardon them."[43]

CHAPTER FIVE

— *The Whirligig of Politics* —

COLONEL COOPER HAD BRAGGED to Katrina Williamson that only one day would be required for him and his son to be found innocent. Now they stood convicted of murder. Over dinner one spring evening at the mansion, Governor Patterson gave Katrina Williamson to understand "that if it came to the worst, he would intervene."[1] Yet the colonel knew better than anyone the ramifications if the governor undid the verdict. Cooper was staking his friend's political future, as well as his own liberty, on the appeal.

The arguments in the celebrated murder case began before the Supreme Court of Tennessee on February 1, 1910. The courtroom in the State Capitol had no jury box, only a low platform and a table with chairs for five. There sat the justices who would decide this case: William D. Beard, Bennett D. Bell, William K. McAlister, Matt Marshal Neil, and John K. Shields.

Before this high court the burden of proof shifted to the defendants. Under Tennessee law and settled precedent, that body could not disturb a verdict of guilty upon the facts where any material evidence sustained it. Therefore, the Coopers had to show that the trial court erred in conducting the case. The law required the justices to assume that the Coopers were guilty. The question before them was, Did the criminal court follow due process of law?[2] To uphold their conviction, at least three of the justices had to answer in the affirmative.

Robin Cooper strolled leisurely into the room that Monday morning, accompanied by his brother William. One reporter thought he looked heavier and in better spirits than on the day he testified that he had shot Carmack to death because he was sure that Carmack was about to kill him.

Duncan Cooper came to court in the company of his nephew Albert Stockell, and his sons-in-law, Dr. Lucius E. Burch and attorney Charles N. Burch. One by one the defendants' lawyers arrived: John M. Anderson, M. Henry Meeks, William H. Washington, and James C. Bradford. In preparation for their second trial, the Coopers added another lawyer to this

Luke E. Wright, for the defense. Source: *Tennesseans, Nineteen Hundred and One and Two*
(1902).

phalanx. In the McKinley and Roosevelt administrations, Luke E. Wright
had served as governor general of the Philippine Islands and secretary of
war. In his hometown of Memphis, he was counsel to the local monopoly
that owned the street railways and power and light utilities. Wright belonged among Southern expansionists, those who dreamed dreams of empire. Like Colonel Cooper they imagined making fortunes from shipping
lines or mining lodes. But vast sums ever eluded Cooper, while Wright
received a fraction of every nickel deposited in the farebox on the streetcar
or draft payable to the electric company. To retain this man to appeal his
case, Cooper defied the powerful sentiment among Tennessee people who
hated the trusts and the railroads as much as they hated the saloons.

As a director of the *Commercial Appeal*, Wright had refused to support
Carmack's course in renouncing Josiah Patterson and the gold standard.
Carmack helped elect Wright's law partner, Thomas B. Turley, to the U.S.
Senate in 1898; and from these associations Wright knew Carmack's tem-
perament. Writing on the letterhead of Wright and Turley, the latter once
had to reassure Carmack over some unknown incident that nothing occurred

The Supreme Court of Tennessee. Source: *Nashville American* (Feb. 4, 1910).

Chief Justice John K. Shields. Source: *The* [Nashville] *Democrat* (Jan. 24, 1913).

"to place you in any wrong light or subject you to any misunderstanding."

The defendants and their attorneys took seats at a long table to the right of the bench. Colonel Cooper leaned his chair against a column, sitting almost with his back to the bench.[3]

The table to the bench's left was reserved for the state. Besides William W. Faw, an assistant attorney general, Judge Sam Holding of Columbia sat

Charles T. Cates, for the State. Source: *Tennesseans, Nineteen Hundred and One and Two* (1902).

Attorney General Cates arguing the State's case. Source: *Nashville Banner* (Feb. 3, 1910).

there. He had stood by Dr. McPheeters Glasgow, who performed an autopsy on the exhumed body of the late senator. Holden had reportedly assented to the doctor's observation that Carmack must have fired first for any shot that struck him would have been fatal.[4] But for Holden that fact did not exonerate the defendants. Ready to present the state's case was Attorney General Charles T. Cates, Jr.

Presiding over this second trial of the Coopers was Chief Justice William D. Beard, seventy-three. Appointed in 1890 to fill a vacancy on the Supreme Court, he served for a few months before resuming his law practice. The following year, Governor Buchanan named him to the chancery court. In 1894 he was elected to the state's highest court, reelected in 1902, and in 1903 became chief justice. He was the last veteran of the Civil War to sit on the Tennessee Supreme Court, and he had less than a year to live.[5]

For his seventeen years of service on the court, Beard's colleague William K. McAlister enjoyed the senior ranking, having been appointed to fill a vacancy by Governor Peter Turney in 1893.[6] Judge McAlister would cast the critical vote in the Cooper case.

Monday and Wednesday belonged to the defense, whose theory of the case held that Carmack forced Robin Cooper to shoot him or be shot. Cates on Tuesday laid out the state's argument that Duncan Cooper, in crossing the street, committed an overt act to carry out his threat and Robin Cooper, taking his father's part, must be judged by his father's act.

Both sides probed the minds of the three men. What did Edward Carmack and Duncan Cooper know or believe about the other's intentions from Sunday night? What led each to act as he did, the other's intemperate words roiling through his thoughts, when they met the next afternoon? What did Robin Cooper intend as he left the curb and started after his father?

Rage clouded Duncan Cooper's thoughts after he read "Across the Bloody Chasm" on Sunday morning, Wright acknowledged. The editorial implied to him that he was a grafter. That evening he cursed Carmack to Ed Craig. But, Wright claimed, the colonel had not known that Craig conveyed his words about the town not being big enough for both men if his name appeared again in the *Tennessean*. "He did not dream that Craig had told Carmack that he, Cooper, would kill him," Wright argued. He did not know that Frank Lander had poured into Carmack's ear Mrs. Burch's fears that her father would shoot the editor on sight. And not knowing those things, "it was only natural that he thought he could talk to Carmack." From the defendants' standpoint, "where was the wrongful aggression in this case?" asked Anderson. Wright gave the appellants' answer:

> Cooper was angry at having Carmack spit in his face every
> morning, using indiscreet words. But [he was] willing to have

the matter amicably settled, asking only that his name be left out of the newspaper. Carmack, cool, arming himself, declaring there was nothing to do but to place Cooper's name in the paper again. What was that but challenge, defiance, forcing the issue? It meant that Carmack proposed to put Cooper to the test.

All day Monday Robin had tried to prevent his father and the editor from meeting one another, Wright reminded the court. Fear for his father's safety gave color and meaning to his every act; it alone impelled him across Seventh Avenue. And then Carmack shot him, and there was no more time to think, only to return the fire, to kill or be killed.

Relying on Mrs. Eastman's testimony, the state held that Robin Cooper had walked down the street, circled around Carmack, and shot him in the back. "A wild and visionary theory," Wright called it. How is it possible that Carmack could have turned around after he received a bullet through his spine? Lamenting his death, his friends and enemies alike blamed him as "morally responsible, morally the aggressor," he said.

Anderson insisted that in his charge to the jury, Judge Hart had linked father and son in their rights and their responsibilities in Carmack's death, when actually "Robin Cooper killed solely in self-defense, and without personal malice, and was entitled to have that theory presented to the jury."[7]

Anderson and Wright did not address some of the most damaging testimony in the record, that of the newsboy Johnny Tindall, of Carey Folk, and that of Mary Skeffington. As for Mrs. Eastman, the defense lawyers had the difficult task of discrediting her account without disparaging her, a society woman; she was the only adverse witness they could not depict as a liar. They tried to separate what she saw from what she thought happened. But they failed to efface her image of Colonel Cooper bearing down on Carmack, his hand outstretched, his voice angry.

In presenting the state's case, Attorney General Charles Cates called Cooper's words to Carmack "an assault in itself." Cates grew up in Maryville, Tennessee, where he had been born in 1863. He graduated from Maryville College in 1881 and taught for a time in the public schools, while reading law at night in his father's office. Except for his years in public service, he would practice law in Knoxville for the rest of his life. At the time of his election as the state's chief lawyer, he was associated with S. G. Shields and Robert E. L. Mountcastle of that city. All three partners evidently espoused the cause of Edward Carmack for governor, counseling him in the summer of 1907 about the manner and timing of his announcement.

As attorney general, Cates defended the 1907 act that outlawed gambling at race tracks. It would become his duty to argue for the constitutionality of the statutes that prohibited the manufacture and sale of liquor in Tennessee.[8]

On Wednesday morning, Cates placed in front of him pasteboard models of the two telephone poles, the thick volumes of the record from the Criminal Court, and Senator Carmack's collar with the bullet hole in the back. Then he delivered the argument that convicted the colonel of murder for a second time.

"This conflict was precipitated by D. B. Cooper," Cates began, "and his son, deliberately or not, went with him and became the instrument of the death of the man whose life he had threatened." Because he had interfered for his father, Robin's "acts must stand or fall by the acts of his father."

Cates reiterated the possibility that Carmack had lived for a few seconds after Robin's bullet pierced him, long enough to return fire. But even if Carmack shot first, he had a right to, Cates insisted. Consider the effect on Carmack of seeing the Coopers coming across the street at him after the colonel had threatened to kill him. "Would any court not have said that had Carmack shot and killed them both, he acted in self-defense?" But if he was shot first, then the threat had been carried out and the Coopers were guilty of murder.

In a brilliant tactical move, Cates casually dismissed the idea of a grand conspiracy. Now five thoroughly political men could vote to uphold the convictions without implying the guilt of the most powerful politician in the state, Governor Patterson. That is what Cates asked them to do, to affirm the verdict and execute its sentence. "Then will it be shown to all the world that human life in Tennessee is not a pawn or plaything for the man who ruthlessly slays it."

And so the second trial ended. "Pass up the record, Mr. Marshal," intoned Chief Justice Beard at ten minutes before one on the third day. Then he adjourned court. "It will be many long weeks," predicted the *Nashville Banner*, "ere an opinion is handed down in this case."[9] Malcolm Patterson hoped for a quicker decision. If he had to free the Coopers, it would be better done as far as possible in advance of the campaign of 1910, for the governor had decided to seek a third term.

The cold days of February shuffled by. The light grew longer, but nights stayed bitter; water froze in the horse troughs throughout the city. Wind whistled around the pediment of the Capitol and bored through the walls of the tenements in Black Bottom.

March followed, and the seasons began turning on their hinges. On the seventeenth, members of the Ancient Order of Hibernians, the Parnell Branch of the Irish National League, and other Nashvillians of Irish ancestry formed a parade that wound through the streets from the Public Square to St. Patrick's Church in South Nashville. And still the high court was silent.

One Sunday evening, Governor Patterson called on Chief Justice Beard at his home, unannounced. Beard came down to his parlor, and the two exchanged some formalities before Patterson came to the point. He was there, he said, to talk about the Cooper case. Beard drew back, replying that he could not talk to the governor or anyone else about that matter. Patterson said that the case must be decided and decided at once. Beard began backing up the stairs, raising his hands to silence the governor, but Patterson went on: The case must be decided right if the members of the court expected to be reelected.[10]

By the end of March, the state Democratic Executive Committee and the governor could no longer postpone the making of a plan by which the party would choose its nominees in the summer. The panel met at the Maxwell House on March 29 for that purpose. With Patterson Democrats dominating the body, it was expected to conduct the election according to rules that were to his liking. The unanswered question was, Did Patterson want a primary that would choose nominees to *all* offices, not just governor and senator?

Under the gavel of Chairman Austin Peay, the committee appointed a subcommittee to propose a definite plan. Jeff McCarn, an announced candidate for governor, appeared before this panel and urged the party to provide for a runoff should no candidate in that race receive a majority. He took no position on nominating judiciary candidates in the primary. But, the *Banner* reported, "the tip" was abroad that a majority of the subcommittee would recommend that procedure.

That night some two thousand people rallied at the Ryman Auditorium under the banner of the Law Enforcement League of Davidson County. Bishop E. E. Hoss and other temperance speakers denounced Criminal Court Judge William Hart for choosing grand juries who refused to indict sellers of liquor and for flippancies toward the ladies of the W.C.T.U. Then Joel O. Cheek, the maker of Maxwell House coffee, took the podium and nominated McCarn to oppose Hart in the coming election.

Called to the platform, McCarn said he had never thought of a judgeship, that he was too narrow and intolerant, that he could not see but one side of a lawsuit "when right was on that side and wrong on the other." He wanted to be governor, he told them. "But I can't refuse this honor. . . . If I am elected, no whiskey will be sold openly in Nashville. The question is, do you want it done?"

"Yes! Yes!" came the calls from all over the house.

"Then, by the grace of God and the good citizens of Davidson County, it shall be done!" McCarn answered. He then made his way to his seat amid wild cheering, having refused the laurels of the state's highest office to shut off the taps at the Utopia if he could beat the genial Judge Hart.

The next day, the state executive committee fixed a delegated primary for June 4. As in 1908, voters would cast their ballots directly for candidates, and the candidate with the plurality in each county was entitled to the votes of the county's entire delegation to the state convention where the nominees would be named. As before, Tennessee Democrats would choose their candidates for governor, United States Senator, state treasurer, and railroad commissioner. But for the first time, the ballot would list candidates for five more offices—the seats on the state Supreme Court.[11]

On that particular of the plan, the party shattered. Within a few days, Justices Beard, Shields, and Neil announced they would not submit their names to the primary but would go before the voters as independents in the August election. Several judges of the civil appeals court likewise declined to be candidates in the June balloting, saying that races for judgeships should be kept separate from political or factional contests. In joining the protest, State Treasurer Reau E. Folk and U.S. Senator James B. Frazier denounced the provisions of the plan that allowed the state committee to select the actual delegates. The rules obligated them to vote for the candidates who carried their county—but the administration's allies on the executive committee were bound to pack the convention with delegates who would write a platform pleasing to Patterson.[12]

The most tumultuous springtime in the political history of Tennessee had begun. Within a few days after that announcement, Beard prepared an opinion in the Cooper case and presented it to his colleagues. But a majority of the court directed Shields to write another, reflecting the views and votes of each justice. One account says that Patterson received word of what the verdict would be and that Luke Wright was preparing to rise and dismiss the appeal so that the reasoning of the justices need not be aired. Patterson would then issue his pardon.[13]

The court may have learned of the plan. On Wednesday morning, April 13, at 9:40 A.M., the marshal brought down the gavel and the spectators stood as the court entered. According to one reporter, "a hush like the stillness of death" fell upon the courtroom. Shields disposed of another case, then launched into the reading without giving counsel for the defense time to rise, if that indeed were their plan. For two hours and twenty-five minutes, he continued. Early in the reading, the Coopers knew the trend of the opinion was not in their favor. The colonel several times spoke to his daughter, Mrs. Burch, sitting back of him.[14]

In all his public career, this may have been the most attentive audience Shields ever had; he was not gifted as a public speaker. Yet in a forceful, sometimes eloquent decision for the majority, he succeeded in depicting Colonel Cooper as the wrongful aggressor in the affair.

Shields told the crowded courtroom that Cooper knew his sudden appearance, his arm outstretched, his voice full of hate, would cause the editor to believe that the colonel's deadly threats were about to be executed.

Even if Cooper had suddenly changed his intentions, resolved to have the personal interview, but advanced on Carmack and denounced him as a coward, "the approach under the circumstances [was] in itself an overt act," giving Carmack the right to defend himself.

But had the accused ever experienced a change of heart from his homicidal resolve of Sunday night? Shields thought not, since both father and son continued carrying arms and Robin went with the colonel expecting difficulty. Besides, a new, pacific attitude would be "inconsistent with the character of Colonel Cooper and contrary to the experience of men in such affairs." The Coopers contended, said Shields, that one could threaten a man's life if a certain thing happened, then within hours of that thing actually happening, approach him for a discussion without communicating a change of mind and in a hostile way and kill him with impunity when he undertook to defend himself. "Such a doctrine would be monstrous," Shields intoned. "It is not the law of Tennessee."

The Coopers' right of self-defense could not rest on whether they had intended to kill Carmack before approaching him, the majority opinion argued. Rather, that right rested on whether, in crossing the street and confronting Carmack, they gave him reason to believe that he faced grave peril. "All [Colonel Cooper's] conduct unquestionably made a case which warranted Mr. Carmack in believing that his life was in danger and about to be taken, and he had the right under the law to kill his adversary in his own defense." Every man, intoned Shields, must "contemplate the reasonable and natural result of his conduct and must answer for such result, especially when the injured party is without fault."

The justice acknowledged that the appellants presented a strong argument that Robin Cooper merited a separate defense because he tried to prevent his father from meeting Carmack and only went across Seventh Avenue to protect him. Yet he supported the murder conviction of Robin Cooper, citing case after case to show that one who interferes to assist another, even a close relative, can use no more force than the person he assists would be entitled to use and that no interference was justified at all when the party to whose aid he came was the aggressor. Shields's colleague Matt M. Neil concurred.[15]

Chief Justice Beard's separate opinion, in which Justice Bell joined, would have given both men a new trial. While praising Carmack as without peer in the public life of Tennessee for half a century, he implicated him in the events that led to his death: "The frequent use of Col. Cooper's name by this greatly gifted man at least remotely led to the deplorable tragedy of November 9th."

The two justices believed that Colonel Cooper had put aside any intention of shooting Carmack on sight when he broke from Robin's grip and started across Seventh Avenue. The colonel's approaching Carmack may have been inconsiderate and imprudent, Beard acknowledged. Yet it was not menacing or aggressive. He did not declare to Carmack that he had the drop on him; rather, he addressed him as "Mr. Carmack," and in an instant the editor drew his pistol and began firing.

Beard quoted Cooper's own testimony as proof that he had made no hostile movement and had no purpose of shooting. If the Coopers committed no assault nor menaced none, they could lawfully claim self-defense. The criminal court judge had the duty to so instruct the jury, said Beard and Bell, which he had not done.

None of their colleagues joined them in this conclusion. McAlister concurred that Duncan Cooper had murdered Edward Carmack, and thus the court upheld the colonel's conviction. But McAlister did not agree with Neil and Shields as to Robin Cooper. He voted to sustain the defense's assertion that the trial court erred when it did not charge the jury that Robin Cooper had a right of self-defense. As to Colonel Cooper, Beard and Bell were a minority; with McAlister's vote they formed a majority as to Robin Cooper. The trio overturned his conviction and sentence and sent his case back to the criminal court.

This majority—Beard, Bell, and McAlister—reasoned that if Robin believed when his father broke away he was going to have a talk with Carmack, and if believing that Robin followed him and met Carmack, who immediately began firing upon Robin, the law gave him the right to shoot and kill Carmack. That was true, the three justices insisted, even if Duncan Cooper intended to provoke a difficulty.[16]

Judge Beard finished reading at one minute before two, and the court adjourned. Friends of the Coopers gathered around them, offering congratulations to Robin. Shortly after the hour, a marshal of the court and a deputy sheriff of the county started for the jail with Colonel Cooper in custody. They reached there at about 2:20, joined by Dr. and Mrs. Burch, Mrs. J. C. Bradford, and Robin.[17]

While Cooper was standing by the jailer, waiting to be taken to a cell, the telephone rang. On the other end of the line was the clerk of the Supreme Court with word for the sheriff. No further steps were necessary, Colonel Cooper could be released. Governor Patterson had pardoned him.

The group of family and friends had narrowly missed receiving the news while still at the Capitol. Addressed to the prison commissioner and the warden of the penitentiary, the pardon was presented for registration at 2 P.M., at the moment when the justices were stepping down from the bench. More than one copy of the pardon document exists. The one bearing the notation "Presented for registration at 2:00 P.M." can be found in Colonel Cooper's papers. At the end of the published report of the case, the reporter noted that Patterson pardoned Cooper "while the court was still sitting."[18]

The colonel showed no surprise and made no statement; privately to Austin Peay, he expressed concern about the possible consequences to the governor. Peay assured Cooper that "the manhood of the state will endorse and sustain" Patterson. Other friends of the administration shared Peay's ebullience. Many doubted that Robin would be tried again; merely to secure a jury could take months. Robin posted bond in the amount of $10,000 and, evidently believing that his new trial would not take place soon, prepared to leave for Europe on holiday.[19]

On the night of the day after Duncan Cooper went free, some citizens of Athens, Tennessee, burned him in effigy. The blaze spread from coast to coast as editors denounced the governor. To the New York *Evening Post*, the case could not have been clearer. "Carmack was brutally shot down in the street—as brutally as was Stanford White by Harry Thaw. The Governor's action will stimulate the gentle and extensive Southern pastime of shooting editors...." The *Washington Post*, which had called Carmack such an ornament in Congress as Edmund Burke had been in Parliament, described the pardon as "a flagrant injustice to the people" of Tennessee.

Patterson received telegrams and letters from around the state and the nation commending his action. And he found support among some Southern editors. They observed that the pardon repaid past favors and old courtesies, as presumably the killing had repaid old injuries. The *Florida Times-Union* wrote, "Mr. Patterson would never have been governor but for Col. Cooper's influence. It was hard for the Governor to forget the friend who probably did more than any other to make his political life." From Mobile, the *Register* observed, "a rough and ready justice . . . the aged defendant is fully entitled to executive clemency." But even in the South, the press generally condemned Patterson. "Another chapter in the sad history of the reign of the pistol in Tennessee," was how the *Birmingham Ledger* saw the case. Its editorial writer added dolefully, "Too many personal and political quarrels have ended in death." The *Atlanta Constitution* agreed: "Every thoughtful American citizen must hail the course of Governor Patterson with disapproval and grave misgivings. . . . A great commonwealth has placed a premium upon bloodshed and violence."

The *New York Times*, ever condescending to Dixie, was practically stupefied that "only a few small fist fights have thus far been reported as a result of the heated discussions on the streets." In the same edition an editorial writer described the Coopers' view of their relations to society and to their victim as "worthy of an Apache or a head-hunter of Borneo." The pardon was "lamentable evidence of the persistence of the barbaric spirit in the South." Later that summer, the *Times* observed, "Tennessee is still a rude state, a state of turmoil, of grudges, of feuds, of embittered hostilities, and of violent, passionate vindictiveness in politics." Other editors saw what Colonel Cooper apparently feared. "Governor Patterson's political career may be ended," the *Arkansas Gazette* speculated. The Lincoln, Nebraska, *Star* concurred: "It looks like a case of political suicide."[20]

A week after he pardoned Duncan Cooper, Patterson announced his candidacy for a third term. Patterson defended the high number of pardons he had issued, lately the subject of attack in Luke Lea's *Nashville Tennessean*. And he offered to submit to a gubernatorial primary against any opponent that dissident Democrats cared to name. Few would be reconciled by the gesture. After a Patterson campaign aide reportedly offered Justices Beard, Shields, and Neil a separate nominating convention and assurance that they would be named, provided only that they would end their independent campaign, the governor seemed more cynical and manipulative than ever.

Instead, the judicial trio recruited two ticket mates to stand with them and form a full slate. Dick L. Lansden of Sparta, a judge of the Chancery Court, had tried and failed to win a seat on the Supreme Court in 1908. Lansden suggested Nashville lawyer Grafton Green for the fifth seat, and he agreed to the race. A convention made up largely of members of the state bar met in Nashville and endorsed the ticket. Someone coined the slogan that caught the popular imagination and by which the campaign would ever be remembered: "A free and untrammeled judiciary."[21]

Beard, Shields, and Neil answered Governor Patterson's conciliatory offer by charging that he tried to influence the court to reverse the conviction of the Coopers. They had been well on the way to reelection, they pointed out, when the appeal came to trial. Across the state their friends had been holding county conventions to name delegates to the state judicial convention where the nominees should be chosen. It was only left for the state executive committee of the party to fix a date when the convention would meet. At that point, they charged, Governor Patterson called together the committee and instructed that nothing be done until the court settled the Cooper case. "It became an open secret," the trio said, "discussed in the corridors of the hotels, in the cars, and on the streets of Nashville that the Cooper case was the pivot upon which the action of the committee was to turn." Dick Lansden alleged an offer from the governor to Judge Shields to postpone a decision in the state committee for a few weeks, provided the court would in that interval decide the Cooper case. When Shields refused, he claimed, the state committee proceeded to call a general primary. They had been given to understand, so they claimed, that they must reverse the conviction or risk the disapproval of the voters in a primary election.[22]

Patterson replied that the court, not he, had been engaged in coercion, delaying the decision until he agreed to support the traditional, separate judicial convention. The justices, he pointed out, had kept the case until after the executive committee met and after three of them had repudiated its plan for conducting a primary that included judicial offices. All he wanted was to allow other candidates for the supreme bench to enter the contest, not just these who inspired the call of the local nominating conventions. Judge Shields had always been "notoriously unfriendly" toward him, Patterson lamented, and "a most active partisan and liberal contributor to the campaign fund of Senator Carmack in the last campaign." Patterson blamed Shields for insisting that the committee be called before the Cooper case was decided. And it was Shields who refused any compromise plan, leading the state executive committee to include the judiciary in the election.

The committee soon approved a unilateral compromise, giving voters in the June 4 primary the right to actually select their county's delegates to the state nominating convention. But the action failed to stanch the defections from the Patterson ranks or to silence the *Tennessean's* villification of the governor. On May 18 five thousand cheering Democrats gathered in the Ryman Auditorium and, under flags draped from the galleries, to the horns and drums of a brass band, lustily denounced Patterson, the executive committee, and all their works. They called for a boycott of the primary and the election of the "free and untrammeled judiciary."

The boycott left most candidates on the June 4 ballot with no opposition and thus assured that voters had little reason to take part. Patterson achieved fewer than one-third of the votes he had received in previous elections. Two weeks later, the state convention dutifully awarded him his third nomination for governor.[23] Day by day his enemies nicked away at that pedestal of support. Duncan Cooper, they were saying by midsummer, was soliciting campaign contributions from liquor interests. Cooper was in truth back at Patterson's side. J. W. Reid of Williamson County wrote him in July, asking for a total of $700 to pay the poll taxes of Patterson supporters. The state committee had sent him only $350 so far, and he warned that "unless we can get more money this county is in danger."[24]

Many who had four short years before looked on Malcolm Patterson as the young knight of reform now saw his shield tarnished, his hauberk rusted, his lance besmirched, some said with the blood of Carmack. The administration never recovered from the campaign of 1908. While losing his own race, Carmack won in helping elect legislators who formed a majority with dry Republicans to enact statewide prohibition. Now Patterson's friendship for the killers, his pardon of Duncan Cooper, his apparent cooperation with the liquor lobby, and his alleged manipulation of the party nominating process combined and brought him down.

On August 4, the independent judiciary ticket swept the state.[25] Its majorities loomed largest in East Tennessee. The Republicans had declined to nominate a slate for the bench in this decisive contest. At the same time, they made clear that they would field a candidate for governor

in November. Having polled 45 percent of the vote in the last two gubernatorial contests and facing a deeply divided Democracy, their prospects
appeared brighter than at any time since they won the statehouse only to
lose it to theft in 1894. Could these avid Republicans find a candidate
whom disaffected Democrats could support? President William Howard
Taft, eager for his party to make inroads into the "Solid South," devoutly
hoped so. He summoned representatives of Republican factions led by
Newell Sanders and loyalists of Walter Brownlow and urged them to agree
on a candidate acceptable to all Republicans and the bolting Democrats.

With the help of a dispenser of patronage from the Taft administration, the Sanders faction controlled the Republican convention when it
met in Nashville on August 16. They defeated party veteran Alf A. Taylor,
the choice of Brownlow's followers, and won the nomination for Ben W.
Hooper. A lawyer and resident of Newport, Hooper had served in the
legislature in 1893, when he was only twenty-two, and again in 1895. He
counted as his most significant service the introduction of a bill to extend
the Four-Mile Law, the statute prohibiting the sale of liquor within four
miles of any institution of learning, to small incorporated towns.

The brutality of his father, a hard-working, generous country doctor
when sober but demonic when he drank, "ground into my very being a
hatred of intoxicants," Hooper wrote. "How many hard punches I have
given King Alcohol." The introduction of his bill, he recalled with pride,
"was the seed from which sprang governors, United States senators, supreme courts, popular upheavals, political murder, nullification of state
laws by municipal bosses, and the final triumph of law and civic decency."
Attaining the rank of captain in the Spanish-American War, Hooper
returned home to practice his profession. In 1906 President Roosevelt appointed him assistant United States attorney for East Tennessee.

Hooper entered the campaign of 1910 with the Republican Party
united behind him. Beginning with his acceptance speech in the convention, he openly appealed to independent Democrats. The platform demanded the enforcement of prohibition and endorsed a judiciary free of
partisan influence. Other language lambasted the Patterson administration
for manipulating the election laws and issuing excessive numbers of pardons. In calling for state bank inspections, worker's compensation, and the
curtailment of convict labor, Hooper's program resembled the mildly progressive ones on which Carmack and Patterson had sought the governor's
office. Thus, he impressed many who had looked first to one then the other
of those Democrats who promised to deliver the state from "machine
politics" and executive abuse of power.

Seeing that he was beaten, Patterson withdrew from the race on
September 11. Three days later, the independent Democrats convened in

Nashville. They endorsed Hooper, statewide prohibition, and more spend-
ing for education, better-run prisons, and the regulation of lobbyists.

A committee escorted the young Newport lawyer from his hotel room
down to the Ryman to meet these new allies. When he reached the rostrum
and stood before the vast audience, the room grew quiet. "They had crossed
the political Rubicon and had cut their bridges behind them," Hooper
remembered. "But there was no wavering, no hesitance, no looking back
over the shoulder — they marched like an army, with banners, instinct with
purpose and might."

The candidate depicted scenes of rural Tennessee, where most of the
delegates lived, and spoke of the "simple, wholesome, sincere way of life"
that the average citizen followed, respecting the constitution and the law.
He believed that Democrats like those before him abhorred the nullification of the statewide prohibition statute in the cities. He pledged to stand
on the platform that the independent Democrats had written, to restore
the supremacy of the law, and to conduct a nonpartisan administration.
"This was a simple speech," Hooper wrote many years later. "But it was
what the convention wanted to hear, and they must have been deeply impressed with the sincerity and determination of the speaker.... These
words were not the evanescent frothings of a mere vote seeker. Behind
them lay a purpose that could never be deflected and a resolution that
could never be shaken." When Hooper was done, a wild demonstration
erupted throughout the hall. As he took his seat on the platform, a friend
sitting beside him asked if he could see a certain large man in the audience,
waving his coat around his head. Hooper replied that he could. His friend
grinned and said, "That is my presiding elder."[26]

That minister, that audience, stood squarely within the great ferment
of Progressivism. The reform-minded, public-spirited citizens caught up in
its sweep viewed their times with discontent; yet their belief in the possibilities for a better world remains inspiring, even if our more cynical age
see ironies in their means to that end. Many who cheered Hooper were
anxious to improve the lot of men for their own good but not necessarily
with their consent; ready to smite the enemy, and grind in justice with their
heel, to let the glory out.

The strength of the movement astonished some Patterson allies, now
without a candidate. Recently beaten in his bid for election to the Supreme
Court because he participated in Patterson's primary, R. M. Barton wrote
Duncan Cooper:

> We are in the midst of a very peculiar time and conditions.
> There is a strange atmosphere pervading this state and affec-
> ting many of its people. As I look at matters, a very consider-
> able number of our people are practically insane....

Robin's trial, he advised, "should be pushed and gotten over with before the election and in time to allow the Governor to act if he should be defeated." Katrina Williamson shared none of Barton's perplexity. "This 'independent' bolt could not have been avoided by any concession on earth," she raged. "It is simply the conclusion of a deal the legislature made with the Republicans through their managers, Shields and Cates, for their assistance in private schemes of these *immaculates* and to vent their personal hatred of Patterson."[27]

Other loyal Democrats doubted the depth of the independents' convictions. Hadn't the party faced and overcome the farmers, the populists, and the alliance between industrialists and Republicans? Now, as then, wasn't the answer a candidate around whom every one could rally, cheering, singing, tapping his feet?

These party faithful nominated Senator Bob Taylor at their convention on October 6. They and not the visionary independents were the true Democracy, they claimed. Their platform declared, with a novel evasion, that the regulation of alcoholic beverages was an economic, not a moral question. As for the election laws, let the voters choose the local election commission, and corruption from above would be ended.

Taylor had, of course, never stood for anything, but won elections by his personal style. The platform planks marked the intellectual summit of his campaign. On the stump he appealed, as he so often had before, for "the boys" to "come on home." Impervious to the irony of his imagery as he sought to succeed a man implicated by many in murder, Taylor told the crowds: ". . . I have got a revolver in each boot leg and a bowie knife down my back, and I haven't killed a Republican in three days. I believe in temperance and good government."

Desperately, the campaign turned to the rock of ages, the race issue. The only hope for preventing a return to carpetbag rule and the elevation of blacks was the election of Bob Taylor as governor, said his supporters in the press. As it had done in every election that the Republicans had contested since Reconstruction, the Democratic Party wrapped itself in the silken robes of redemption and declared itself the party of the white man alone. Luke Lea led the charge of this brigade from the editorial pages of the *Nashville Tennessean*. "If you want the criminal negroes to hold the balance of power in Davidson County and Tennessee," the editor told readers, "vote for the Patterson ticket throughout. That's the way to invite a repetition of the horrors of Reconstruction."

This time the strategy failed. Hooper made public morality the cornerstone of his campaign. He defined Malcolm Patterson as the issue and claimed that the campaign of Republicans and independent Democrats was "a voluntary uprising of the better elements . . . to free this commonwealth from the clutches of a criminal despotism that has disgraced it in the eyes of the world." Polite and affirmative on the stump, Hooper in his autobiography portrayed Patterson as a sniveling, impotent servant of liquor lobbyists.

The Republican candidate garnered the support of many notable, disillusioned Democrats. Attorney General Charles T. Cates campaigned for Hooper, depicting the issues as "genuine democracy and good citizenship against the forces of lawlessness and disorder." Prohibitionists, notably the Women's Christian Temperance Union, enlisted in Hooper's column. Said the candidate to a Memphis audience, "I know that I am but an atom, so to speak, borne upon the crest of a political revolution."

Hooper remembered the whirling campaign as filled with dramatic incident. Traveling with supporter Jeff McCarn through West Tennessee, the nominee gathered a crowd at one stop, only to have the city government try to disrupt his speech by sending the fire brigade past the speaking. At Columbia, an old Confederate veteran, preparing to say a good word for the candidate, fainted and fell on the platform, then revived and finished his speech.

That same day, a little boy knocked on the door of Hooper's hotel room. "I am Ned Carmack," he said, and handed the candidate a note. It was from the widow of the senator. Illness prevented her attending the speech, she wrote, but she extended her best wishes.

Hooper defeated Taylor 133,074 votes to 121,694. The victor won twenty thousand more votes than the Republican candidate had in 1908, and the loser received eleven thousand fewer than Patterson tallied that year. Most Democrats remained loyal to the party standard, but enough of them deserted it to give Hooper his slight majority. In Middle and West Tennessee, Hooper won between 30 and 40 percent more votes than the Republican candidate had in 1908.[28] The killing of Carmack, the pardon of his killers, and the Patterson administration's overweening exercise of power gave Tennessee its second Republican governor since Reconstruction. The voters returned a small Democratic majority to the State Senate and sent to the House enough independent Democrats to allow them to form a working coalition with the Republicans.

In the race for Criminal Court Judge in Nashville, Jeff McCarn charged his opponent, William Hart, with selecting for the grand jury persons whom he knew would not indict violators of the prohibition law. The "funny judge," McCarn labeled Hart. The attorney general vowed he would have the whiskey sellers "on the rock pile or in Hopkinsville," the southern Kentucky town that served as a distribution center for importers of liquor into Nashville. In the campaign, Hart referred to his opponent as "Governor McCarn," and on election day in early August smartly beat him 10,000 votes to 7,000.

The former attorney general returned to the practice of law and in 1912 worked in the successful reelection campaign of Governor Hooper. The following summer, President Woodrow Wilson named him United States Attorney for the Hawaiian Islands, where he served for two years. In 1916 McCarn returned to private practice in Nashville. He died in 1942, and obituary writers recalled his role as prosecutor in the Carmack murder case.[29]

Judge Hart spent the weeks after his reelection at his farm near Gallatin, resting for the coming term of court that included the case of Robin Cooper. "If I can just stay here until frost," he told a friend, he would be relieved from the attacks of neuralgia that had plagued him during the campaign. On Sunday, September 4, the day before he was to have taken his oath of office and convened court, he died. By law the responsibility fell to Governor Patterson to make a temporary appointment to the court.[30]

The new General Assembly had the duty of filling the U.S. Senate seat falling vacant in 1911. Senator James B. Frazier, whose election in 1905 angered Robert Taylor and impelled him to challenge Carmack, declared as a candidate to succeed himself. Former Governor Benton McMillin wanted the place in satisfaction of a long-held ambition. So did B. A. Enloe, just elected railroad commissioner on the ticket with Governor Hooper.

For days and days the balloting went on, Enloe at one point coming within three votes of election. Finally, Luke Lea sought out the governor. The Memphis delegation, he said, pledged him their votes for a single ballot. Would Hooper ask his old ticket-mate, Enloe, to stand aside for just that one round? Enloe grudgingly did, and it was enough; Lea took the prize that surely would have been Carmack's had he lived. At age thirty-one Lea became the youngest member of the United States Senate.[31]

Lea denied to Mrs. Carmack that he attended a harmony meeting between warring Democrats in the fall of 1910 knowing that J. C. Bradford would be present. The widow and the politician remained implacable in defense of the man they had loved and supported. Cobey Carmack credited Lea with crushing the Patterson organization, driving from power the man she held responsible for her husband's death.

For the rest of their lives, Luke Lea and Cobey Carmack showed each other deference and forbearance. Soon after her husband's death, the press reported her as likely to become postmaster at Columbia. But the president named another candidate, presumably one favored by the member of the House of Representatives representing the town. Did Taft prevail upon the congressman? Why did Lea refrain from upholding confirmation by the Senate? We do not know. But to widespread approval, President Wilson named Mrs. Carmack to the post in the summer of 1914.[32]

Congressman Kenneth McKellar's challenge to Senator Lea in 1916 forced Mrs. Carmack to choose between two personal and political friends of her husband. She loyally supported Lea, because he had been there, "at my boy's and my side, helping me to get justice." Nonetheless, McKellar won the Democratic nomination by a plurality, Memphis putting him ahead of the field of candidates that included, besides Lea, Malcolm Patterson and George L. Berry, labor's candidate. In November, McKellar defeated the Republican nominee, Ben W. Hooper.

In 1915 Mrs. Carmack wrote her brother-in-law, Sam, of her battle, "fighting thoughts, forgetting as far as possible the past." She survived her husband by forty years, increasingly isolated by deafness. In the senator's papers is her brief account of the campaign of 1908, which concludes: "A few days after the election, on November 9, he was assassinated on the public streets of Nashville by Duncan B. Cooper and his son, Robin Cooper." The last prepositional phrase is marked through with slashes.[33]

Senator Robert L. Taylor died on the last day of March 1912, a year before his term was to expire. Governor Hooper had the duty of filling the post, an appointment that was fraught with political risk. In an adroit maneuver, Hooper chose Newell Sanders, who had played the kingmaker in the Republican convention of 1910, and wrung from him the promise that he would serve only until the General Assembly of 1913 elected his successor.

In the election of 1912, Hooper beat the Democratic nominee, Benton McMillin. Once again, the voters returned to the legislature enough independent Democrats willing to continue the working coalition with Republicans. The first order of business before the General Assembly in January was the filling of Taylor's seat in the U.S. Senate. Chief Justice John K. Shields and Railroad Commissioner B.A. Enloe dominated the contest through several days of balloting, with most Republicans and independent Democrats supporting Enloe.

After Shields won sixty-four of sixty-six votes needed for election, the coalition with Luke Lea, working among his friends, turned its support to Attorney General Charles T. Cates. They could not prevail. On the next ballot, Shields, the leader of the untrammeled judiciary movement and a Carmack Democrat, won the election with the support of Democratic legislators who were not part of the so-called "fusionist" movement. The following day, the General Assembly honored Carmack's old teacher, W. R. "Sawney" Webb, with election to the Senate to fill out the two months remaining in Taylor's term.[34]

Senator Shields would cast the deciding vote in committee that sent to the floor with a favorable recommendation Woodrow Wilson's controversial nomination of Louis D. Brandeis as associate justice on the Supreme Court. Yet the president believed that Shields never liked him, and he admitted that the antipathy was mutual. As the Great War drew to a close, and Shields's contest for election was at hand, Wilson threatened to write an open letter to Tennessee Democrats, appealing to them to support the senator's opponent. "I want a senator who will uphold my plan of securing a permanent world peace," Wilson told Kenneth McKellar. "Mr. Shields will not be for me." McKellar later claimed he persuaded Wilson not to write the letter, and his colleague won reelection by ten thousand votes. But from that time on, Shields fought Wilson and his League of Nations. The letter Wilson did not write in 1918 he did write in 1923. Shields, he said, had been during his administration one of the least trustworthy of his professed supporters. Luke Lea gladly published the former president's letter as an advertisement in his *Tennessean.* The following year, Shields went down to defeat. McKellar credited Wilson's letter with being decisive.[35]

Like Hooper, Shields loved the highlanders of his native East Tennessee, and he returned to his homeplace, Clinchdale, some thirty miles north of Knoxville. Generations of his forebears lay buried in the graveyard there. Thoughts of the family plot may have influenced one of his opinions as a justice of the Tennessee Supreme Court, which enjoined a railroad from cutting a track through a cemetery. In 1941, the Tennessee Valley Authority opened Cherokee Dam on the Holston River, flooding Clinchdale. Before the waters came rushing over his estate, project managers disinterred what was left of the late senator and his family and moved them from their ancestral burial ground.[35]

To the east, the road between Johnson City and Elizabethton runs through Happy Valley. Sitting on the porch of his home, Alf Taylor reminisced for a visitor about his race for governor against his brother Bob in 1886, recalling the processions, the comical speeches, the practical jokes and furious fiddle-playing. The gift Tennesseeans denied him that year they gave him in time. In 1920, disillusioned with Wilson and the war, they voted for Warren G. Harding for president and Alfred A. Taylor for governor. He defeated the incumbent, Albert H. Roberts, by forty thousand votes. Carmack, Hart, Shields, and Taylor, all had looked to the Tennessee countryside for their health or the well-being of their state. "The only real happiness is in home, fireside, and family," Alf Taylor told the visitor to Happy Valley. "The truth of the matter is, that's all there is worth living for."

In Governor Taylor's reelection campaign of 1922, his three sons entertained the crowds with religious hymns and mountain folk tunes. The Democratic nominee, Austin Peay, promised to build highways, improve public education, and lower taxes, pledges that extended the original vision of his mentor, Malcolm Patterson. When Peay invoked Edward Carmack's name in the closing days of the campaign, Job Garner telegraphed the candidate deploring his right to do it.

The people cheered Taylor, but as the sound of his fiddle faded into the autumn night, they voted for Peay by a majority of forty thousand. With the valiant support of Luke Lea's *Tennessean*, Peay in two more successful biennial campaigns denounced urban bosses Ed Crump of Memphis and Hilary Howse of Nashville for dominating the state at the expense of the rural counties. Peay served until his death in 1927, having won a third term the year before, the first governor to do so since Isham G. Harris.[36]

Malcolm Patterson, who sought that distinction in 1910 and failed of it, wrote a note of sympathy to Duncan Cooper on the death of a brother in the summer of 1911. In the days of their power, they must have spent constant hours together. Now, Patterson informed Cooper, "As you can see, I am a lawyer again." He had returned to private practice in Memphis. Gradually, the friendship resumed. That fall, Patterson contemplated a challenge against Governor Hooper in 1912, asking Cooper's advice. In the same letter, he confided that he had to travel at once to Seattle to rescue Malcolm, Jr., from serious trouble. If the trouble was a bout with alcohol, as rumored at the time, the young man may have come by the disposition through inheritance. Katrina Williamson observed to her friend Colonel Cooper that for Governor Patterson, "drinking at all is most perilous."[37]

In July 1913, the former governor was arrested in a brothel in the slums just north of the Capitol. His friends believed that his political enemies had arranged the affair. The city court judge agreed, and dismissed the case. But Patterson made no excuses for himself. While waiting to transact some legal business, he recounted to the press, "I began to drink and continued until all sense of responsibility was gone."

Patterson from that moment swore off whiskey. "Liquor and I have parted company forever," he wrote Duncan Cooper a month after his arrest. The following spring, from the lecture circuit as a speaker for the Anti-Saloon League, he declared to his old friend, "Daily I am more pleased with this change. Now I am *free—and right.*"

Defeated for the Democratic nomination to the U.S. Senate in 1915, Patterson never abandoned the quest for vindication nor, apparently, the zeal of his convert's view. Governor Peay appointed him to the circuit court in Memphis in 1923, assuring the new judge that he need only remove himself for a time from public attention and voters would be in a different mood concerning his return to politics.

Patterson bided his time. For the Memphis *Commercial Appeal*, he wrote a column, "Day by Day with Governor Patterson," that presented his views on current affairs and public events. On December 20, 1925, he assured his readers, "If I had the power not another drop of liquor would ever be made or sold on earth. Law has not destroyed it, perhaps never will. Every man must write his own law of prohibition before the statutory one becomes wholly effective." And in words that echoed a passage in Edward

Carmack's lecture "Character," Patterson wrote, "I would like to know that I could keep even one boy from taking his first drink."

In the darkest days of the Great Depression, Patterson once again sought the governorship. "Back to the Good Old Days" was his campaign theme, that year of 1932. At his rallies, friends passed out sheets that bore the lyrics to popular songs. To the tune of "It's a Long Way to Tipperary," audiences sang, "It's a good thing to be a booster / It's the best thing I know."

Patterson made the race with the support of the outgoing administration of Governor Henry H. Horton. Horton was Luke Lea's man, his and Rogers Caldwell's, a business associate of Lea's. Caldwell and Company, an investment bank interested mainly in the bonds of Southern municipalities, had formed the Bank of Tennessee. There, the company placed its own deposits and, after Horton took office, an ever-increasing share of the capital assets of state government. With the crash of the stock market in October 1929, the Bank of Tennessee failed, and Horton faced charges of impeachment in the legislature. The move failed, but the governor left office in disgrace. His organization's support of Patterson had little effect. The Crump machine in Memphis delivered the election to Hill McAlister, demonstrating the Bluff City boss's domination of state politics.

In May 1934, following his conviction on bank fraud charges, Luke Lea entered prison. The following autumn, Patterson retired from the bench. On March 8, 1935, he died. Luke Lea, Jr., wrote a note of sympathy to Mary Gardner Patterson, on behalf of his father and himself.[38]

There was during these years a great gathering of souls involved in the affair between Duncan Cooper and Edward Carmack. In early March 1936, the Washington newspapers noted the death at Memphis of Katrina Williamson. As reported in the *Evening Star*, Mrs. Williamson was taken from her residence at the Stoneleigh Court apartments to a sanitarium in Memphis.

Many years later, Peter Taylor, her relation, described the last days of the woman who had befriended, advised, and perhaps loved Duncan Cooper, and who had spent the afternoon of Carmack's death with him. She appears as "Lottie Hathcock" in Taylor's story, "Their Losses." The narrator, Hathcock's niece, is bringing her dying aunt home to Tennessee from Washington and laments that Hathcock's passing "will be a loss to us all, for through her wit and charm she was an influence on Capitol Hill." The tables in her apartment "were covered with framed photographs of the wives of Presidents, Vice Presidents inscribed to Lottie Hathcock." Like her fictional counterpart, Katrina Williamson returned to Tennessee accompanied by a special nurse. "My aunt is a mental patient," Taylor's narrator tells a friend on the train. "She doesn't even know me." Mrs. Williamson died the day after reaching home.[39]

In the marriage of LaFollette's daughter, Kate, and Cooper's son, William, came a confluence of blood. When two of their children happened to fall in love, the grand old friends and political warhorses became ordinary in-laws. The days of LaFollette's fortune were behind him. Hard times beset the coal industry in the years after the First World War, and many miners fled the fields for opportunities in the North. He was forced to file for bankruptcy in 1924, his principal creditor holding notes and mortgages on properties LaFollette owned in Georgia and Tennessee. He remained in business in New York City. During a trip to the far West in 1929, he died and was buried in Colfax, Washington, where he was visiting relatives.[40]

Within weeks after his conviction for murder, Duncan Cooper was mulling over a return to the insurance business. In the summer of 1911, he inquired about writing health and accident policies on employees of the L & N Railroad, exchanging correspondence with the president of the line, Milton H. Smith. He eventually persuaded the company and the NC & St. L. to grant to certain insurance companies he represented the franchise for writing health and accident policies on their employees. Once he learned that the agent for one of the companies had "ideas in relation to labor organizations" not in harmony with those of the railroads, he urged a change. "I *can not* be placed in a position in any manner hostile to my friends," he declared.

By the summer of 1914, Cooper had established himself in Syracuse, New York, as general agent of the Connecticut Mutual Life Insurance Company. On June 25, Cooper wrote Theodore Roosevelt and pleaded with him not to run for governor but to save himself for the presidential contest of 1916. And he saluted, one old soldier to another:

> I voted for Lincoln the second time while I was in the Army, and have voted the Republican ticket straight until last year when I voted the Progressive ticket, so I may be said to be loyal to the interests of the country.[41]

Three days later, Archduke Ferdinand was shot to death as he rode through the streets of Sarajevo, and the world would never be the same.

Writing to his father from Karlsbad in August 1910, Robin Cooper included the itinerary for the rest of his European trip. The young lawyer planned to visit several towns in south Germany before going on to Paris. From there he would return home, stopping first in New York for a few days.

Robin's letter alluded to his plans to marry Evalee Smith in the fall. He was "looking with entire dependence," he wrote, to money his father had promised him since he had "practically no income from practice now" and did not expect to make a living for at least two years.

The news of his son's nuptials hardly surprised Duncan Cooper. Evalee Smith had visited Robin in confinement during the months after he killed Carmack. And Duncan Cooper probably knew full well of the matter that followed in the letter. "I am proceeding on the assumption," Robin wrote, "that Anderson and Hart will do as they indicated and put an end to my case."[42] "Anderson" presumably referred to Arthur B. Anderson, who had succeeded Jeff McCarn as attorney general in the general election of August 1910. But Hart had only a few weeks to live.

In his memoirs, written many years later, A. B. Neil insisted that Patterson named him criminal court judge without so much as mentioning the Cooper case. There is no reason to doubt that. Patterson would have considered only candidates who wholeheartedly shared his view that the Coopers committed no crime in killing Carmack. Carmack's old allies in the Anti-Saloon League regarded Neil as one of the "chief officers of the crime trust" in Nashville.[43]

Nor can there be much doubt of collusion in the events that then took place. On Monday evening, November 14, the *Banner* reported that Cooper's case, scheduled for the next morning in the Criminal Court, had been postponed. Two deputies in the office of Criminal Court Clerk Vernon Sharp apparently provided the information to the newspaper.

Luke Lea's reporters at the *Tennessean* and *American* tried to confirm the *Banner* story. Until after midnight on Monday, they called the homes of both Judge Neil and Attorney General Anderson. Neither came to the telephone; neither returned the calls. The editors evidently decided to rely upon the unconfirmed *Banner* story. Tuesday's edition of the morning paper announced that the Cooper case had been postponed, and no date set.

Guston Fitzhugh arrived in Nashville as the *Tennessean* reached the streets. He went immediately to Lea's office. The Memphis lawyer wanted to make absolutely certain of the report. He asked a stenographer to telephone the criminal court clerk. The party on the other end of the line assured Lea's aide that the Cooper case would not be heard that day. Satisfied, Fitzhugh went about other business.

About thirty minutes after court convened, Sharp, the clerk, called the Cooper case. The defendant was present, and, as though expecting the state in force, so were his attorneys: John M. Anderson, William H. Washington, Charles N. Burch, M. Henry Meeks, and James C. Bradford. Attorney General Arthur Anderson requested a jury for the disposition of the case, and twelve men filed into the box. The courtroom fell silent as he addressed the bench. Briefly he reviewed the two trials, then offered his views of the evidence.

Arthur B. Anderson. Source: *Nashville American* (Aug. 6, 1910).

Albert B. Neil. Courtesy *Nashville Tennessean* (Sept. 15, 1933).

> I do not only believe that Robin Cooper was not proved guilty, but I believe his innocence was established ... I could not conscientiously prosecute a man whom I believe to be innocent and will not go through the farce of arguing against conscience.

A new trial was bound to end in acquittal, the attorney general argued, and it was his duty to save public money and time by ending the matter now. "This case was set for trial today, which fact has been widely publicized," he observed. Yet in the two-and-a-half months since taking office, he had heard nothing from those attorneys who obtained Cooper's conviction. Under all these circumstances, the chief prosecutor concluded, "I desire to recommend to the court that a verdict of not guilty be entered."

Judge Neil turned to the jury. In view of the statement of the attorney general, he said, and of the fact that no further effort was being made to prosecute the case, the jury would return a verdict of not guilty. And the jury did as it was told. Robin Cooper left the courtroom in the company of his lawyers, a free man. With the impaneling of the jury, he had been placed in jeopardy of his life for murdering Carmack. Under the Fifth Amendment to the Constitution, he could never be tried again on the charge.

"Justice can only bow her head and weep," Fitzhugh told reporters, when the public prosecutor would not prosecute and the governor had ready another pardon. Attorneys for the state, representing the Carmack family, petitioned the court to declare the proceedings illegal and void on the grounds that prosecutors had received no notice. The petition bitterly arraigned Attorney General Anderson and accused him of plotting with Robin Cooper and his lawyers. Judge Neil refused to allow the petition to be filed.[44]

Robin Cooper and Evalee Smith, daughter of L & N President Milton Smith, married in Louisville on December 15, 1910. Returning to Nashville after a wedding trip to Panama, the couple made their home for the next eight years on Twenty-fourth Avenue, South, in the Murphy Addition near Vanderbilt University. Mrs. Cooper's brother-in-law, Thomas Felder, had developed the area (naming it for his foster parents). Nettie Bell Smith, when she decided to marry Felder, sent word to another suitor requesting the return of her letters. Appearing at her door, the boy shot himself and fell dead at her feet. She reached down to the corpse, took the letters from the coat pocket, and only then called for help.

Three sons were born to Evalee and Robin Cooper. They named Milton for his maternal grandfather, a man widely despised in Nashville for his line's monopoly over the shipping business. Robin, Jr.,'s name would memorialize his father, and William's his venerable great-uncle.[45]

In the years after his trial, Robin Cooper resumed his legal career in association with his uncle, J.C. Bradford. The two appeared together in Chancery Court from time to time, with Bradford listed in the rule docket as the chief counsel. After Bradford's death in 1914, Cooper went on developing a practice that grew in prestige. He represented among others the Gerst Brewing Company, the Metropolitan Life Insurance Company, and the noted Nashville builder, the Foster Creighton Company. The Martindale Company evaluated Cooper's legal ability as "very good" and reported that he received "very high" recommendations, which were its most estimable professional ratings.

Cooper's part in Carmack's death did not hinder his status in the community. He belonged to the Belle Meade Country Club, the social center for upper-class Nashvillians, and to the older downtown Hermitage Club, the finest in the city. Mrs. William M. Geraldton listed him and his wife in her blue-covered "Social Directory" of the city, published in 1915. In June 1919, the Cooper family moved into a Tudor house on Leake Avenue, a road also known as the golf club lane because it led from Harding Road to the Belle Meade course.[46]

That same month Robin Cooper sailed on the *Mauretania* for France, there to represent the American heirs of his cousin, Baroness Antoinette de Charette, for whom his father had once named a falls on a wild, roaring river. Young Cooper encountered a Europe on the edge of collapse. A member of the British Parliament pointed out to his colleagues that all the people east of the Rhine, not only in Germany but in Russia, Rumania, Austria, and Bohemia were in danger of starvation. Ninety percent of the sales in many women's shops in Germany comprised mourning clothes because throughout the former Kaiser's domain the children were dying. It was a deliberate policy of the victorious allies that not even they should have any help. "We are enforcing the blockade with rigor," wrote Winston Churchill, the assistant secretary of state.

On June 23, two hours before the allied armies' deadline for beginning an invasion into Germany, its government surrendered. In Paris soldiers and their girls danced in the grand boulevards. Searchlights and lamps lit the city as brightly as noon. Robin Cooper of Nashville must have shared in the honor done Americans wherever they went. He returned home to a changed land. On July 1, prohibition took effect throughout the United States. The law forbade the manufacture of alcoholic beverages made from grains, cereals, or fruits, some of those essential foodstuffs denied the starving children of Europe. After June 30, it became illegal to sell liquor or transport it across state lines. Anyone who wanted to drink in his own home could do that, if he could obtain a supply.[47]

On Sunday evening, August 24, Evalee Cooper, with her firstborn son, boarded a train at Nashville's Union Station, bound for Evanston, Illinois, to visit relatives. The newspapers later quoted unnamed sources as saying that Robin Cooper entertained guests that evening. On Monday night, so the police understood, a quiet poker game took place. (Relatives insisted that the game had been whist bridge.) One servant said the play, whatever it was, continued on Tuesday and Wednesday night.[48]

Cooper reportedly arose on Thursday morning at his usual hour, ate breakfast with William and Robin, Jr., then drove into town. His office, which he shared with brother attorney Albert W. Akers, was on the seventh floor of the Stahlman Building.

About nine o'clock, he went down to the first floor. There in the lobby, he spoke for a few minutes with Jim Jacobs, Jules Lusky, and Paul Eldridge. A newspaper account subsequently described the conversation as an argument. Cooper returned upstairs.

Near eleven o'clock he left his office again, going down one floor to the suite of G. Bibb Jacobs, a lawyer and brother of Jim. Bibb Jacobs, the press reported later, was out of the city. Again Cooper spoke with Eldridge and Jim Jacobs. Reginald Stonestreet joined the three men for this meeting.

At noon Cooper went to the Hermitage Club, where he lunched with insurance broker Tom Morris, Jr., and other friends. Afterwards the party drove out to the Belle Meade Country Club. They spent the afternoon on the links.

Cooper reached the eighteenth hole first and, without waiting for the others, returned to his home nearby. He left a word for Morris with the clerk at the clubhouse desk, asking his friend to telephone him. Morris, returning to town, decided to make the call from the Hermitage Club. But he sat down to dinner and apparently forgot the message until about nine, when he rang the Cooper home. Robin told him, "I wanted you to have dinner with me, nothing important."[49]

Sometime later — first reports put the hour at about 10 P.M. — servants heard a man's voice calling from the front lawn, "Cooper, Cooper!" Close acquaintances called one another by their surnames in those days. Cooper came to the door, but he did not invite this caller inside. "Do you have a car here?" servants heard the voice ask.

"Yes," Cooper said.

"Then get it."

Cooper closed the door and, putting on his straw hat, went upstairs to kiss his sons goodnight.

Back downstairs, he started toward the front door, then changed his mind. He took off his hat, hung it on a hatrack in the hall, and went out the back door. The donning, then doffing of the hat suggests that Cooper first planned to go out at the behest of his visitor, but changed his mind and was preparing to refuse whatever further entreaties were made.

Maude Perkins, a housegirl apparently attending the children, went to a window overlooking the front porch when she heard the stranger calling. She saw a "large square-jointed man" standing in the dark and talking with her employer. Apparently the visitor walked around the house to the garage after Cooper shut the door.

Dennis Metcalf, the gardener, occupied a room in one of the outbuildings. On this humid late summer night, he had opened his window. When Cooper came out the back door, he and the visitor resumed their conversation. Metcalf claimed he heard only one phrase distinctly. Cooper told the other man, "You could have had more if you'd asked for it." The two of them got into the car and drove off, heading west on Leake Avenue toward Harding Road. One of the servants remembered that the clock struck nine a few minutes after the visitor came.[50]

An hour later Walter O. Parmer, who owned the farm between Harding Road and the Cooper home, heard a shot ring out. "That sounded like a German pistol, and it hit something," he remarked to his brother, Samuel. Josie Starnes, a servant in the Parmer home, lived in a cabin just thirty-five feet from the golf club lane. She also heard the pistol report.[51]

Neither she nor the Parmers went out into the night to investigate. Over the city and countryside, the rain was pouring down.

CHAPTER SIX

The Murder of
Robin Cooper

BETWEEN THE TIME ONE OF HIS KILLERS swung a long flat rock against Cooper's head and the discovery of his body, a day and a half passed. No one at the household reported his absence. Passersby later mentioned seeing his Overland automobile parked by the road with headlamps ablaze, but none investigated.

About 7:30 on Saturday morning, Samuel Parmer drove over the bridge on Leake Avenue that spanned Richland Creek. The car, its lights still burning, remained on the grassy shoulder of the road's right lane. The transmission had choked in reverse gear. Parmer saw some newspapers lying on the seats. They were stained with blood. More blood was splattered on and just under the windshield and marred the upholstery on the ceiling.[1]

On the back seat lay a billfold, belonging to Cooper. Inside were a check for $10.42, a poll tax receipt, and requisitions from the Nashville Golf and Country Club. The lawyer's notebook, also found in the car, contained notations of lawsuits and letters and memoranda about Cooper's passage to France.[2]

Resting against the right rear door, nearly perpendicular with the floor, was the murder weapon: a large stone, fifteen inches long, six inches wide, and two inches thick. It was streaked with blood.

Parmer's call to the police brought the chief of the force, Alex Barthell, and the chief deputy sheriff, Robert Moore. By nine o'clock officers were combing the lane and the woods near the car.

The *American* printed an extra edition, and the curious flocked out Harding Road to the scene. As the auto in which he was riding crossed the tracks of the Belle Meade street car line, Harry Argo was looking out the window on the passenger side. Railroad tracks ran parallel to the highway some sixty-five feet to the north. When the car passed over Richland Creek, flowing under Harding Pike, Argo thought he saw something. His companion, George Blackwood, stopped. Argo alighted, clambered down the bank, and strode into the knee-deep water.

The roiling current pinned Robin Cooper's corpse fast against the railroad trestle with only the right shoulder visible above the water. Argo dragged the body to the bank, where Blackwood stood waiting. There they remained until Chief Barthell arrived. He hefted the body into his car and drove it to Dorris, Karsch, and Company, undertakers, where a coroner's jury convened.[3]

When he died Cooper was wearing a lightweight summer suit, silk shirt, and tan shoes. His coat had been almost torn from his body. The left pockets of his trousers, front and rear, were turned inside out. In the right front pocket was a silver pocketknife on a chain and $2.02 in change. As the undertaker removed his shirt, a crayfish skidded from beneath the folds and fell to the floor.[4]

First reports of a bullet wound in the head proved unfounded. But an autopsy revealed six open lesions there. From the eyes up, Cooper's face was beaten in. The stone had crushed the skull all around and fractured it at the base. The ring finger of the left hand was broken and the knuckles of that hand were badly torn, which led some to believe that Cooper had vigorously resisted his assailant. The coroner's jury concluded that Cooper had died from wounds inflicted with a blunt instrument by a party or parties unknown. Among the physicians present at the inquest was the dead man's brother-in-law, Lucius E. Burch.[5]

Rites for Robin Cooper, led by the Episcopal bishop of Tennessee, took place at midday Monday at Christ Church. ("They who are known as the 'quality' of Nashville attended," an out-of-town correspondent wrote.) The mourners sang "Brief Life Is Here Our Portion" and prayed the prayers of the new liturgy. Then they accompanied Cooper's remains to Mount Olivet Cemetery.[6]

Within hours of the discovery of his body, the police were saying that a quarrel over bootleg whiskey had cost Robin Cooper his life. Their sources told them that he had borrowed a supply from a friend to entertain a guest, a Mr. Walker, whom he had met on his trip to France. Promising to pay back the loan on Thursday or Friday, he contracted for delivery at the isolated spot on the road near his home. According to this theory, the bootlegger came to his door and demanded more money before turning over the shipment. Cooper replied with the exasperated remark that the gardener overheard. Alex Barthell sketched the rest of the scene. "When they got to the place where the whisky was to be delivered," he surmised for a reporter from Cincinnati, "the bootlegger figured that the opportunity was at hand to get the money and keep the whisky as well."

Slain Attorney, Death Car And Murder Scene

The car in which Robin Cooper died and the rock with which he was bludgeoned. Source: *Nashville American* (Aug. 30, 1919).

In an interview with the same correspondent, Lucius Burch pronounced this the most logical explanation of the crime. Wasn't this how bootleggers worked, meeting their customers along a side road? And did not the fact that every bone in Cooper's skull was fractured mean that the criminal was a man "of very low order?" Burch asked. "The murderer of Robin Cooper," he observed, "struck again and again until the last spark of life had been struck out."[7]

Tennessee's "bone dry" law of 1917 had made it illegal to ship liquor into the state or even to possess intoxicants. Nonetheless, cars and trucks creaking under the weight of barrels of Kentucky whiskey made the run from Hopkinsville and other Kentucky border towns to Nashville. Local entrepreneurs concocted several cheaper, but potent, varieties of moonshine. The coming of national prohibition failed from the start to halt the consumption of intoxicants in Nashville. Chief Barthell cracked down on bootleggers and other vice peddlers, leading to more than sixteen thousand arrests in 1919. District Attorney General G. B. Kirkpatrick railed against the "reservoirs of liquor" in the city.[8]

The police clung for several days to the idea that bootleggers had killed Cooper. They reportedly questioned every man who made and sold whiskey, but they brought charges against only one. J. F. Feuston had the reputation of dealing in liquors of a high grade and numbering clubmen of the city among his clients. On his arrest, in the company of a companion, Miss Casey Jordan, he was carrying 150 quarts of whiskey in his automobile. The police did not want Feuston, or Miss Jordan, or the moonshine; they wanted the name of Cooper's liquor dealer. Feuston's answer was apparently, Not me, and I don't know who. Agents of the U.S. Department of Justice acknowledged late Monday that they had seen Feuston on the southbound train from Louisville on the night of the murder.[9]

Some argued that the man who had come to Cooper's door had spirited him away intending to rob him. On the day his body was pulled from Richland Creek, the newspapers reported that Cooper had recently taken out a bank loan of ten thousand dollars. Rumors of gambling losses at the poker parties were heard on the street. Yet Albert Akers, who claimed to know his law partner well, dismissed the idea that Cooper was troubled by debt. Later published accounts put the bank loan at four thousand dollars, of which only two hundred dollars had been withdrawn. Not known for carrying large sums of money on his person, Cooper apparently left home on the fatal ride without stopping to gather up a bundle of cash.[10]

On Tuesday morning, reporters asked Chief of Detectives Robert Sidebottom what theory the police would proceed on now. "There's no telling," he said with a chuckle.[11]

Twenty-four hours later he declared, "the police are on the right clue." Chief Barthell added, "We have just begun today to get valuable information pertaining to the Cooper murder case," referring to facts developed by Emergency Officer Joseph D. Ferriss. Based on this newly discovered evidence, the *Banner* expected the momentary arrest of two men and a "sensation transcending the crime." It quoted an unidentified physician as saying, on the day Cooper's body was found, that he was killed "as a result of a business transaction and because he knew entirely too much." In particular, he had once threatened to "expose something concerning his

alleged dealings with a concern selling stocks which he is believed . . .
to have bought and subsequently discovered to be worthless." His murder,
the report continued, had been linked "to local channels of speculative
finance."

That same afternoon the *American* named the four men — Jim Jacobs,
Reginald Stonestreet, Paul Eldridge, and Jules Lusky — with whom Cooper
held two conversations on the last morning of his life. Barthell was quoted
as saying that the Pinkerton detectives on the case "had a line" on another
person connected with the corporation from a previous investigation.[12]

"Police have questioned three prominent businessmen who were
associated in stock transactions with Robin Cooper," the *Cincinnati Post*
reported. The men, whom it did not name, acknowledged the conference.
Such conferences took place almost daily, they said, and that far from being
dissatisfied, Cooper was pleased with the way affairs of the company were
proceeding. "The par value of the the stock was fifty cents a share," the
newspaper reported, and quoted the men as telling police that Cooper had
declared he would not sell his for five dollars apiece. "Our relations were
of the friendliest," they added.

The police obviously gave the story about the stock dealing to the
press, only to retract it within hours. By Wednesday evening, Sidebottom
was denying that he had "made any statement reflecting on prominent
businessmen of Nashville," a denial carried in Thursday morning's *Tennessean*. That afternoon, the *Banner* printed no story at all about the Cooper
case. And the *American* noted that the police had thoroughly investigated
and "cast aside as worthless" the theory that the tragedy grew out of a conventional business misunderstanding. Sidebottom, evidently reined in by
his chief, did not talk to the press for several days. Most out-of-town newspapers withdrew their correspondents after the police discarded the latest
theory.[13]

From then until the end of the comedy, Luke Lea's newspapers, the
Tennessean and the *American*, the latter abruptly cut off from its sources,
were reduced to comments on the case from actresses, idlers, and the
district attorney. E. B. Stahlman's *Banner*, when next it took up the story,
reported in headlines that the family of Robin Cooper had concluded that
"there is nothing which would establish a motive for the crime." Since
Milton Smith thought that no one had cause to murder his son-in-law, Major Edward B. Stahlman, former vice president of the L & N, most assuredly
agreed.

Stahlman's newspaper had in 1917 supported the reelection of Mayor
William Gupton, challenged by Hilary Howse, the former mayor who had
refused to enforce prohibition. Alex Barthell was identified with the reform
element that in the *Banner*'s words wanted to "clean house" of the "lawlessness, graft, and flamboyant vulgarity" that had characterized the Howse

Dennis E. Metcalf. Source: *Nashville American* (Sept. 26, 1919).

years. The "good government" ticket won, and so owed something to Stahlman and the merchants and manufacturers for whom his paper largely
spoke.

Smith's words about no motive probably carried some weight with
Barthell, who had gotten work on the line as a detective after he shot down
a local labor leader during a heated political dispute in 1896. Barthell
remained the railroad's faithful employee for more than ten years, then
entered politics.[14] If Smith had Pinkerton detectives employed on the case,
as Barthell told the press, they surely knew what Joseph Ferriss knew, or
soon learned whereof he spoke. And the information was Smith's to use,
his and Lucius Burch's.

For unknown reasons, Sheriff Joe W. Wright kept secret the recovery
of a pair of blood-stained overalls on the day Cooper's body was found.
These belonged to the gardener, Dennis Metcalf. When officers announced

the find on Thursday, it diverted attention from the facts and speculations in the previous day's press.

Officers were also now putting hopes in an analysis of bloody finger-prints left in the car where Cooper died. Two sets of marks, one of them near the handle, marred the left rear door. A fingerprint expert, Captain Robert S. Dunning of the Cincinnati police department, spent a day in con-sultation with Sidebottom. They removed the door, dusted the marks with powdered aluminum, and studied them with a magnifying glass. Dunning also examined the bloody newspapers taken from the car.

Bound for home on the northbound Pullman on Saturday night, Dun-ning discussed his findings with a reporter. "There is a difference between fingerprints and impressions," he explained, "and the marks left in blood on the rear door of the car were impressions and badly smudged." As for the newspapers, their texture could not take a print. The same applied to the rock since "it is practically impossible to get any fingerprints on stone unless it is a smooth finish." But his examination of the rock led him to believe that a big man had done the deed. "It took a large hand to use such a weapon," he said. Dunning concluded that the Robin Cooper case was "one of the great murder mysteries of the country."[15]

As the expert left the city, Barthell authorized the statement that after a week's investigation the police were no nearer a solution to the crime than the morning the body had been found. "There has never been a case into which more real work has been put," he told reporters. Fourteen police and detectives were assigned to the case. They had interviewed some one hundred and seventy-five people, securing written statements from most of them. Three automobiles had been constantly in service, chasing down leads that had come to them from the interviews, letters, and telephone calls. More than thirty people had been taken within hearing distance of the family servants, who listened as these suspects called out, "Cooper, Cooper."

His officers, according to Barthell, had established certain facts. Cooper was killed while sitting at the steering wheel of his car. The time of death was around eleven o'clock on Thursday night, two hours after he and the unknown party rode off in the rain down Leake Avenue. Cooper knew the man who came to the door and, although annoyed, did not leave home in apprehension of his life. And, according to the *Banner*, "certain statements have been made that lead the officers to believe that perhaps two men were implicated in the crime."[16] Stahlman's newspaper reported the police chief's fulsome account of his department's labors in a tone that agreed with his conclusion: We have done all we can, and we have no reliable clues nor any apparent motive.

One person who saw Cooper's killers told police there were two of them. Steve Fulghum, a black man whose name Walter Parmer gave to the police, had taken a late streetcar from town to the end of the line and was riding out into the country on the horse that he had left tied in Belle Meade Park. At the lane leading left to the golf club, he noticed two men, one about a head taller than the other, standing by the stone wall there and an automobile parked on the right shoulder. One report said that Fulghum saw the pair get into a roadster and speed east from the scene toward Nashville. Another news story indirectly quoted Fulghum as seeing the car being backed off Harding Road onto Leake Avenue. By this account, a short time passed before one man jumped out of the stalled car, walked back to Harding Road, and climbed into a vehicle waiting for him. According to both reporters, Fulghum placed the time as about 10 P.M.[17]

And there, it seems, the police investigation of the case stopped. The few facts that Barthell and Sidebottom laid out were all they would ever have. A reward for information leading to the arrest of the murderer totaled $1,500: $500 apiece from Governor Albert Roberts, Dr. Lucius Burch and friends, and a like amount from members of the bar. The sum would never be paid. "Any way you look at it," commented a thirty year veteran of the police department, "the Cooper case is the greatest criminal mystery Nashville has ever had."[18]

Two weeks after the murder of Robin Cooper, divekeeper Sol Cohn was accosted in the garage of his home and relieved of a diamond stud. "Without a clue, the police worked for several days," according to one newspaper account, before two men were arrested by Chief of Detectives Sidebottom and his officers. All shared in the five hundred dollar reward.[19] The police had much richer information with which to pursue the murderers of Robin Cooper than they had to accuse the muggers of Cohn. But when the fingerprints in the death car proved useless, the hope among police for conclusive evidence seemed to vanish. They abandoned the field, and left the intriguing case to those with peculiar powers.

Nashville's "Seer of the Unseen," Mrs. Anna W. Littleton, declared that "I feel yet that I shall go out to the creek, wet my handkerchief, wipe the blood from the car, and walk up to the man who killed Cooper and say, 'I have brought you something.'" Dusting just a drop of snuff into her nostrils, she shuffled her cards, and produced her revelations. Two men killed Cooper, she said, one stocky and dark, the other tall and light. The dark man had already left town, but the light one remained behind. He is "something of a politician," and works in a public building, Littleton revealed. He was worried because Cooper shot him, burning his cuffs and wrist. The pistol was still in the creek.

Littleton had the audacity to go to the Cooper home and ask to see the widow, who gave her an audience. The police dismissed the seeress's theories altogether. But three days after her first interview in the newspapers, they were dragging rakes over the bed of Richland Creek for a gun.[20]

On September 26, on a warrant sworn out by Gabriel Hansen, a self-styled "psychoanalytic detective," sheriff's deputies arrested Dennis Metcalf for the murder of Robin Cooper. Hansen, whom the newspapers called the "dream sleuth," arrived in Nashville from his home in Memphis and, amid the frustration of officials, promoted himself into the leading authority on the case. Supposedly he had once helped find some lost Mexican bonds and now operated a business that sought misplaced valuables and missing persons. He reportedly carried letters from a former judge, a representative of the U.S. Department of Justice, and others.[21]

Hansen claimed that during a "psychological demonstration," he saw Metcalf kill Cooper in his garage while seated in the car. The body was then drawn over the seat into the back. The killer drove to the bridge nearest the railroad trestle and placed Cooper's remains on the creekbank. The rain swelled the creek, and the rising water picked them and carried them to the pylon. "I have solved the Cooper murder," Hansen told reporters. "I know by past experience that what I have seen is the truth." Anna Littleton, who had earlier pronounced Metcalf innocent, realized Hansen had stolen the footlights from her. "I knew it all the time," she said with a sage nod to a reporter.[22]

Also arrested on Hansen's warrant was Nora Lee Jones, a cook for the Cooper family, charged with being an accessory before the fact. A newspaper account of an interview between Jones and one of the investigating officers linked her with Metcalf. The policeman went into the kitchen after the overalls were seized and remarked to the cook, "You must have lots of good food out here. Do you have chicken often?" "Yes," she replied, "we had a chicken Thursday night. Metcalf went out and killed us a chicken."[23]

At the preliminary hearing for Jones and Metcalf, attorney Roscoe Bond entered their pleas of not guilty. "This is the twentieth century," he observed to reporters. "The days of witchcraft and spells and mystic incantations are over." On Sunday, the prisoners went free on bond.[24]

Now the authorities turned over to Dr. William Litterer of Vanderbilt University Medical School the pair of blood-stained overalls they had held since the day Cooper's body was pulled from the creek. The gardener explained that the stains came from slaughtering a chicken or maybe from swatting horseflies. The tests to distinguish human blood would take a long time, the press was given to understand.[25]

The police had questioned Metcalf earlier, but allowed him to go. Chief Barthell commented that Hansen had never furnished him any evidence, "but he did ask that the Negro woman be arrested, claiming that she knew all about the murder. I asked him to 'cite me,' and he said it was only his theory." The sheriff's deputy who had actually found the overalls, Robert A. Moore, wanted to wait until the results of Litterer's tests became known. Hansen's warrant compelled him to act; thereafter he and his department left the dream sleuth to twist slowly in the wind.[26]

A man of about fifty years, with little formal education, Metcalf insisted he had never had a cross word with Robin Cooper. He told reporters that he came to work for the household in June. Before that, he and his wife had farmed on an Alabama plantation. She left there and came to Nashville, where she found work in the household of the family from whom the Coopers bought their home. Joining her in the city, Metcalf took work as a mechanic. His wife helped him obtain his place with the Coopers, then departed for Chicago seeking better wages. Police first questioned him on the morning after they found Cooper's body, when he quoted the reply that his employer made to the caller, "You could have had more if you had asked for it."[27]

Hansen constructed his case against Metcalf and Jones relying upon popular prejudices of the hour, created by the newspapers, then aped by others. The bigoted *Tennessean* reported that Metcalf spoke with an accent and noted that he had a foreign-born wife, this at an hour when the attorney general of the United States, A. Mitchell Palmer, was rounding up Americans of foreign extraction and jailing them as spies and terrorists without proof. Was not Metcalf the last man to see Robin Cooper alive, except his murderers? Was he not one of "a very low order?" As for the servants, their failure to report their employer's absence all day Friday might persuade a jury that they were not eager for his whereabouts to be discovered. A "prominent businessman" was quoted as saying that he had telephoned the house on Friday night. The voice on the other end of the line told him that Cooper had not been at home all day, laughed, and hung up.[28]

A week after Metcalf and Jones posted bond, the psychic detective put some new evidence before Attorney General G. B. Kirkpatrick, the amount of the gardener's bond was raised, and deputies returned him to jail. That same day, Friday, October 4, Hansen swore out a warrant for Thomas E. Jennings on the charge of being an accessory to the murder of Robin Cooper. The *New York Times* identified Jennings as a "capitalist" because he told the papers that he lived on his investments. An eccentric character, he reportedly inquired of Hansen about some anonymous letters that the detective had received. That aroused Hansen's suspicions. Percy Warner, president of the Nashville Railway and Light Company and real estate magnate — a genuine capitalist — went surety on Jennings' bond. No more was heard of him in connection with the case.[29]

Kirkpatrick liked Hansen. "One of the smartest men I ever met," the attorney general told the *American*. "He has given the best practical analysis of the case I have ever heard." Hansen also claimed credit for finding suspicious letters in a trunk kept in a room that Metcalf rented downtown. Kirkpatrick repeatedly allowed Hansen extensions in presenting his evidence to the grand jury.[30]

Roscoe Bond aggressively countered the dilatory tactics of the state. After Metcalf was imprisoned the second time, Bond obtained a writ of habeas corpus. But the following Tuesday, Metcalf's bondsman withdrew, and he voluntarily surrendered to police. For the third time, he was locked up.[31]

"'This looks bad for Metcalf,'" the *American* quoted an anonymous source supposedly close to the grand jury. "'Gabriel Hansen has some very material evidence besides the letters and the bloody rags.'" But Bond argued that if the grand jury failed promptly to indict his client, he was entitled to his freedom. Hansen failed to appear before the panel on October 7, and the lawyer sought a second writ of habeas corpus. The judge of the circuit court denied the plea. But this time the jury, led by foreman Sam Borum, got down to business.

On the morning when the court heard Metcalf's petition, jurymen opened a new investigation of the Robin Cooper murder case. Although the *Banner* credited the grand jury with exploring the mystery "from all angles," it is not clear that the panel did any such thing. None of the witnesses whose names were printed in the newspaper was in a position to know of Cooper's dealings with the men he argued with twelve hours before he died.

Among those giving testimony—published reports put the number at between thirty and seventy-five—was Steve Fulghum. A salesman from Castner-Knott testified that Metcalf had been in the department store the day after the murder displaying bills of large denominations. William Litterer appeared before the panel, saying his tests had thus far found no human blood on Metcalf's overalls, and he appealed for more time to complete the work. The dead man's father also gave evidence. "I will prosecute anybody the jury indicts and thinks murdered my son," declared Colonel Duncan Cooper.[32]

Sam Borum had worked for a time as Wright's deputy. In the spring of 1919 Wright fired him for allegedly taking on a hunt for blockade runners two men who were not deputized and then shooting up an automobile that held no liquor but did belong to a reputable citizen. On his dismissal, Borum accused Wright of giving protection to a ring of boss bootleggers. Chief Deputy Robert Moore led the sheriff's defense. Wright and Moore's case against Metcalf, resting on some blood-stained rags, a few letters of a barely literate man, and Gabriel Hansen's trances, went to a grand jury whose foreman bore no affection toward the sheriff's department.[33]

On October 30, the grand jury returned a no true bill, and Dennis

Metcalf walked out of jail a free man. Hansen, his accuser, had left town. "I hope Gabriel Hansen don't return to Nashville with any more of his dreams," Metcalf muttered.[34]

All his life, Edward Carmack, Jr., claimed that he murdered Robin Cooper and thus avenged his father. The young man's name was on many lips in those late summer days, as the case seized the local headlines and held briefly the attention of the nation. Carmack's lawyer and lifelong friend, Jordan Stokes, III, always believed that Carmack wielded the rock that bludgeoned the life out of Cooper. So did the police, or so they said to Carmack when they picked him up for questioning. Stokes recalled the scene many years later: "They told him, 'We know you did it, you might as well confess.' And Ned answered, 'If you know I did it, prosecute me.'"[35]

About to resume a pinched life as a third-year law student at Cumberland University in Lebanon, Tennessee, Carmack was staying in Nashville on August 28, 1919, at the Phi Delta Theta house on the Vanderbilt campus. Ned belonged to the fraternity, and local chapters extended that courtesy to brothers from other campuses.[36]

Carmack had lately seen something of the world. He graduated from Columbia Military Academy in 1916, and his aptitude and good record won him admission to Vanderbilt University. Apparently he did not do well there. He transferred to Cumberland and completed courses that qualified him for admission to law school. He pursued legal studies at the University of Chicago for a time before returning to Cumberland. In 1918, the nation at war, he enlisted. Yet he bridled at the military life, and fortunately for him his active service was short. That fall his orders took him as far as Camp Perry, Ohio. With the Armistice he waited there for demobilization and received his pass home before Christmas.

In his twentieth year Ned Carmack possessed no power of judgment or degree of patience beyond his age. He was courting Charlotte Lockridge, and no matter how much he loved her, he doubted both her ardor and her fidelity to him. He lived all that spring and summer of 1919 in terrible anger, and more than once he nearly severed the ties between them.[37]

To Jordan Stokes and other friends, Ned Carmack gave a detailed account of how he would have accomplished—the conditional tense was his—the murder of Robin Cooper. "'I would have gone upstairs that evening,'" Stokes recalled Carmack saying. "'People would have seen me go up, wouldn't see me come down. I would have climbed out the window and down a trellis. I would not have gone out the road [West End Avenue and Harding Road] where I might have been seen. I would have walked along the railroad, to Belle Meade.'"

Did you really do it, Ned, Stokes once asked his friend. And Carmack answered, "Don't you ever tell anybody I didn't."[38]

Carmack gave Stokes the poem he wrote in which Cooper's spirit appears to him, "Begging the crumbs of memory that fall / From life's loud feast. . . ." Does he also come to challenge to a duel in the hereafter? Carmack asks.

> Will that other be there also—
> Why comes he not?—to hold the front
> While you strike from behind?

And the poet boasts, "In that grim foursome / I shall not fight alone."
Carmack taunts and insults his spectral visitor:

> Where are your bosom's pals,
> Your sons that I have seen
> Clamber your knees so fondly,
> Your mare-faced wife
> Whose father's money bought you?

He asks of all these loves of Robin's life, does not one remember? Does only his enemy not forget?

> Would God that I could give you breath again
> That I might snuff
> That whimpering breath.[39]

Carmack's lines called Robin Cooper back from the grave so that he and not some other could send him there again. An imaginative, even visionary man, he longed to round out a tale begun long before his birth, the story of landed aristocrats who had tried to deny his father his dreams of building a purer world by murdering him, only themselves to die under his son's blows, leaving children as he, Ned, had been left.[40]

But Ned Carmack did not kill Robin Cooper. Trustworthy evidence puts him in the company of a good friend near the time the Parmers and Josie Starnes heard the pistol shot from the direction of Harding Road.

Andrew Ewing, who later became a senior partner in the prominent Nashville law firm of Dearborn and Ewing, had in August 1919 just graduated from Vanderbilt University. He was working to save money for law school and living on Terrace Place, in the shadow of the campus. On the afternoon of August 28, Ewing, a Phi Delt like Carmack, met Ned at the fraternity and invited him to spend the night in his quarters.

"Ned was interested in girls and chasing everything in skirts," Ewing recalled over sixty years later. "He had a date with some floozy that night." Young Carmack's rakish ways that summer either repaid Charlotte Lockridge in kind, or else he projected onto her his own promiscuity. A profoundly insecure young man wrote those letters. If plotting the great and terrible avengement of his father's death, he could scarcely have let it pass or failed to at least allude to it once done. Oftentimes Ned reproached Charlotte in violent anger over the affairs he believed she was having. Not once did he refer to Robin Cooper in the torrent of bullying and demanding and jealous words.

Carmack accepted Ewing's offer of his place to stay overnight. "He did come by, between ten and eleven o'clock, and I went to the front door and let him in," Ewing remembered. "He was composed and quite natural, no blood stains, nothing unusual in his demeanor. It is impossible to believe that he had just committed a bloody murder."

Ewing's phrase "between ten and eleven o'clock" undoes all the confessions Carmack ever made, all his importunate tellings to friends, whom he held with a glittering eye. Twice the police questioned Ewing and concluded from his account of the time that Carmack had nothing to do with the murder.

Indeed, if Cooper had been murdered on the stroke of ten and Carmack arrived on Terrace Place on the hour of eleven, he would have had to traverse five miles, through the rain, in an hour. He was no athlete, and he had no automobile. Would he have dared take a late evening streetcar back to town wearing clothes spattered with viscera? And how could he have changed from them in time to appear, so collected and self-possessed, at Ewing's gate? In fact, the police placed Cooper's death at about 11 P.M., by which time Ned was regaling his friend about his conquest of the evening. Carmack's hands may have carried the scent of cheap perfume, while the murderer was scrubbing Robin Cooper's blood from his knuckles.

Carmack's further fantasy must finally put to rest his claim of vengeance. He also murdered Duncan Cooper, he confessed to friends, slipping into the colonel's bedroom and smothering him with a pillow as he lay dying in November 1922. "Utter nonsense!" Lucius Burch, Jr., retorted. "My grandfather died in the upstairs bedroom at Riverwood, and my mother and father were both at his bedside. They came into my room and told me of his death moments after it occurred." In his diary, Dr. Burch noted that the colonel "passed away without a struggle."[41]

Who murdered Robin Cooper, if not a bootlegger, not Dennis Metcalf, and not Ned Carmack?

Along with letters and business records, the heirs of Duncan Cooper saved a carefully clipped rectangle of paper, seven inches by two inches. Written on it are two names: "Dr. Stonestreet, deceased" and "Bibbs Jacobs, deceased." "Some members of my family believed that Robin Cooper was killed by Dr. Stonestreet," Lucius Burch, Jr., recalled. "We always heard that Robin had been involved in a business venture, discovered it was corrupt, and was going to expose it."[42]

Born in Cape Town, South Africa, on April 28, 1864, Reginald Stonestreet received his early education in England. At age eighteen he came to the United States and by 1886 was clerking in Nashville, on South Market Street. The next year, Edward B. Stahlman, vice president of the L & N Railroad and publisher of the *Banner*, employed young Stonestreet as private secretary. He remained in that prestigious and sensitive position for several years. When he was about twenty-five, he married Elizabeth Blackman, daughter of Dr. W. C. Blackman, and subsequently entered medical school at the University of Nashville. In the early nineties, he received the M.D. degree there.[43]

In June 1907 Stonestreet's daughter, Wilhelmina, wed Albert Hutchison, a partner with his brother Thomas in a brick business. With the help of Duncan Cooper, Thomas received an appointment, perhaps ceremonial, as colonel and ordnance officer on Governor Malcolm Patterson's staff. Thomas Hutchison loaned Cooper the pistol that he carried on the fateful walk across Seventh Avenue.[44]

Stonestreet lived in Glendale Park after 1912, near this outing spot that street railway companies built to encourage patronage of their lines. Despite the ambition for riches of Glendale's builders, affluent Nashvillians did not flock to the area as they had to Belle Meade when entrepreneur Luke Lea opened it in a similar venture. In 1918 Stonestreet's immediate neighbors included a freight agent, restaurant operator, bookmaker, and salesman for a lumber company.[45]

Stonestreet was credited with effective work among victims of the influenza pandemic of 1918-19. He also had the reputation of being the town abortionist. Upon his death in the spring of 1921, six siblings survived him, including three brothers scattered throughout the British Empire.[46]

Who was Bibb Jacobs (for the name was "Bibb" and not "Bibbs" as the scrap of paper had it)? What else links him with Stonestreet beyond that strange document and the fact that Jacobs' brother, Jim, argued with Robin Cooper twelve hours before he was murdered?

In a family photograph taken in 1916, the six children of John and Belle Kelly Jacobs regard the camera with formal but pleasant stares. Bibb's expression comes closest to a smile, and his outsize, drooping bow tie suggests that he is a showman. He and brother Jim, James Madison Jacobs, sit side by side, both of them devastatingly handsome men. Jim is the larger of the two, with burly shoulders. In his fine suit, he sports an insignia, perhaps a pin from the Benevolent and Protective Order of Elks to which he belongs. This moment before the camera is one of the rare times when he is not smoking his pipe, which he usually keeps in his mouth. Standing behind Bibb is their one sister, Hattie Isabella, a woman of astonishing beauty

G. Bibb Jacobs. Source: *Nashville Banner* (July 15, 1914).

and the very model of propriety. She once refused to accept a newspaper from a gentleman stranger on a train, thinking the offer forward.[47]

Belle Kelly on her death in 1905 left her modest estate to Hattie, and she explained why. "Believing my beloved sons — whom I love very dearly — are capable to care for themselves and that my daughter is not so well prepared to fight life's battles, is the reason I make this will." The Jacobses were a striving family, and a proud one. They had bought a home in the respectable Waverly Place suburb, moving there from Magazine Street, which overlooked the railroad tracks and was near black settlements that the racial segregation of Nashville was establishing. A block away from the Jacobses' new address, on Eighth Avenue, Dr. Reginald Stonestreet lived between 1906 and 1912.

As to Hattie, Belle Jacobs was wrong. This lovely, strong-willed woman must have had her chances for romance and marriage. She chose instead a vocation. She won a degree at George Peabody College and taught English literature in Nashville public schools for forty-six years. For more than half a century, until her last illness, she lived at the Beech Avenue address with a brace of kinsmen. During the greatest part of that time, the household comprised her and Jim Jacobs' widow, whose name was also Hattie.[48]

Dr. Reginald Stonestreet. Courtesy *Nashville Banner* (Mar. 15, 1921).

As to Jim and Bibb, Belle Jacobs' prediction of their prospects in life proved right for a time. Bibb demonstrated his family's earnestness, "always interested in politics and making money," a niece recalled. Born in 1885, he was managing the cigar stand in the Capitol when he was just fourteen, the year Edward Carmack was elected to the U. S. Senate. One may imagine the legislators on the winning side buying their stogies from the youngster with the engaging smile.

When still a boy, Bibb Jacobs won the attention and affectionate interest of Mr. and Mrs. Leslie Warner. Warner was connected with his father, James Cartwright Warner, in the latter's extensive coal, iron, and railroad interests. In ill health, Leslie Warner retired about his fortieth year and devoted the rest of his life to amassing a collection of fine art. He exhibited his treasures in his opulent downtown residence, once described as the "center of Nashville culture."

The Warners gave birth to three children, but all died while still young. Their grieving parents buried them in Mount Olivet Cemetery and placed over their grave life-size statues of them in the embrace of Jesus. The lonely couple's eyes fell on the sweet, handsome lad Bibb Jacobs. One account says they raised him and gave him an education. When the actor

Joseph Jefferson visited Nashville to play the lead in "Rip Van Winkle" in the early 1890s, he stayed in the Warner home. Jefferson employed Bibb in one of the scenes, carrying the boy on his shoulders.[49]

From a concessionaire, Bibb Jacobs became an insurance salesman. It was work that allowed many a man with engaging ways to set himself up with a title and a calling card, aiming for rewards built on his energy, his enterprise, his contacts. Duncan Cooper, another charming man of entrepreneurial bent, never abandoned the insurance business for long.

In 1908, Jacobs graduated from Cumberland University's law school, that great progenitor of the Tennessee bar, and set up his practice in downtown Nashville. By 1915 he had offices on the seventh floor of the Stahlman Building.

He had come a long way. Perhaps he gazed out the window toward the Capitol, where he had listened to the oratory and heard the cheering and imagined someday being a man of influence. So he was, on the fringes of politics. In 1914 he chaired the Davidson County campaign committee for Judge Samuel Cole Williams, candidate for reelection to the Tennessee Supreme Court. Williams carried the county by nine hundred votes, providing him an important margin in his narrow statewide victory.

Bibb Jacobs and his wife, Marjorie, boarded with Mr. and Mrs. Jim Jacobs, the latter setting a sumptuous table. Bibb proudly identified himself as counsel to the Empire Realty and Mortgage Company and the First Amortization Mortgage and Bond Company, a single firm lending money on real estate. The company's officers included several Nashville businessmen of means and standing. In a suit in Chancery Court in 1914, Robin Cooper had represented a related corporation, the Standard Home Company of Birmingham. The following year its officers were indicted, prosecuted, and convicted of mail fraud.[50]

Thus trouble came to Bibb Jacobs, about the time he posed for the family portrait. Empire Realty fell under the scrutiny of the Justice Department, the United States Attorney finding that the company was conducting a business similar to that done by the Standard Home Company and was perhaps connected to it. Empire Realty's treasurer destroyed large amounts of records, presumably to conceal evidence. Receivership followed, and by 1918, the company's affairs were in the hands of trustees in bankruptcy. Bibb Jacobs left his prestigious downtown address. And he began calling himself a mining engineer.[51]

His brother Jim worked hard, "capable to care for" himself. In the salesman's creed was quintessential American loneliness and ferocious independence. "For a salesman, there is no rock bottom to life," proclaimed Charley years later in Arthur Miller's tragedy. "He don't put a bolt to a nut, he don't tell you the law or give you medicine. He's a man way out there in the blue, riding on a smile and a shoeshine." Jim Jacobs worked as a commercial traveler, a life lived on riverboat and rail, sustained with fine clothes, clever patter, an infinite resilience, spontaneity, superficiality — all to the point of taking the order. By 1906, about the time the family moved to Waverly Place, he worked repairing typewriters. Later, he sold for the Smith Premier Typewriter Company, with offices in the Arcade. Was he listing the next day's prospects that Monday afternoon in 1908, when the Coopers and Sharp met below, turned, and stepped out into the dark street?[52]

As America prepared to enter the war, Jim Jacobs began selling automobiles for the Case Company of Racine, Wisconsin. The company upgraded its line in 1918. But so many strained to afford food in the face of wartime inflation, and they stopped smiling back.[53]

Perhaps it was through their common interest in business and politics that Paul Eldridge became acquainted with Bibb Jacobs. From the early 1890s Eldridge worked in several of the packing and milling firms that gave the city its sobriquet, the "Minneapolis of the South." Trained in accountancy, he served them as secretary and treasurer. Then young Eldridge became an insurance agent, about the same time that Bibb Jacobs did. The Eldridge family lived in Waverly Place, and Paul belonged to the Elks and worked actively in county Democratic circles.

When war came, Eldridge was an officer at the Tennessee Burley Tobacco Company. Son Paul, Jr., worked as cashier for Davis, Bradford, and Company, insurers, whose senior partners were Paul M. Davis and James C. Bradford, Jr. But the senior Eldridge either lost his job or left it to become a bookkeeper for a real estate, insurance, and loan company located in the Stahlman Building. In 1919 he also held the post of secretary at the Consolidated Graphite Mining and Milling Company.

The president of Consolidated Graphite, Dr. Paul DeWitt, practiced medicine at the Hitchcock Building on Church Street, the same professional address as Reginald Stonestreet. Not just fellow businessmen, they were friends. When Stonestreet died in 1922, his family named DeWitt an honorary pallbearer, along with Major Edward B. Stahlman. DeWitt's brother, John, actually helped carry the doctor's coffin to the grave.[54]

There was another in the party accosting Robin Cooper on the morning before his death. Like Stonestreet and Jacobs and Eldridge, Julius Lusky could remember what it had been to live better than present circumstances permitted.

Julius's father, Morris, had arrived in Nashville in the 1850s and died when the boy was still young. Jules, as he was sometimes known, found his way clerking and selling in the dry goods houses on the Public Square. A conservative, Protestant, Anglo-Saxon city gave its patronage to Rosenheim's fabulous department store there. Lusky Brothers, a more modest establishment managed by Julius and his brother Herman, closed with the latter's death in 1902. Thereafter, Julius managed a pawnshop on Cedar

Street in the black business district. Five years later success purchased him an office on Union.

In time Lusky became partners with Clarence Bernstein, a jeweler who catered to rich and fashionable Nashville society. Bernstein built and managed splendid apartment houses in West End and lived there, as prestigious an address as there was in the city. At Bernstein and Company, Lusky ought to have had a future. Perhaps he did and rejected it to strike out on his own. By 1918 he had returned to Cedar Street, operating a furniture company. But the work did not last for him. At fifty-eight, the oldest among the four who met Robin Cooper in the Stahlman Building's lobby, Lusky had little to show for himself.[55]

Diminished circumstance united all of them, Lusky, Eldridge, the Jacobs brothers, and Dr. Stonestreet. During the second week of May 1919, Bibb Jacobs leased space for his law office on the sixth floor of the Stahlman Building. That week Consolidated Graphite Mining and Milling Company opened its doors on the same floor. In violation of Tennessee law, it never filed a charter.[56]

America was awash in phony stock, many schemers trading their worthless paper for Liberty Bonds, the government issues that funded the war. Promoters aped the pleas of Treasury officials that the war required patriotic citizens to lend their money for exploration for oil or minerals needed by the fighting machine. In the winter of 1919, the Nashville City Bank urged American investors to buy foreign securities so that the nation might "keep up its international financial position."[57]

Bibb Jacobs and Jim Jacobs moved easily among their townsmen, with beguiling smiles and ready greetings. To reach the office of Consolidated Graphite Mining, they rode the elevator with lawyers in Chancery practice, leading architects, accountants, physicians, and railroad managers. Bibb Jacobs had no credentials at all as a mining engineer. But the brothers of Reginald Stonestreet did.

Eldridge, Lusky, Stonestreet, and Jim Jacobs met with Robin Cooper on the morning before he died and demanded something of him. Was it money? Or was it to keep silent, as agents moved upon the company? Barthell told reporters that the government had been investigating a foreign corporation with which Cooper was known to have been connected. According to Mrs. Cooper her late husband had made two trips during the winter of 1919 in the interest of an unknown corporation. About that time the Federal Trade Commission asked attorneys throughout the country to voluntarily send in names and prospectuses of stock peddlers who offered to exchange questionable securities for Liberty Bonds.[58]

No one now knows, or ever will again, what led to the confrontation in the Stahlman Building on August 28. But if Robin Cooper learned that he had promoted a worthless stock sale, he was faced with a question of

Dr. Paul DeWitt. Courtesy Special Collections, Vanderbilt University Medical Center.

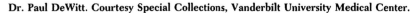

his personal honor. His esteem and prestige, won in the arena among the influential men of the town, stood at stake.

The perpetrators of the fraud also faced the judgment of the community where their loyal, proud, clannish family had won respectability, which was honor bought by money and circumspect behavior. Two of the men who confronted Robin Cooper that morning could not stand disgrace, and he having hold of them both, they whirled asunder and dismembered him.

It served the interest of many people that they were never arrested, indicted, or tried. Called to testify, prominent men of Nashville would have had to acknowledge wartime speculations and other excruciatingly private dealings. And none of that sordid spectacle, his family knew, would bring Robin back.

Paul DeWitt, president of Consolidated Graphite, had been awarded the Founder's Medal in his class at Vanderbilt Medical School, the highest honor given a graduate. Thus he earned the respect of the school's dean, Lucius Burch. DeWitt and the rest who promoted the stock of Consolidated

Edward B. Stahlman. Courtesy *Nashville Banner* (Nov. 19, 1922).

Graphite must have shivered in horror, and none had the wish or the will to see any of it come out.

Whether Stonestreet and the Jacobs brothers traduced him or not, Victor Emmanuel Shwab was such a man of standing. His palatial home stood on West End, across from Clarence Bernstein's apartment house and Jules Lusky's residence. The personification of the term "liquor interests," Shwab founded the Cascade Distillery Company and George A. Dickel and Company. He was one of a number of wealthy and enterprising German businessmen, including Edward B. Stahlman, whose capital and social position advanced their countrymen into positions of influence in Nashville.

Shwab's sister, Augusta, married Paul M. Davis, cofounder of First American National Bank, associate of James C. Bradford, Sr., and Jr., and by way of them the Coopers. Robin Cooper represented both men in lawsuits; Duncan Cooper had called upon the distiller's largess for political war chests. Shwab's brother, Felix, loved Paul Eldridge, naming a son for him.[59] Suspicion of Eldridge because of the newspaper coverage of the case must have deeply distressed the compatriot of Stahlman, while Davis's

Dr. Lucius E. Birch. Courtesy *Nashville Banner* (Dec. 14, 1928).

friendship with the Cooper family went back, down, and deep. After the *Banner*'s story of September 3, did Shwab and Davis converge on the publisher's office?

The Department of Justice had six months before quietly closed its investigation of Edward B. Stahlman as a possible enemy alien. The inquiry followed bitter allegations in Luke Lea's *Tennessean* that Stahlman, the son of German immigrants, had never been naturalized. Reginald Stonestreet, private secretary to Stahlman when he held his greatest influence over political affairs in Tennessee, was quoted in reports sent to the attorney general that the publisher was capable of accepting money to spread German propaganda. In the end, the probe produced no evidence that Stahlman was other than a loyal, bona fide citizen.[60] But Milton Smith knew that the trial of Stonestreet for the murder of Robin Cooper would reopen Stahlman's past and his fierce, at times unscrupulous pursuit of the interests of the L & N Railroad. What if the publisher's former secretary were indicted for a murder that grew out of sales of stock in a bogus corporation supposedly engaged in mining a vital war material? Would A. Mitchell Palmer reopen the loyalty case against Stahlman?

When Mrs. Leslie Warner died in 1923, she left her brother, Lucius Burch, enough money to pay the mortgage on the old ancestral home of William and Duncan Cooper. "It makes me very happy to note that

Milton H. Smith. Courtesy L & N Collection, University of Louisville Archives.

Riverwood is free," the doctor wrote, and he noted that his dear sister remembered "all of her relatives and close friends."[61] Notably absent from Katherine Burch Warner's beneficiaries is her surrogate son, George Bibb Jacobs. Once she had loved him, and through her estate she had the power to grant him his dreams of wealth. That she did not do, but her erstwhile sponsorship may have saved his life. How could Dr. Burch prosecute the murderers of his brother-in-law when his beloved sister had brought one of them into the home circle?

The hand that put an end to the case also touched the obscure life of policeman Joseph Ferriss. Ferriss had been a stockman, a pressman, and a brakeman on the railroad before joining the force about 1910. He seemed to have found his work there; never in his life would he remain with any other job for as long.

Six months before Robin Cooper's murder, Ferriss met trouble. Police Chief Alex Barthell charged him before the city commission with deliberately letting a car of "blockade runners" escape. Barthell's witnesses were the occupants of the fleeing automobile, which was eventually captured. When Ferriss's turn in the disciplinary hearing came, he brought forward

Mrs. Leslie Warner. Source: *Nashville Banner* (Mar. 27, 1909).

county officials and coworkers who testified that he never failed in his duty to enforce the law. In the end, the attorney for the city found that no proof showed Ferriss guilty of any criminal intent but allowed he might have been more diligent. The commissioners suspended him for sixty days.

When an opportunity came to show how persistent he could be, Ferriss did so—and he learned the truths of the Robin Cooper murder case. Did he leave the police force under duress or in disgust? It cannot be known, but he did leave. By 1922 he was working as a salesman for the Stockell Motor Car Company, owned and managed by a nephew of Duncan Cooper.[62] And nothing more was printed in the *Banner* about the connection he had found between the murder and phony securities.

After the killing of Robin Cooper, James M. Jacobs moved his family to Indianapolis for a time, then returned to Nashville. In December 1920 he was diagnosed as having cancer of the tongue and he died in September 1922. He lies by his wife, mother, and sister in Nashville's great necropolis, Mt. Olivet Cemetery, a hundred yards from the grave of Edward B. Stahlman.

Bibb Jacobs relocated permanently to New York City before the end

Thomas E. Matthews. Source: *Nashville Banner* (Aug. 6, 1910).

of 1919. He lived in older, apparently seedy housing, on the eastern fringe of tough Hell's Kitchen. Farther to the west, Manhattan's piers, freight yards, and warehouses employed the residents of this working class, largely Irish neighborhood. The gangs that had once terrorized the area had diminished, but Prohibition and the docks still gave some a lucrative, illegal livelihood and places to congregate. As one walked east he came to brightly lit marquees and the beginning of the theater district.

In 1924 at age thirty-nine, Bibb Jacobs died of septic endocarditis, an infection of the heart valves that was generally fatal in the days before antibiotics. His death certificate listed his occupation as "mining engineer." With a judge, an editor of the *Banner*, and the son of a former Congressman serving as pallbearers, Jacobs was buried in Nashville's Calvary Cemetery near the circle of priests of the Catholic diocese. Although he had taken his wife's faith, neither she nor any other member of his immediate family lies in rest near his grave.[63]

"It is at least as old as the Roman poet Horace—'the spoken word flies away, but the written word remains,'" Judge Thomas Matthews wrote some years later to a friend, Mrs. Leonard Bond. In his letter he promised that when he saw her again he would tell her the names of the two men who murdered Robin Cooper.

Matthews was born in 1854 in Plaquemire, Louisiana. His family later moved to Nashville, where he attended Montgomery Bell Academy. He studied at the University of Virginia and when Vanderbilt University established its law school, he enrolled there. In 1876, he graduated first in his class, the Founder's Medalist.

In Nashville's general election of 1908, voters made Matthews judge of the circuit court. He served on the bench for eleven years. In his retirement, at the request of the Daughters of the American Revolution, he wrote a biography of his grandfather, James Robertson, one of the founders of Tennessee.

"'The Judge,'" a reporter once observed, "exemplified the traditions of a time that has passed." Tennessee Supreme Court Justice Grafton Green regarded Matthews as "a gentleman of broad culture and of the highest character." And John H. DeWitt thought Matthews "a gentleman of very unusual intellectual power." DeWitt knew "no citizen of this section who bears a better reputation for personal integrity, for culture, for dependability.... He is one of the leading citizens of our City and our State."[64]

In his letter to Mrs. Bond, Matthews paraphrases conversations with third parties and alludes to people quoting still other people. Yet this witness of impeccable character and distinction as a jurist, lawyer, and historian corroborates the work of Joseph Ferriss, who spent most of his life selling cars.

The letter begins in the middle of things. No, the name Mrs. Bond had heard had not been told to Matthews. "Only two names were mentioned," he wrote, "and those were the names of the actual killers."

The judge had heard one of the names before. A woman friend of his, visiting New York City, had been escorted there by one of the men. Under the influence of liquor, he told her about his part in the crime.

Then Matthews turned to his source for the names, a physician. He related to the doctor, whom he does not name, the story of the bibulous confession.

"'Was that So & So?'" the doctor asked Matthews, who answered that it was.

"Then he spoke the truth, for he was one of the criminals."

Matthews' friend went on. The brother of one of the murderers, living in Canada, had had an interest in the stock selling. But that brother knew nothing "about the crime of blood that issued out of the sales of the fraudulent stock."

Matthews declared he would not write the names of the killers. "It is not that I do not trust either your honor or your discretion," he assured Christine Bond, but a letter often "reaches readers for whom it was never intended by losing and finding, also by prying curiosity." Matthews was a historian himself; he had no sources except by such caprice. And for someone, at some time, he sent what he knew into the future. The handwriting on the scrap of paper bearing the names Bibb Jacobs and Reginald Stonestreet matches the handwriting in his letter to Mrs. Bond.[65]

Along with the appeals for pardons, and schemes for wild riches, and declarations of love, the papers of Duncan Cooper hold both these documents. In 1970 Mrs. Lucius Burch, the colonel's daughter, gave her father's manuscripts to the Tennessee State Library and Archives. The scrap of paper and the judge's letter provided that the truths about Robin Cooper's murder might be told, after she and Duncan Cooper, the Jacobs brothers, and Dr. Stonestreet were all dead, every one.

The Days of
Ninevah and Tyre

THE PEOPLE WERE STILL gathering on the steps below the Capitol, shaking hands and asking after families, as Tony Rose's Booster Band struck up "Bohemian Girl." At the top of the curved steps, leading up the hill from Charlotte Avenue, stood a veiled statue and to either side of it an honor guard of marines and national guardsmen. As the instrumentalists swung into a medley of old time tunes, Ned Carmack, Jr., and his mother, Cobey, took seats near the lily-like trumpets of the loudspeakers.

The day before, Friday, June 5, 1925, the trains to Nashville had brought Frank D. Lander, from Birmingham, and former U.S. Senator Sawney Webb of Bell Buckle. And there came members and officers of the Women's Christian Temperance Union, all to honor Edward Ward Carmack. Within days of his death, seventeen years before, friends of Carmack had announced a campaign to build this monument to his memory. Donations flowed into the coffers, and the same General Assembly that enacted statewide prohibition authorized the erection of the statue on the Capitol grounds. Governor Malcolm Patterson signed the resolution, which commended Carmack's "lofty character," "sterling worth," and "wise and patriotic public services."[1]

Allen G. Hall, a Nashville attorney, collected the money, and he and his memorial committee contracted for construction of a base. They also commissioned a model for a statue of Carmack, but fire destroyed the building where it stood, and it was lost. Hall died not long afterward, and the movement lagged.[2]

In 1919, Carmack's old friend Edward B. Craig revived the goal of a statue for the empty pedestal and reassembled supporters to raise the money. Five years later, in February 1924, they awarded the commission to Nancy Cox-McCormack, a Tennessean, whose work included war memorials and religious sculptures. She immediately began work in her

Building the base for the Carmack statue. Source: *The* [Nashville] *Democrat* (July 3, 1912).

studio in Rome. By the winter of 1925 the bronze likeness of Carmack stood against the bare trees and white sky of Capitol Hill. Craig's committee made plans for the dedication the following summer.[3]

When the day came, Craig was too sick to attend; perhaps his doctor feared for his safety in the awful heat, which had claimed three hundred lives around the nation. A trace of rain fell in the early morning and again at noon, like blessings on old friends and old enemies of the dead man, mingling.

For the dedication, the statue stood concealed from view by flags suspended from pulleys. Little Mamie Craig Howell, granddaughter of the chairman of the memorial committee, drew the rope that whisked these drapings aside.

Guston T. Fitzhugh, fourteen years before the able prosecutor of Duncan and Robin Cooper, presented the monument to the state. No one ever depicted the martyred man with more power, nor with greater love. His oration related the Carmack legend and remains the finest expression of it.

Here was the man, Fitzhugh told his listeners, who "made every home and fireside within the borders of Tennessee his everlasting debtor."

> With the zeal and courage of a crusader, he made the fight
> against the entrenched forces of evil, and though he fell, the
> hosts of faithful men and women who had followed his stain-
> less flag continued to press the battle for cleaner politics and
> happier homes.

Still he had made "no attacks from the rear," said Fitzhugh, alluding to the old prosecutorial theory of the case. Instead, Carmack "hurled his shining lance full and fair in the face of his opponent."

At an impressionable age, Carmack had endured the sorrow, suffering, and humiliation of Reconstruction. "Is it strange," Fitzhugh continued, "that his soul was steeped in a love of the South, which became a passion and made him the most invincible champion of her cause?"

Yet in the land where all things were possible, tradition offered the only real hope for any man. Fitzhugh quoted his friend, the reformer:

> When you have destroyed popular reverence for the old con-
> servative faiths and traditions, you appeal against the moods
> and passions of the hour. If we would resist the forces of dis-
> order, we must preserve intact and unbroken the walls
> which our fathers raised and stand last by the citadel of the
> Constitution as by the ark of the covenant of the Living God.

Forget the "great dead," Fitzhugh warned, and the institutions that the living build will perish. The speaker wished that every public official and private citizen who passed the statue might feel "a stronger determination to walk erect the pathway of truth and duty and honor." In this apotheosis, Carmack called Tennesseeans to greatness.

Mrs. Carmack had refused to set foot on the Capitol grounds if Governor Austin Peay took part in the unveiling. Respecting her wishes, the organizers of the day arranged for her friend Luke Lea to accept the statue for the state. Peay nonetheless decided to come. When Mrs. Carmack saw him, she had her chair taken from the platform to the lawn in front of the statue and turned so that her back was to His Excellency. There she sat throughout the ceremony, where she could hear Lea's speech but not see Peay.

"As we stand here today," Lea proclaimed, "Tennessee's heroes seem to pass in review." Sevier and Sam Houston were marching in line, followed by Old Hickory, James K. Polk, and Sam Davis. Then Lea conjured "a stalwart figure, straight and erect, confident in right, shaking his head as we loved to see him do." And Lea gave his old friend a voice that revised and extended his pledge to the South:

Former U.S. Senator Luke Lea addressing the crowd. Courtesy *Nashville Tennessean* (June 7, 1925).

> Peace I seek, peace for myself, peace for all. . . . I would wait here upon these steps for resurrection's call . . . I would face the South, my South, whose fibre is woven into the very warp of my being; the South of yesterday that gave this nation birth; the South of today that is this nation's anchor; the South of tomorrow that will be this nation's hope.[4]

Tell us the names of the ten "greatest Tennesseans," the editors of the *Nashville Banner* invited its readers in the summer of 1931. Andrew Jackson received the most votes, followed by John Sevier and James K. Polk. Nathan Bedford Forrest, Sam Houston, and Andrew Johnson were ranked fourth, fifth, and sixth. Standing seventh was Edward Ward Carmack. Sam Davis, James Robertson, and Isham G. Harris completed the pantheon. Carmack deserved everlasting fame in the annals of American life, Fitzhugh told the audience at the dedication. But by the bicentenary of the

Opposite: The Unveiling. Courtesy *Nashville Banner* (June 6, 1925).

Ned Carmack. Courtesy *The* [Memphis] *Commercial Appeal* (July 26, 1942).

republic, he was virtually forgotten. In a "Greatest Tennesseans" poll that the *Banner* conducted in 1976, his name did not appear even among the first thirty-five citizens receiving votes.[5]

As Fitzhugh spoke, the world where values had any objective meaning was passing away before the insights of Freud and Heisenberg. Southerners, especially, might glance back "with knowledge carried to the heart." But words like "noble" and "knightly" disappeared from the vocabulary of their public life, as no one could pretend that most who attained public office stood far above the shoulders of those who elected them. And the idealistic cause for which Carmack stood in his last campaign, the prohibition of liquor, proved impossible to enforce when it became the law of the land. For a modern man, "making the most of himself" no longer meant self-denial, discipline, and restraint, as it had to many nineteenth-century Americans, but stretching out one's arms toward the beckoning green light.

For a time Ned Carmack followed that dream of riches. Abandoning the practice of law, he became a speculator in the Florida land boom of the twenties. With his partners, he bought and sold, sold and bought, generating paper, and lawsuits, and deal after deal.

It was a life for which he was honorably unsuited, and he repaired to work as editor of the Murfreesboro *Daily News Journal*. He wrote like an angel. He wrote with courage by his lights when in 1928 he renounced Al Smith as a tool of Tammany Hall and called upon Tennesseeans to desert the Democratic Party and vote for Herbert Hoover. He wrote with courage by any measure when in 1934 he denounced the lynching of a black man, Dick Wilkerson, who had defended his wife and friends from a gang of drunken white men. Although Carmack would not abjure the Ku Klux Klan, since he believed its organization of rural people counterbalanced the power of city machines, he would not join it either. As time went by, he became an increasingly vocal opponent of Ed Crump and the influence of his Shelby County organization in the politics of the state.[6]

Carmack tried to acquire the *Nashville Tennessean*, which on petition of one of Luke Lea's creditors went into receivership in 1933 and floundered there for four years. He apparently had standing to enter the lawsuit owing to the stock his father had left him and his mother. In March of 1937, the federal district judge ruled that Nashville banker Paul Davis had validly purchased the property at auction the previous winter. At the same time the court dismissed Carmack's petition to reorganize the publishing company.[7]

Having failed to succeed his father at the helm of the *Tennessean*, Carmack three times in the next ten years sought election to the United States Senate. In 1938 he entered the Democratic primary but was forced to withdraw when a pair of hitchhikers to whom he gave a ride beat him into insensibility and left him permanently injured in his legs. The disability prevented him from getting into the war, which he desperately sought to do, in part to enhance his attractiveness as a political candidate. Even Senator Kenneth McKellar's contacts with the War Department availed Carmack nothing. Franklin D. Roosevelt led the armed forces as commander in chief while confined to a wheelchair, but Ned Carmack was not even allowed a desk job because of the brace on his leg.[8]

Even without a war record, Carmack apparently defeated incumbent Tom Stewart in the Democratic primary of August 1942. As the count moved from east to west, he led the incumbent going into Shelby County by eighteen thousand ballots. But Memphis belonged to Crump, and Carmack did not. The organization turned out nearly forty-three thousand votes to eight thousand for Carmack, giving the county and the election to Stewart.

Four years later Carmack tried again, this time against McKellar, the old friend of his father's who fifty years before had managed his defense against Josiah Patterson on the floor of the House of Representatives. In a marginal note in his copy of McKellar's book about Tennessee's U.S. Senators, Ned Carmack wrote, "I find as I read that I rather like old Senator

McKellar. . . . I ran against my father's old friend with only half a heart, for I was never deeply ambitious for public office. But I thought the Crump tyranny must be broken and as Estes had a Congressional seat to risk if he made this dangerous race, he, Silliman Evans, and I decided that I should take on the old champion. (Gore wouldn't try McKellar that go-round.)" McKellar, and Crump, won again. It was their last victory. Carmack had helped prepare the way for the successful challenge, two years later, by U.S. Representative Estes Kefauver against Stewart. Kefauver's election broke Crump's long domination of Tennessee politics, and in 1952 Congressman Albert Gore brought down Kenneth McKellar.[9]

By that time Carmack had abandoned a temperate life and started to drink. He read widely, wrote engaging letters, and made money as a developer and land speculator, but lost it indifferently. Creditors called at the door of his now seedy mansion. Still dressed in pajamas and tattered robe, and being chauffeured about by Charlotte in a creaky maroon Cadillac, he created a spectacle in the streets. Yet even after an afternoon and evening in his cups, he would rise in the morning and compose poems or work at a play.[10]

Charlotte Lockridge Carmack died in 1968. Ned acknowledged remembrances of her on a printed card in his hand, dated November 9, the anniversary of his father's death. He lived on in the house, surrounded by memorabilia of the senator's life.

Some who knew and loved Ned Carmack felt that he never found his purpose in life. He may have agreed. He once wrote his friend Jordan Stokes about going to the fair as a little boy and standing before a booth displaying "wondrous, gleaming silver-handled knives." He did not really want such a knife, yet he felt glum because he did not have it. Later the mature man looked back on his young self:

> He sensed, I believe, the truth of which that experience was symbol—that he could go through life, or a big part of it, spending himself, trying futilely to capture things he didn't really want—because he felt a restless energy that he must do something but there was never any buddy by to tell him really what. And there was that blind spot in his vision—he could never draw a bead—must just fire randomly in a general vague direction because he was never to see an object worth his fire, never but once, and that he would hit, quite literally; but sadly, without joy, without acclaim.

Stokes believed that in the last sentence Ned referred to his murder of Robin Cooper. Perhaps for Carmack, all else that he attempted and attained seemed slender and small because other men carried out that work that he thought should have been his.[11]

Ned Carmack fell dead beside the desk in his library on September 18, 1972. Many believed he was a wealthy man—some who knew him well said that he had made at least three separate fortunes since 1950—and the press took an interest in the provisions of the will. But Carmack's affairs were in utter disarray. Debts, litigation, and tax liens threatened to reduce if not liquidate the assets. The executors Carmack named obtained release from service, and court-appointed administrators felt impelled to raise some cash to satisfy the most pressing obligations. The winter after he died, they decided to put the century-old Carmack residence in Murfreesboro and all its furnishings on the auction block.[12]

Ned had bought his home in 1942 and brought his mother and his aunt Lucille Dunnington there to live. They filled the rooms with china, silver, furniture, and books. Both women had died in the house, and now their relics came into the auctioneers' hands. Here was the scrapbook that Captain John Dunnington, Miss Lucille's uncle, kept about his voyages across the Atlantic and the Pacific in the 1850s. The old lady had pasted sentimental poems over its pages. Here were Cobey Carmack's violins, charcoal sketches, and a letter from her to Ned, dated 1929, admonishing him against thinking thoughts of revenge against his father's killers.

The auctioneers combed over the house from icy front steps to the sooty attic, tagging items for sale. Climbing ladders, they took down sconces and chandeliers, while out on the lawn workmen sawed limbs off the trees to make room for the sale tent.

The buyers flocked to the sale and lavished their money away. Senator Carmack's billfold brought $37.50, and a plaster bust of him went for $30. His top hat, which Ned had worn to parties, sold too.

The finest piece of furniture from the house, a late eighteenth-century cherry sideboard, inspired a winning bid of nearly $3,000. But absolute junk went for unexpectedly high prices. A pasteboard box of pieces of wire, string, doorknobs, and chips of wood sold for $29. Bidders paid between $2 and $30 for stacks of books that they scarcely examined. The owner of an antiques store spent $175 for an old brass bathtub. She told reporters she planned to use it as an advertising gimmick.

Noon Saturday was the hour set for the sale of the house. Auctioneer Fred Brown worked the microphone, determined to get the price the administrators wanted.

The bid stood at $58,000, when Army Lieutenant Colonel James R. Dismukes raised it to $58,500.

"Are you all done? Are you all done?" cried Brown.

They were not. A bidder called out "$59,100," then another "$59,500," then still another "$59,750."

"Are you all done?"

Dismukes bid $60,000. "Sell it! Sell it! Sell it!" yelled Johnny Jones, a floorwalker standing over Dismukes.

The auctioneer rolled into his chant.

"Sixty and it's going one time.

"Sixty and it's going the second time. Today's the day, tomorrow's too late.

"Going, going. Are you all through?"

"Sell it! Sell it!" Jones yelled.

"She's going. She's going. She's all gone," Brown declared. Colonel Dismukes and the crowd sagged in their seats.

Altogether the shrewd and foolish buyers paid over $40,000 for Ned Carmack's personal effects. With the sale of the house and the disposition of other real property, that "should clear the Tennessee debts," the administrators announced. In fact they strained to conceal their glee over the high proceeds the auction brought.[13]

Some present at the sale imagined Ned's shade standing by, as his father's effects passed into the streams of petty capitalism or into ornamented rooms where the name of Edward Carmack had been forgotten. Those same friends saw him laughing out loud. "What is the soul," he once reflected, "but the thing in us that remembers? . . . Only the joy that we have shared, the dance, the game, the feast has the power to live in us again after its little actual day is one with the days of Ninevah and Tyre."

No memory save one was as dear to Ned Carmack as the one he invented, that of standing over Robin Cooper after he struck him lifeless. Edward Carmack—his voice, his touch, his gestures— belonged to those who had known him best and who lived out their lives grieving over his death. They were Ned, who found no place in the world, Cobey, who had lost her hearing, and Miss Lucille, who could no longer see.

Ned once described watching his old aunt's

> time-eaten face beneath the white cloud of her hair, empty and remote like a forgotten rock on the side of a lonely hill. Then suddenly her blind blue-bright eyes will lighten as though a sun shaft had smitten that old rock face. Her gray lips will sweeten with the wan ghost of a smile . . . And when she speaks it is always of an experience of life shared and intermingled. "Cobey," she will say, "do you remember the time that you and Ned and Mai and Will Caperton and I went on a picnic out to Morgan Hall and Will fell in the spring?"

As she laughed and told the story, his father and companions seemed for Ned to live again in that world of long ago. "Perchance they do," he wrote, "and fully as we enter the lives of others do we have immortality."[14]

NOTES

Chapter One

1. Henry Goodpasture, "Memoirs of Henry Goodpasture," mimeographed (Nashville: privately printed, 1979), p. 17, available at the Tennessee State Library and Archives, Nashville. A contemporary report put the number of saloon proprietors in Nashville at 141. *Nashville Tennessean*, December 20, 1908. Most such establishments were concentrated in a few square blocks in the downtown.

2. C.D. [pseud.], "The True Story of the Carmack Tragedy," *The Taylor-Trotwood Magazine* 9 (1909): 68–69.

3. William Waller, ed., *Nashville 1900 to 1910* (Nashville: Vanderbilt University Press, 1972), pp.75–78, 177, 191, 213, 215, 326.

4. *Nashville Banner*, November 9, 1908; *Duncan B. Cooper and Robin J. Cooper, in Error, vs. The State of Tennessee*, Digest of Testimony, p. 242: testimony of J. B. Lewis. Students of the case must cite the digest for testimony that was originally recorded in Volume VIII, which is missing from the transcripts. The eight-volume record and digest was the transcript of the trial in the Criminal Court, filed at the Tennessee Supreme Court when the Coopers appealed their conviction. The seven surviving volumes and the digest are now in the holdings of the Tennessee State Library and Archives.

5. *Nashville Banner*, November 10, 1908; *Cooper vs. State*, Vol. I, p. 116: testimony of Mrs. Charles Eastman.

6. Cash book of the Nashville *American* for 1886, entry for February 3, in the Duncan Brown Cooper Papers, Manuscripts Section, Tennessee State Library and Archives; *Cooper vs. State*, Vol. III, p. 853: testimony of Duncan B. Cooper; William R. Majors, *Editorial Wild Oats; Edward Ward Carmack and Tennessee Politics* (Macon, Ga.: Mercer University Press, 1984), pp. 17–50; idem, *Continuity and Change; Tennessee Politics Since the Civil War* (Macon, Ga.: Mercer University Press, 1986), pp. 18–20; Robert E. Corlew, *Tennessee; A Short History*, 2nd ed. (Knoxville: The University of Tennessee Press, 1981), pp. 372–84.

7. *Nashville Tennessean*, October 21, 1908; Will Dunn Smith, "The Carmack-Patterson Campaign and Its Aftermath in Tennessee Politics" (M.A. thesis, Vanderbilt University, 1939), p. 77.

8. *Daily American* (Nashville), February 12, 1892.

9. *Nashville Tennessean*, November 8, 1908.

10. *New York Times*, November 12, 1908; *Cooper vs. State*, Vol. III, p. 953: testimony of Duncan B. Cooper.

11. *Cooper vs. State*, Vol. I, pp. 86–87: testimony of Edward B. Craig; Vols. III and IV, pp. 936–41 and 1176–77: testimony of Duncan B. Cooper.

12. *Ibid.*, Vol. I, pp. 94–108: testimony of Edward B. Craig; Vol. III, pp. 938, 944: testimony of Duncan B. Cooper; Vol. V, pp. 1513–14: testimony of Thomas S. Hutchison.

13. *Ibid.*, Vol. V, pp. 1412–26: testimony of William O. Vertrees.

14. *Nashville Tennessean*, November 9, 1908.

15. *Cooper vs. State*, Vol. IV, pp. 1324–43: testimony of Duncan B. Cooper; Vol. II, pp. 500, 519–22, 646–47.

16. *Ibid.*, Vol. II, pp. 540–49: testimony of Robin J. Cooper.

17. *Ibid.*, Digest of Testimony, p. 243: testimony of John A. Witherspoon.

18. *Ibid.*, Digest of Testimony, p. 244: testimony of Frank D. Lander.

19. *Ibid.*, Vol. III, pp. 949–53: testimony of Duncan B. Cooper; Vol. V, pp. 1497–1500: testimony of Sandy Brown.

20. *Ibid.*, Vol. I, pp. 390–92: testimony of Donie Braxton (house servant at the Burch residence).

21. *Ibid.*, Vol. VI, pp. 1830–31: testimony of James C. Bradford; Vol. III, pp. 953–54: testimony of Duncan B. Cooper. This text of Colonel Cooper's note is from a copy that Bradford made and gave to reporters shortly after the killing. The original then disappeared, with prosecution and defense in the trial each blaming the other side for losing it. See *ibid.*, Digest of Testimony, p. 232. A milder version of the note is in the Duncan Brown Cooper Papers.

22. *Cooper vs. State*, Vol. V, p. 1582: testimony of Malcolm R. Patterson; Vol. VI, pp. 1826–27: testimony of James C. Bradford; Vol. II, pp. 549–51: testimony of Robin J. Cooper; Vol. III, pp. 718–23: testimony of John Sharp; Katrina Williamson to Duncan B. Cooper, letter, November 14, 1908, in the Duncan Brown Cooper Papers, Manuscripts Section, Tennessee State Library and Archives.

23. *Cooper vs. State*, Vol. V, p. 1595: testimony of Malcolm R. Patterson; Vol. V, pp. 1413–16: testimony of William O. Vertrees.

24. *Ibid.*, Vol. VII, pp. 1997–99: testimony of James C. Bradford; Vol. VII, pp. 2045–48: testimony of John J. Vertrees.

25. Katrina Williamson to Duncan B. Cooper, letter, November 14, 1908, Duncan Brown Cooper Papers.

26. *Cooper vs. State*, Vol. I, pp. 381–86: testimony of Daisy Lee.

27. *Ibid.*, Vol. VI, pp. 1834, 1840: testimony of James C. Bradford; Vol. VI, p. 1822: testimony of Tully Brown; Vol. II, pp. 574–77: testimony of Robin J. Cooper; Vols. III and IV, pp. 1011–14: testimony of Duncan B. Cooper.

28. *Ibid.*, Vol. VI, p. 1779: testimony of R. L. Thompson; Digest of Testimony, p. 246: testimony of C. H. Farrell; p. 247: testimony of Mrs. G. H. Williams; p. 238: testimony of Jordan Stokes.

29. *Cooper vs. State*, Vol. I, pp. 183–95: testimony of John Tindall; Vols. III and IV, pp. 1019–22: testimony of Duncan B. Cooper; Vol. II, pp. 574–80: testimony of Robin J. Cooper; Vol. III, pp. 724–25: testimony of John Sharp.

30. *Ibid.*, Vol. II, pp. 583–84: testimony of Robin J. Cooper.

31. *Ibid.*, Vols. III and IV, pp. 1024–28: testimony of Duncan B. Cooper.

32. *Ibid.*, Vol. I, pp. 122–30: testimony of Mrs. Charles Eastman; Vols. III and IV, pp. 1030–31, 1358–65: testimony of Duncan B. Cooper; Vol. II, pp. 602–04, 608–17, 677–78 and Vol. III, p. 768: testimony of Robin J. Cooper.

33. *Cooper vs. State*, Vol. V, pp. 1613–38 and VI, pp. 1651–57: testimony of McPheeters Glasgow; *Nashville Banner*, November 10, 1908.

34. *Cooper vs. State*, Vol. V, pp. 1515–46: testimony of Leigh Thompson.

35. *Ibid.*, Vol. I, p. 135: testimony of Mrs. Charles Eastman; Vol. III, p. 1033: testimony of Duncan B. Cooper; *Nashville Banner*, November 10, 1908.

Chapter Two

1. *Duncan B. Cooper and Robin J. Cooper, in Error, vs. The State of Tennessee*, Vol. V, pp. 515–46: testimony of Leigh Thompson; idem, pp. 1394–97: testimony of Winston Pilcher; *Nashville Banner*, November 10, 1908.

2. *Cooper vs. State*, Vol. V, pp. 1335–66: testimony of Richard Dake; *Nashville Banner*, November 10, 1908.

3. *Cooper vs. State*, Vol. II, pp. 451–61: testimony of Rufus E. Fort; idem, Vol. I, pp. 307, 311: testimony of Theresa McKeon and Spurgeon Van Deren; *Nashville Banner*, November 10, 1908; *Nashville American*, November 10, 11, 1908.

4. *Cooper vs. State*, Vol. II, p. 433: testimony of Robert Vaughn, February 18, 1909; *Nashville Banner*, November 10, 1908.

5. *Nashville American*, November 10, 11, 1908; *Nashville Banner*, November 10, December 23, 1908; *New York Times*, December 10, 1908.

6. *Nashville Banner*, November 10, 1908; *Nashville American*, November 10, 1908; *Nashville Tennessean*, November 10, 1908. In the weeks after Carmack's death, souvenir hunters carved gashes out of the utility poles through which he had fired on Robin Cooper. Finally, an enterprising local citizen bought one of the poles, removed it from the curb, and took it away to manufacture memorabilia. *Cooper vs. State*, Vol. V, pp. 1492–93: testimony of A. H. Wright; *Nashville Tennessean*, December 10, 25, 1908.

7. *Nashville Banner*, November 12, 1908; *Nashville American*, November 11, 24, 1908.

8. *Nashville Tennessean*, November 13, 1908; C. D. Johns, *Tennessee's Pond of Liquor and Pool of Blood* (Nashville: C. D. Johns and Co., 1912), pp. 73–74; *Nashville Banner*, November 10, 1908.

9. *Nashville Banner*, November 12, 1908.

10. *Nashville American*, November 13, 1908; *Memphis News-Scimitar*, November 15, 1908.

11. *Cooper vs. State*, Vol. I, pp. 196–206: testimony of James Wittenberg.

12. *Nashville Banner*, November 12, 1908; *Nashville American*, November 13, 1908; *Commercial Appeal* (Memphis), November 13, 1908.

13. *Nashville Banner*, November 10, 11, 1908; *Daily Herald* (Columbia, Tenn.), November 10, 1908; Jordan Stokes, III, to Gary Blackburn and James Summerville, interview, August 12, 1985, Nashville.

14. *Nashville Banner*, November 11, 12, 1908; *Nashville American*, November 11, 1908.

15. *Commercial Appeal* (Memphis), November 12, 1908; *Nashville Banner*, November 11, 12, 1908. The *Banner* story about Carmack's rites was written by staff correspondent Joseph B. Wilson, brother of Woodrow Wilson.

16. J. Walker Green to Mrs. Edward W. Carmack, letter, November 12, 1908, in the Edward Ward Carmack Papers, Southern Historical Collection, University of North Carolina at Chapel Hill. Photocopies were consulted at the Tennessee State Library and Archives. Citations hereafter are to the Edward Ward Carmack Papers.

17. *Daily Commercial* (Memphis), May 4, 7, 1893; Thomas Harrison Baker, *The Memphis Commercial Appeal; The History of a Southern Newspaper* (Baton

Rouge: Louisiana State University Press, 1971), pp. 163–64; Paul R. Coppock, *Memphis Memoirs* (Memphis: Memphis State University Press, 1980), pp. 50–51; William R. Majors, *Editorial Wild Oats; Edward Ward Carmack and Tennessee Politics* (Macon, Ga.: Mercer University Press, 1984), pp. 51–59; C. Vann Woodward, *Origins of the New South, 1877–1913* (Baton Rouge: Louisiana State University Press, 1951), pp. 158–60. Edward Carmack, Jr., noted the eventuating friendship between his father and Collier in a handwritten note in his copy of Kenneth McKellar's *Tennessee Senators*. Gunplay regularly marked public life in the South during these years. See Dewey W. Grantham, Jr., "Goebel, Gonzales, Carmack: Three Violent Scenes in Southern Politics," *Mississippi Quarterly* 2, no. 1 (Winter 1958), pp. 29–37.

18. *Commercial Appeal* (Memphis), May 23, 24, 25, June 13, 14, 1895.

19. Baker, *Commercial Appeal*, p. 170; Coppock, *Memphis Memoirs*, pp. 51–52; Clyde J. Faries, "Carmack v. Patterson: The Genesis of a Political Feud," *Tennessee Historical Quarterly* 38, no. 3 (Fall 1979), pp. 332–45; Marilyn J. Hutton, "The Election of 1896 in the Tenth Congressional District of Tennessee" (Ph.D. diss., Memphis State University, 1976) pp. 45–128.

20. Carmack's speech in defense of his seat is reprinted in Paul Franklin Bumpus, *Carmack; The Edward Ward Carmack Story* (Franklin, Tenn.: privately printed, 1977), pp. 25–37. An able summary of the floor action in this election contest can be found in Faries, "Carmack v. Patterson." See also Majors, *Editorial Wild Oats*, pp. 76–81. The congratulations came from F. G. Pettus to Edward W. Carmack, telegram, April 23, 1898, in the Edward Ward Carmack Papers.

21. Guston Fitzhugh to Edward W. Carmack, letter, September 20, 1989; Kenneth D. McKellar to Edward W. Carmack, letter, August 31, 1900, both in the Edward Ward Carmack Papers; *Nashville Banner*, July 10, August 2, 3, 11, 16, 1900; *Senate Journal of the 52nd General Assembly of the State of Tennessee*, 1901 (Nashville: Brandon Printing Company, 1901), p. 51; *House Journal of the 52nd General Assembly of the State of Tennessee*, 1901 (Nashville: Brandon Printing Company, 1901), p. 64; Majors, *Editorial Wild Oats*, pp. 83–84.

22. *New York Times*, January 29, 1906.

23. Majors, *Editorial Wild Oats*, pp. 88, 96–97; Richard H. K. Vietor, "Businessmen and the Political Economy: The Railroad Rate Controversy of 1905," *Journal of American History* 64, no. 1 (June 1977), pp. 48–53.

24. Richard E. Welch, Jr., *Response to Imperialism; The United States and the Philippine-American War, 1899–1902* (Chapel Hill: The University of North Carolina Press, 1979), pp. 62–71; Nell Irvin Painter, *Standing at Armageddon; The United States, 1877–1919* (New York: W. W. Norton, 1987), p. 147. For an account of the hearings before the Senate committee on the Philippine repression, see Daniel B. Schirmer, *Republic or Empire; American Resistance to the Philippine War* (Cambridge, Mass.: Schenkman Publishing Co., 1972), pp. 234–40.

25. Carmack's speeches in the House and Senate are reprinted in Bumpus, *Carmack*, pp. 37–129. Other sources supporting this discussion are Edward W. Carmack to Cobey D. Carmack, undated letter, 1903, in the Edward Ward Carmack Papers; Frank Embrick Bass, "The Career of Edward Ward Carmack in Congress" (M. A. thesis, George Peabody College for Teachers, 1930), pp. 64–89; Robert Franklin Crutcher, "The Career of Edward Ward Carmack and the Cooper-Sharp Trial" (M. A. thesis, Western Kentucky University, 1932), pp. 23–30 and Majors, *Editorial Wild Oats*, pp. 99–100. N. O. Robbins attributes to Roosevelt the praise of Carmack in Robbins's letter to Carmack of January 22, 1907, in the Edward Ward Carmack Papers. Most scholars of today who came of age during the

Second Reconstruction look back on T. R.'s reaction to the Brownsville affair as a sorry episode in his presidency. The work that led to the posthumous exoneration of the black soldiers is John D. Weaver, *The Brownsville Raid* (New York: W. W. Norton Company, 1970).

26. Paul Deresco Augsburg, *Bob and Alf Taylor, Their Lives and Lectures; The Story of Senator Robert Love Taylor and Governor Alf Alexander Taylor* (Morristown, Tenn.: Morristown Book Co., 1925), pp. 32–33, 43–49, 65–72; Daniel Merritt Robison, *Bob Taylor and the Agrarian Revolt in Tennessee* (Chapel Hill: The University of North Carolina Press, 1935), pp. 32–33, 43–44, 56–72; Robert E. Corlew, *Tennessee; A Short History*, 2nd ed. (Knoxville: The University of Tennessee Press, 1981), pp. 373–80; Majors, *Editorial Wild Oats*, p. 39.

27. Corlew, *Tennessee*, pp. 384–87; Robison, *Bob Taylor*, pp. 196–99; Augsburg, *Bob and Alf Taylor*, pp. 146–47; J. B. Scott to Edward W. Carmack, letter, May 17, 1906, in the Edward Ward Carmack Papers.

28. Majors, *Editorial Wild Oats*, pp. 108–09; idem, *Continuity and Change; Tennessee Politics Since the Civil War* (Macon, Ga.: Mercer University Press, 1986), pp. 106–07; Corlew, *Tennessee*, pp. 419–21.

29. Majors, *Editorial Wild Oats*, p. 108; "Center Shots in the Senatorial Campaign; Plain Truths Plainly Told" and other campaign circulars in the Edward Ward Carmack Papers; untitled manuscript in box 8, folder 6, the Edward Ward Carmack Papers; *Nashville Banner*, June 6, September 20, 1905; letters of the Republican senators named to T. Leigh Thompson, box 8, folder 6, the Edward Ward Carmack Papers; Joe Michael Shahan, "Politics and Reform in Tennessee, 1906–1914" (Ph.D. diss., Vanderbilt University, 1981), p. 65; "How Governor Taylor Tickled the Republicans Under the Ribs," Carmack campaign tract, in box 8, folder 6, the Edward Ward Carmack Papers; *Lebanon Democrat* (Lebanon, Tennessee), February 14, 1906; Corlew, *Tennessee*, p. 421; Bumpus, *Carmack*, p. 71; *Nashville American*, October 8, 1905.

30. John I. Cox to Edward W. Carmack, letter, July 21, 1904; S. A. Bowman to Edward W. Carmack, letter, May 13, 1904; Edward W. Carmack to Frank M. Thompson, letter, May 26, 1906; Reese V. Hicks to Edward W. Carmack, letter, May 15, 1906, all in the Edward Ward Carmack Papers; Shahan, "Politics and Reform," pp. 70–71, 76, 92.

31. *Memphis News-Scimitar*, editorial, n.d., in box 1, folder 6, Edward Ward Carmack Papers; Louis Brownlow to Edward W. Carmack, letter, January 21, 1908, in the same collection.

32. The author's analysis of the 1906 senatorial primary is based on returns published in the *Nashville Banner*, May 17, 1906. For a discussion of the profound effect of the popular primary as it was adopted across the South in this period, see Dewey W. Grantham, *Southern Progressivism; The Reconciliation of Progress and Tradition* (Knoxville: The University of Tennessee Press, 1983), p. 11.

33. R. N. Hutton to Edward W. Carmack, letter, May 14, 1906; J. S. Cooper to Edward W. Carmack, letter, May 14, 1906; George Armistead to Edward W. Carmack, letter, May 17, 1906, all in the Edward Ward Carmack Papers.

34. Edward W. Carmack to W. G. Rainey, letter, May 16, 1906; Edward W. Carmack to August Belmont, letter, May 16, 1906; Edward W. Carmack to J. W. Emison, letter, May 21, 1906; Edward W. Carmack to J. W. Bonner, letter, May 26, 1906; Edward W. Carmack to John P. Hickman, letter, May 26, 1906; Edward W. Carmack to Joe Jones, letter, June 15, 1906; Edward W. Carmack to George H. Armistead, letter, n.d., Edward W. Carmack to unknown correspondent (letter fragment, n.d., 1906?), all in the Edward Ward Carmack Papers; Shahan, "Politics and Reform," pp. 79–80.

35. George H. Armistead to Edward W. Carmack, letter, December 26, 1906; J. C. Beene to Edward W. Carmack, letter, February 10, 1907; Dan Carpenter to Edward W. Carmack, letter, May 23, 1906; author unknown to Edward W. Carmack, letter fragment, January 26, 1907, all in the Edward Ward Carmack Papers.

36. Edward W. Carmack to the Reverend A. H. Hughlett, letter, March 13, 1907, in the Edward Ward Carmack Papers; Shahan, "Politics and Reform," pp. 122–24; William D. Miller, *Memphis During the Progressive Era, 1900–1917* (Memphis: Memphis State University Press, 1957), pp. 136–47; idem, *Mr. Crump of Memphis* (Baton Rouge: Louisiana State University Press, 1964), pp. 50–70.

37. Edgar Estes Folk, "Senator Edward Ward Carmack; A Life Sketch," *Baptist and Reflector* 20, no. 21 (January 14, 1909), pp. 2–4; Edward B. Craig to Edward W. Carmack, letter, February 4, 1907, in the Edward Ward Carmack Papers; Majors, *Editorial Wild Oats*, p. 120.

38. *Nashville Banner*, November 13, 1908; *Harper's Weekly* 51, no. 2636 (June 29, 1907), pp. 942–44.

39. E. C. Faircloth to Edward W. Carmack, letter, May 14, 1906; R. E. L. Mountcastle to Edward W. Carmack, letter, August 2, 1907; W. O. Mims to Edward W. Carmack, letter, August 19, 1907; Ernest H. Boyd to George H. Armistead, letter, September 9, 1907, all in the Edward Ward Carmack Papers; Shahan, "Reform and Politics," pp. 138–39.

40. Malcolm R. Patterson to Mary Gardner, letter, August 25, 1907, in the Malcolm Rice Patterson Papers, Manuscripts Section, Tennessee State Library and Archives, Nashville.

41. A careful student of the turn-of-the-century reform movement in the South notes that "the question of railroad monopoly in Tennessee remained relatively unimportant, despite the agitation of anti-corporation politicians like Carmack. In most states of the region, the carriers employed lobbyists, owned newspapers, fended off regulation through litigation, and made alliances with governors." See Grantham, *Southern Progressivism*, pp. 146–47.

42. Paul E. Isaac, *Prohibition and Politics: Turbulent Decades in Tennessee, 1885–1920* (Knoxville: The University of Tennessee Press, 1965), p. 127; B. A. Enloe to Edward W. Carmack, n.d., the Edward Ward Carmack Papers.

43. Majors, *Editorial Wild Oats*, pp. 125–26.

44. *Ibid.*, pp. 123–37; James H. Timberlake, *Prohibition and the Progressive Movement, 1900–1920* (Cambridge, Mass.: Harvard University Press, 1963), pp. 9–15; Jack S. Blocker, Jr., *Retreat from Reform; The Prohibition Movement in the United States, 1890–1913* (Westport, Conn.: Greenwood Press, 1976), pp. 133, 166–67; Norman H. Clark, *Deliver Us From Evil; An Interpretation of American Prohibition* (New York: W. W. Norton, 1976), pp. 1–66; and Grantham, *Southern Progressivism*, pp. 5–64, 161–77.

45. Majors, *Editorial Wild Oats*, p. 125; Isaac, *Prohibition and Politics*, pp. 107–08.

46. Isaac, *Prohibition and Politics*, pp. 106–11, 116–20, 151; Will Dunn Smith, "The Carmack-Patterson Campaign and Its Aftermath in Tennessee Politics" (M. A. thesis, Vanderbilt University, 1939), pp. 42–43; *Nashville Tennessean*, March 16, 17, 1908; Shahan, "Politics and Reform," pp. 106–07, 147–49; Edward W. Carmack to James C. Beck, letter, May 16, 1906, in the Edward Ward Carmack Papers; Majors, *Editorial Wild Oats*, p. 128.

47. Edward W. Carmack to members of the state Democratic Executive Committee, form letter, n.d., 1908?, in box 2, folder 22, Edward Ward Carmack

Papers; *Nashville Banner*, February 19, 1908; Smith, "The Carmack-Patterson Campaign," pp. 142–45.

48. "Regulations for the Primary of June 27, 1908 and the Convention of July 14, 1908 Prescribed by the Democratic State Executive Committee," in Manuscripts Section, Tennessee State Library and Archives; *Nashville Banner*, February 21, April 24, 1908; Isaac, *Prohibition and Politics*, p. 143; Shahan, "Reform and Politics," pp. 145–53.

49. Thomas Fauntleroy, "History Made in 54 Debates by Patterson and Carmack," n.p., n.d., fragment, in "Scrapbook—Prohibition, 1887–1940," in Manuscripts Section, Tennessee State Library and Archives, Nashville; J. G. Rice to George H. Armistead, letter, April 2, 1908, and W. G. M. Thomas to Edward W. Carmack, letter, April 1, 1908, both in the Edward Ward Carmack Papers; *Nashville Banner*, April 17, 20, 27, 1908; *Memphis News-Scimitar*, March 15, 1908; Shahan, "Politics and Reform," pp. 152–53.

50. Majors, *Editorial Wild Oats*, p. 135; Shahan, "Reform and Politics," p. 135. For a cogent defense of Patterson's stance, see "The Position of Governor M. R. Patterson and the Democratic Party on the Temperance Question" (n.p., n.d., 1908?), in the James Douglas Anderson Papers, Manuscripts Section, Tennessee State Library and Archives, Nashville.

51. *Nashville Banner*, April 16, 17, 18, 22, 27, May 1, 2, June 16, 17, 1908; J. M. Mays to Duncan B. Cooper, letter, May 13, 1908, in the Duncan Brown Cooper Papers, Manuscripts Section, Tennessee State Library and Archives, Nashville; *Nashville Tennessean*, May 19, 1908; Smith, "Carmack-Patterson Campaign," pp. 38–41, 50–57; James M. Brice, *I Had a Real Good Time; The Making of a Country Editor* (Union City, Tennessee: privately printed, 1984), p. 73.

52. Majors, *Editorial Wild Oats*, pp. 134–37; Shahan, "Politics and Reform," pp. 157–59; Edward W. Carmack to Guston Fitzhugh, letter fragment, February 10, 1908, in the Edward Ward Carmack Papers.

53. Shahan, "Politics and Reform," pp. 161–64; *Nashville Tennessean*, July 15, 1908.

54. *Nashville Tennessean*, August 20, September 19, 27, October 15, 21, 22, 23, 1908; Casper B. Kuhn to Duncan B. Cooper, letter, November [no further date; 1908?] and J. M. Mays to Duncan B. Cooper, letter, September 19, 1908, both in the Duncan Brown Cooper Papers; Edward W. Carmack to James C. Bradford, letters, October 21, 23, 1908; James C. Bradford to Edward W. Carmack, letter, October 23, 1908, all in the Edward Ward Carmack Papers; Smith, "Carmack-Patterson Campaign," pp. 76–77.

55. Silena M. Holman to Mrs. Edward W. Carmack, letter, November 13, 1908, in the Edward W. Carmack, Jr., Papers, Manuscripts Section, Tennessee State Library and Archives, Nashville.

56. *Nashville Tennessean*, November 8, 1908.

57. J. Walker Green to Mrs. Edward W. Carmack, letter, November 12, 1908, and N. W. Baptist to Mrs. Edward W. Carmack, letter, November 27, 1908, both in the Edward Ward Carmack Papers; Edward W. Carmack, Jr., "A Portrait," in Bumpus, *Carmack*, p. 278.

58. Carmack was received into the Linden Avenue Christian Church, Memphis, in 1905. See the Reverend W. H. Sheffer to Edward W. Carmack, letter, January 30, 1905, in the Edward W. Carmack Papers, and Herman A. Norton, *Tennessee Christians; A History of the Christian Church (Disciples of Christ) in Tennessee* (Nashville: Reed and Company, 1971), pp. 221–22.

59. C. E. Merrill to Duncan B. Cooper, letter, November 12, 1908; Will

Armstrong to Duncan B. Cooper, letter, November 15, 1908; R. W. Banks to Duncan B. Cooper, letter, November 15, 1910, all in the Duncan Brown Cooper Papers.

60. *Nashville Banner*, November 16, 1908.

61. James E. Caldwell, *Recollections of a Life Time* (Nashville: privately printed, 1923), p. 72. The best study of Sam Jones's influence on Progressive-era Nashville is James Douglas Flamming's "The Sam Jones Revivals and Social Reform in Nashville, Tennessee, 1885–1900" (M.A. thesis, Vanderbilt University, 1983).

62. This restatement of the reform ideals of the prohibitionists is indebted to Clark, *Deliver Us from Evil*; Timberlake, *Prohibition and the Progressive Movement*; Blocker, *Retreat from Reform*; and Grantham, *Southern Progressivism*.

63. *Nashville Tennessean*, November 12, 1908.

64. William Waller, ed., *Nashville, 1900–1910* (Nashville: Vanderbilt University Press, 1972), p. 78; *New York Times*, September 16, 1903; *Nashville Banner*, November 25, December 28, 1908; *New York American*, January 21, 1909.

65. *New York Times*, November 14, 1908; *Nashville Banner*, November 16, 1908.

Chapter Three

1. Mrs. G. B. West to Duncan B. Cooper, letter, April 25, 1907, in the Duncan Brown Cooper Papers, Manuscripts Section, Tennessee State Library and Archives, Nashville.

2. *William West, in Error vs. The State, Brief and Assignment of Errors*, by Sam E. Young for the Defendant, in East Tennessee Division, Tennessee Supreme Court, January 1905, unpaginated; *William West, in Error vs. The State*, Memorandum Brief for State in East Tennessee Division, Tennessee Supreme Court, n.d., pp. 1–2.

3. Mrs. G. B. West to Duncan B. Cooper, letters, April 25, July 31, August 10, October 16, November 15, December 16, 1907, March 25, July 14, 1908; Katrina Williamson to Duncan B. Cooper, n.d., all in the Duncan Brown Cooper Papers. Patterson, like other Tennessee governors of the time, reaped political benefits in issuing pardons. See W. R. Boone to George Armistead, letter, September 11, 1907, in the Edward Ward Carmack Papers, Southern Historical Collection, University of North Carolina at Chapel Hill. (Photocopies consulted at the Tennessee State Library and Archives.) Patterson lieutenants advised the governor of the probable consequences of granting or withholding a given pardon. See Lake Erie Holladay to Malcolm R. Patterson, letter, February 18, 1908, in the Malcolm Rice Patterson Papers, Manuscripts Section, Tennessee State Library and Archives, Nashville, and P. I. H. Morris to Duncan B. Cooper, August 9, 1908, in the Duncan Brown Cooper Papers. Students of politics and the clemency power in this period have a mother lode of material in the Patterson pardon files. For 1907 alone there are eighteen files of petitions. One file chosen at random holds forty-six petitions.

4. William S. Speer, comp., *Sketches of Prominent Tennesseans* (Nashville: Albert B. Tavel, 1888), p. 13; Lesbia Word Roberts to James Summerville, letter, July 9, 1989. All students of the Cooper family are indebted to Mrs. Roberts' definitive study, *Hugh Cooper (1720–1793) of Fishing Creek, South Carolina, and His Descendents* (Fort Worth: privately printed, 1975).

5. Goodspeed Publishing Co., *History of Tennessee From the Earliest Times to the Present* (Nashville: Goodspeed Publishing Co., 1886), p. 776; Robert E. Corlew, *Tennessee; A Short History*, 2nd ed. (Knoxville: The University of Tennessee Press,

1981), pp. 137–38; Jill K. Garrett, ed., *War of 1812 Soldiers of Maury County, Tennessee* (Columbia, Tenn.: Daughters of the American Revolution, n.d.), p. 36; Lesbia Word Roberts to James Summerville, letter, July 9, 1989.

6. Speer, *Prominent Tennesseans*, p. 13; William Bruce Turner, *History of Maury County, Tennessee* (Nashville: Parthenon Press, 1955), p. 263; Duncan B. Cooper to William F. Cooper, letter, September 12, 1902, in the Cooper Family Papers, Manuscripts Section, Tennessee State Library and Archives, Nashville; Lesbia Word Roberts to James Summerville, letter, July 9, 1989.

7. Speer, *Prominent Tennesseans*, p. 13; Virginia Wood Alexander and Jill Knight Garrett, comps., *Maury County Tennessee Marriage Records, 1838–1852* (Columbia, Tenn., n.p., 1963), p. 22; "Cooper Family of Maury County, Tennessee," in the Duncan Brown Cooper Papers. (This last source, a genealogical chart, is inaccurate in certain dates and should be used with caution.)

8. Charles Albert Snodgrass, *The History of Freemasonry in Tennessee, 1789–1943* (Chattanooga: Masonic Historic Agency, 1944), pp. 80–81, 174–75; *Columbia Herald*, June 16, 1871; *Columbia Herald and Mail*, December 4, 1874; Speer, *Prominent Tennesseans*, p. 13; Roberts, *Hugh Cooper*, pp. 619–22.

9. Paul A. W. Wallace, *Pennsylvania; Seed of a Nation* (New York: Harper and Row, 1962), p. 101; *Catalogue of the Officers and Students of Jefferson College for the Academical Year, 1859–60* (Canonsburg, Pa.: Jefferson College, 1860), pp. 13, 19; Duncan B. Cooper to Matthew D. Cooper, letter, October 24, 1859, in the Cooper Family Papers.

10. Frank H. Smith, *History of Maury County, Tennessee* (Columbia, Tenn.: Maury County Historical Society, 1969), pp. 105, 223; Jill K. Garrett and Marise P. Lightfoot, *The Civil War in Maury County, Tennessee* (Columbia, Tenn.: privately printed, 1966), pp. 122, 223.

11. Thomas L. Connelly, *Civil War Tennessee; Battles and Leaders* (Knoxville: The University of Tennessee Press, 1979), pp. 13–14; Garrett and Lightfoot, *Civil War in Maury County*, p. 62; *Nashville Banner*, March 3, 1897.

12. Garrett and Lightfoot, *Civil War in Maury County*, pp. 154, 157. The role of guerrillas like Cooper in the Civil War in the midstate is interpreted in Stephen V. Ash, *Middle Tennessee Society Transformed, 1860–1870* (Knoxville: The University of Tennessee Press, 1988), pp. 147–48.

13. William M. McCarren to Duncan B. Cooper, letter, April 14, 1910; Mary P. Webster to Duncan B. Cooper, letter, May 12, 1909, both in the Duncan Brown Cooper Papers.

14. Francis C. Ward, letter to the editor, *Table Grove* [state?] *Herald*, January 7, 1909; Francis C. Ward to Duncan B. Cooper, letter, November 29, 1894, both in the Duncan Brown Cooper Papers; Garrett and Lightfoot, *Civil War in Maury County*, pp. 159, 192–93.

15. Lucius Burch, Jr., to Gary Blackburn and James Summerville, interview, October 29, 1985, Nashville.

16. J. A. Woollard to Duncan B. Cooper, letter, November 13, 1908, in the Duncan Brown Cooper Papers. I have preserved Woollard's original spelling.

17. W. R. H. Matthews to Duncan B. Cooper, letter, April 6, 1910; Bedford Matthews to Duncan B. Cooper, letter, October 15, 1910, both in the Duncan Brown Cooper Papers.

18. C. E. Merrill to Duncan B. Cooper, letter, April 8, 1909; Katherine M. LaFollette to Duncan B. Cooper, letter, November 10, 1908, both in the Duncan Brown Cooper Papers; "Duncan Brown Cooper," unpublished biographical sketch, n.d., in the same collection.

19. Lucius E. Burch, Jr., to James Summerville, letter, May 17, 1988; Alexis de Tocqueville, *Democracy in America*, eds. J. P. Mayer and Max Lerner (New York: Harper and Row, 1966), p. 419; Bertram Wyatt-Brown, *Yankee Saints and Southern Sinners* (Baton Rouge: Louisiana State University Press, 1985), pp. 186–87, 215; Frankie Wilson to Duncan B. Cooper, letter, n.d.; Francis B. Ward to Duncan B. Cooper, November 29, 1894, both in the Duncan Brown Cooper Papers.

20. *Nashville Banner*, November 5, 1922; James C. Rembert to Duncan B. Cooper, letter, February 17, 1909, in the Duncan Brown Cooper Papers; Joshua W. Caldwell, *Sketches of the Bench and Bar of Tennessee* (Knoxville: Ogden Brothers and Co., Printers, 1898), pp. 364–65; Speer, *Prominent Tennesseans*, pp. 12–14.

21. Corlew, *Tennessee*, p. 378; *Daily Times* (Chattanooga), November 14, 1908.

22. *Daily Times* (Chattanooga), November 14, 1908. Edward Carmack, Jr., recounted hearing Johnson's words quoted by one present at the speech. Carmack, Jr., made pencil notes on the story at the biographical sketches of Andrew Johnson and Henry Cooper in Carmack's copy of Kenneth D. McKellar's *Tennessee Senators as Seen by One of Their Successors* (Kingsport, Tenn.: Southern Publishing Co., 1942), later acquired by Dr. James High and loaned by him to the author.

23. Louis Torres to James Summerville, letter, August 12, 1986; Roxana Deane, Washingtoniana Division, District of Columbia Public Library, to James Summerville, letter, November 12, 1986; "Letter from W. W. Corcoran, Chairman, Joint Commission for the Completion of the Washington Monument, Transmitting the Annual Report of the Engineer in Charge, for the Year Ending November 30, 1880," in *Senate Miscellaneous Document 9*, 46th Congress, 3rd Session; *Daily Times* (Chattanooga), November 14, 1908; Duncan B. Cooper to William F. Cooper, June 20, 1879, in the Cooper Family Papers.

24. Jill K. Garrett (comp.), *Obituaries from Tennessee Newspapers* (n.p., n.d., Columbia, Tennessee?; reprinted Easley, S.C.: Southern Historical Press, 1980), p. 64; Turner, *Maury County, Tennessee*, pp. 244–57; *Century Review, 1805–1905, Maury County, Tennessee* (Columbia: Mayor and Board of Aldermen, 1905; reprinted: Easley, S.C.: Southern Historical Press, 1980), p. 107; Jill K. Garrett, *Maury County, Tennessee Historical Sketches* (n.p., n.d., Columbia, Tennessee? 1972?), p. 142; William Henry McRaven, "Antoinette Polk, Baroness de Charette," unpublished biographical sketch, in the William Henry McRaven Papers, Manuscripts Section, Tennessee State Library and Archives, Nashville; Louis Brownlow, *A Passion for Politics* (Chicago: The University of Chicago Press, 1955), pp. 314–15.

25. Robert B. Jones, *Tennessee at the Crossroads; The State Debt Controversy, 1870–1883* (Knoxville: The University of Tennessee Press, 1977), pp. 120–21, 132–34.

26. *Daily Times* (Chattanooga), November 11, 1908.

27. Brownlow, *Passion for Politics*, pp. 313–14.

28. Henry M. Doak, letter to the editor, *Commercial Appeal* (Memphis), November 14, 1908; W. I. Cherry to Theodore Duncan Rousseau, letter, January 30, 1909, in the Duncan Brown Cooper Papers.

29. Cash book of the *American*, 1886, unpaginated fragment, in the Duncan Brown Cooper Papers; minutes of the *American* stockholders' meetings, January 9, 1886–August 29, 1895, unpaginated, in the Duncan Brown Cooper Papers.

30. Corlew, *Tennessee*, pp. 384–87; Don H. Doyle, *Nashville in the New South, 1890–1930* (Knoxville: The University of Tennessee Press, 1985), pp. 136, 237.

31. *Senate Journal of the First Session of the Forty-Ninth General Assembly of the State of Tennessee* (Nashville: Franc M. Paul, Printer to the State, 1895), pp. 20, 703–16, and passim; *Acts of the State of Tennessee Passed by the Forty-Ninth General*

Assembly, 1895 (Nashville: Franc M. Paul, Printer to the State, 1895), pp. 32, 36, and passim.

32. "Members of the Open Letter Club, Nashville and New York," unpublished manuscript, in possession of the author; William Waller, ed., *Nashville in the 1890s* (Nashville: Vanderbilt University Press, 1970), p. 23; *New York Times*, August 24, 1897, January 30, 1898, June 13, 1900.

33. Richard Harding Davis, *Three Gringos in Venezuela and Central America* (New York: Harper and Brothers, 1896), pp. 60–61, 75.

34. *New York Times*, January 16, 1897, September 16, 1898, June 13, 1900.

35. Davis, *Three Gringos*, p. 73; *New York Times*, January 15, 1919.

36. Frank Marshall White to Duncan B. Cooper, letter, February 14, 1909; Henry Proctor Waugh to Duncan B. Cooper, telegram, March 20, 1909, both in the Duncan Brown Cooper Papers; *New York Times*, December 30, 1919, November 13, 1924.

37. J. Coleman Drayton to Duncan B. Cooper, May 4, September 27, October 1, 1904; Bruce L. Rice to Duncan B. Cooper, letter, November 10, 1908; E. Bright Wilson to Duncan B. Cooper, letter fragment, n.d.; Edwin Taliaferro to Duncan B. Cooper, telegram, November 10, 1908; Jesse M. Littleton to Martin Littleton, November 27, 1908; John Peacock to Duncan B. Cooper, letter, November 20, 1908, all these missives in the Duncan Brown Cooper Papers; *New York Times*, November 13, 1924, November 12, 1934.

38. C. Vann Woodward, *Origins of the New South, 1877–1913* (Baton Rouge: Louisiana State University Press, 1951), pp. 456–59; Paul Franklin Bumpus, *Carmack; The Edward Ward Carmack Story* (Franklin, Tenn.: privately printed, 1977), pp. 204–05; Grover Cleveland to Duncan B. Cooper, letter, March 31, 1903, in the Duncan Brown Cooper Papers.

39. Taft penned his comments at the top of Van Leer Polk's letter to Theodore Roosevelt dated March 9, 1906, in the Theodore Roosevelt Papers, Library of Congress; *Knoxville Sentinel*, November 17, 1908; E. Bright Wilson to Duncan B. Cooper, letter, n.d., in the Duncan Brown Cooper Papers.

40. These conclusions are based on the author's analysis of returns reported by the Tennessee Secretary of State and printed in the *Nashville American*, November 19, 1896, November 29, 1898, November 30, 1900, December 3, 1902, and December 6, 1904.

41. Corlew, *Tennessee*, p. 380.

42. William Waller, ed., *Nashville 1900 to 1910* (Nashville: Vanderbilt University Press, 1972), p. 36; *Duncan B. Cooper and Robin J. Cooper, in Error, vs. the State of Tennessee*, Vol. IV, pp. 1314–17: testimony of Duncan B. Cooper; Doyle, *Nashville in the New South*, p. 30.

43. Sparrell Hill to Duncan B. Cooper, letters, February 2, May 4, 1906, in the Duncan Brown Cooper Papers. Hill had once been Carmack's friend, offering to help him obtain charge of another paper after he resigned from the *Commercial Appeal*. Sparrell Hill to Edward W. Carmack, April 29, 1896, in the Edward Ward Carmack Papers.

44. Edward W. Carmack to Duncan B. Cooper, letter, December 17, 1904, in the Duncan Brown Cooper Papers.

45. "C.D." [pseudonym] "The True Story of the Carmack Tragedy," *The Taylor-Trotwood Magazine* 9, no. 1 (April 1909), p. 70.

46. William D. Miller, *Memphis During the Progressive Era* (Memphis: Memphis State University Press, 1957), pp. 135–47; *Commercial Appeal* (Memphis), August 23, 25, September 2, 1904.

47. Joe Michael Shahan, "Reform and Politics in Tennessee, 1906–1914" (Ph.D. dissertation, Vanderbilt University, 1981), pp. 70–81.

48. Harvey M. LaFollette to Duncan B. Cooper, letter, May 14, 1907; Malcolm R. Patterson to Duncan B. Cooper, letters, February 1, 13, 1908; Katrina Williamson to Duncan B. Cooper, letter, n.d., all in the Duncan Brown Cooper Papers.

49. Harvey M. LaFollette to Duncan B. Cooper, letters, April 24, 26, 1907, and passim; Katherine M. LaFollette to Duncan B. Cooper, letters, February 19, 1908, and passim; Katrina Williamson to Duncan B. Cooper, n.d., all in the Duncan Brown Cooper Papers; Albert Taylor to James Summerville, letter, November 20, 1986, in the author's possession.

50. Jim Stokeley and Jeff D. Johnson, *An Encyclopedia of East Tennessee* (Oak Ridge: Children's Museum of Oak Ridge, 1981), p. 84; *LaFollette Press*, June 19, 1986; Department of Commerce, Bureau of the Census, *Thirteenth Census of the United States, 1910, Volume I, Population* (Washington, D.C.: Government Printing Office, 1913), Table 59, p. 96.

51. Katherine M. LaFollette and Katrina Williamson to Duncan B. Cooper, letter, n.d.; Katrina Williamson to Duncan B. Cooper, September 11 [no year given]; Katherine M. LaFollette to Duncan B. Cooper, letter, n.d., all in the Duncan Brown Cooper Papers.

52. Harvey M. LaFollette to Duncan B. Cooper, letters, March 27, April 11, 14, October 28, 29, 30, November 4, 1908, in the Duncan Brown Cooper Papers.

53. Harvey M. LaFollette to Duncan B. Cooper, letter, November 4, 1908, in the Duncan Brown Cooper Papers.

54. *Nashville Tennessean*, January 5, 9, 13, 14, 1909; *Nashville American*, January 13, 14, 1909; *Senate Journal of the 56th General Assembly, 1909* (Nashville: McQuiddy Printing Company, 1909), pp. 44, 75–82; Katrina Williamson to Duncan B. Cooper, letter fragment, n.d., in the Duncan Brown Cooper Papers.

55. *Senate Journal, 56th General Assembly*, pp. 23–27. This legislature also outlawed the manufacture of liquor over Patterson's veto. *Ibid.*, pp. 150–54. Estimates held that with the coming of prohibition the state would lose more than one million dollars in revenue from its taxes on saloons and that twelve thousand jobs in breweries and distilleries would disappear. *New York Times*, February 6, 1909. Tennessee's adoption of prohibition was part of a moralistic wave that swept the South between 1907 and 1909. See Woodward, *Origins of the New South*, pp. 389–92, and Dewey W. Grantham, *Southern Progressivism; The Reconciliation of Progress and Tradition* (Knoxville: The University of Tennessee Press, 1983), pp. 160–66.

Chapter Four

1. *Nashville Banner*, January 19, 20, 1909.

2. William Waller, ed., *Nashville, 1900 to 1910* (Nashville: Vanderbilt University Press, 1972), pp. 74–87, 290.

3. Jeff McCarn to Edward W. Carmack, letter, June 5, 1908, in the Edward Ward Carmack Papers, Southern Historical Collection, University of North Carolina at Chapel Hill. The author consulted photocopies at the Manuscripts Section, Tennessee State Library and Archives, Nashville.

4. John Trotwood Moore and Austin P. Foster, *Tennessee; The Volunteer State, 1769–1923*, vol. 4 (Chicago: S. J. Clarke Publishing Company, 1923), pp. 103–04; alumnus biographical file for Jeff McCarn for the "Vanderbilt Directory," in Special

Collections, The Jean and Alexander Heard Library, Vanderbilt University; Albert Bramblett Neil, "My Great World; or Fifty Years on the Bench," mimeographed (Nashville: privately printed, n.d., 1964?), pp. 88–89, unpublished typescript available at the Tennessee State Library and Archives, Nashville.

5. *Chattanooga Sunday Times*, November 15, 1908; Guston Fitzhugh to Mrs. Edward W. Carmack, letter, November 20, 1908, in the Edward Ward Carmack Papers; John Allison, ed., *Notable Men of Tennessee*, Vol. 1 (Atlanta: Southern Historical Association, 1905), pp. 127–28; Southern Biographical Association, *Men of the South* (New Orleans: Southern Biographical Association, 1922), p. 578; Moore and Foster, *Tennessee*, Vol. 3, pp. 48–51; Guston Fitzhugh to Mrs. Edward W. Carmack, November 20, 1908, in the Edward Ward Carmack Papers.

6. *Nashville Banner*, January 21, 22, 25–30, February 12, 14, 1909.

7. *The Taylor-Trotwood Magazine* 9 (April 1909): 70; New York *Herald*, February 17, 1909. An ironic gloss on the jury selection process is an editorial, presumably written by Edward Carmack, "Liberty and Law," in the *Nashville Tennessean*, October 23, 1908: "The rule with respect to disqualifying jurors because of informed opinions is not enforced as rigidly as it once was. . . . In these days of newspapers, every intelligent man must get some information and form some opinion with respect to every important crime."

8. *Nashville Banner*, January 21, 30, February 3, 13, 1909, April 26, 1935, June 19, 1939; *New York World*, February 4, 16, 1909; *Nashville Tennessean*, January 21, 26, 1909, June 19, 1939; John P. Graves, *Northwest Davidson County; The Land — It's* [sic] *People* (Nashville: privately printed, 1985), pp. 41–44, 60. For a study of rural violence in a north central Tennessee setting similar to Paradise Ridge, see William Lynwood Montell, *Killings; Folk Justice in the Upper South* (Lexington: University Press of Kentucky, 1986).

9. *Nashville Banner*, February 16, 1909; *New York American*, February 17, 1909.

10. *Duncan B. Cooper and Robin J. Cooper, in Error, vs. the State of Tennessee*, Vol. I, pp. 122–32, 134–36, 139, 151, 160: testimony of Mrs. Charles Eastman; *Nashville Tennessean*, March 10, 1937. The former is the transcript of the trial in the Criminal Court, filed at the Tennessee Supreme Court when the Coopers appealed their case, now in the collections of the Tennessee State Library and Archives, Nashville.

11. Philip M. Hamer, ed., *Tennessee, A History, 1673–1932*, Vol. IV (New York: American Historical Society, 1933), pp. 789–90; Allison, ed., *Notable Men of Tennessee*, Vol. I, pp. 106–07; Moore and Foster, *Tennessee*, Vol. III, pp. 508–10; Waller, ed., *Nashville 1900 to 1910*, p. 324.

12. *Cooper vs. State*, Vol. I, pp. 149, 153, 157, 160–61, 163–66: testimony of Mrs. Charles Eastman.

13. *Ibid.*, Vol. I, pp. 183–94: testimony of John Tindall; Vol. I, pp. 207–22: testimony of Carey Folk.

14. *Ibid.*, Vol. I, pp. 269–83: testimony of Mary Skeffington; Vol. I, p. 230: testimony of Hugh Morton; Vol. I, pp. 248–49: testimony of W. J. Smith; Vol. I, p. 255: testimony of L. A. Welch; Vol. I, p. 295: testimony of C. B. Horn; Vol. I, pp. 325–29: testimony of Charles Warwick; and Vol. I, pp. 347–49: testimony of George W. Cooper.

15. *Ibid.*, Vol. II, pp. 406–12: testimony of Finley Dorris; Vol. II, pp. 416–27: testimony of William Murray.

16. *Nashville Banner*, February 19, 1909.

17. This correspondence may be found in the James Douglas Anderson Papers, Manuscripts Section, Tennessee State Library and Archives, Nashville.

18. James Douglas to J. M. Anderson, letter, November 13, 1908, James Douglas Anderson Papers; J. D. Anderson, "The Making of a Lawyer; a Biographical
Sketch of J. M. Anderson with Some Facts Relative to Law Practice in Nashville
Between 1882 and 1934," mimeographed (Nashville: privately printed, n.d.), pp. 1–4,
12–17, available at the Tennessee State Library and Archives; Waller, ed., *Nashville
1900 to 1910*, pp. 83–84, 315; Moore and Foster, *Tennessee*, Vol. III, p. 475; *Nashville Tennessean*, December 31, 1933.

19. Robert M. McBride and Dan M. Robison, *Biographical Directory of the
Tennessee General Assembly*, Vol. II (Nashville: Tennessee State Library and Ar-
chives and Tennessee Historical Commission, 1979), pp. 614–15; Moore and Foster,
Tennessee, Vol. III, pp. 349–50; *Commercial Appeal* (Memphis), August 12, 1938;
Nashville Banner, January 18, 1909; Waller, ed., *Nashville 1900 to 1910*, p. 337.
Charles N. Burch, forty, a lawyer from Memphis and Colonel Cooper's son-in-law,
took no active part in examining witnesses nor arguing the case. Other lawyers
assisting the defense were Edmond Baxter, Albert Ewing, Jr., and James A. Ryan.

20. *Nashville Banner*, September 5, 1910; *Nashville American*, September 5,
1910; *Nashville Tennessean*, September 5, 1910.

21. Anderson, "Making of a Lawyer," p. 18; Department of Commerce, *Thir-
teenth Census of the United States, 1910*, Vol. VI, Population — Occupation Statistics,
Table VIII, "Males and Females in Selected Occupations," p. 568; Department of
Commerce, Bureau of the Census, *1980 Census of Population*, Vol. I, Part 44. Popu-
lation Characteristics — Tennessee, Table 219, "Detailed Occupation of Employed
Persons," pp. 44–319.

22. *Cooper vs. State*, Vol. II, pp. 521–23, 525–99, 602 –33: testimony of Robin
J. Cooper; *Nashville Banner*, February 22, 1909.

23. *Cooper vs. State*, Vol. II, pp. 636–42, 659–67, 680–704: testimony of Robin
J. Cooper; *Nashville Banner*, February 22, 1909.

24. *Cooper vs. State*, Vol. III, pp. 718–848: testimony of John Sharp; *Nashville
Banner*, February 23, 1909.

25. Katrina Williamson to Duncan B. Cooper, letter, n.d., in the Duncan
Brown Cooper Papers; *Nashville Banner*, February 24, 25, 1909.

26. *Cooper vs. State*, Vol. III, pp. 849–901; *Memphis News-Scimitar*, March 15,
1908. Colonel Cooper was apparently prepared to present a witness from the *News-
Scimitar* staff who would confirm that Carmack wrote the editorial. W. W. Talbert
to Duncan B. Cooper, February 22, 1909, in the Duncan Brown Cooper Papers.
Gates was industrial and immigration agent for the L & N. See correspondence
from him in the Duncan Brown Cooper Papers about certain 1906 legislative races.

27. *Cooper vs. State*, Vol. III, pp. 849–938, 942–1024: testimony of Duncan
B. Cooper.

28. An investigator who examined the court records found no judgment
against Cooper or his sureties that remained unpaid. E. E. Erwin to Duncan B.
Cooper, letter, February 16, 1909, in the Duncan Brown Cooper Papers.

29. *Cooper vs. State*, Vol. IV, pp. 1037–1383; *Nashville Banner*, February 24,
25, 26, 1909.

30. *Cooper vs. State*, Vol. V, pp. 1584–1608: testimony of Malcolm R. Patterson; *Nashville Banner*, February 27, 1909.

31. *Cooper vs. State*, Vol. V, pp. 1613–38; Vol. VI, pp. 1651–56; Vol. VII,
1871–93: testimony of McPheeters Glasgow; *Nashville Banner*, March 1, 2, 4, 1909.
That Carmack had lived to fire at least one shot was first proposed on the morning
after his death in the newspaper he had edited. See the *Nashville Tennessean*,
November 10, 1908.

32. *Cooper vs. State*, Vol. VI, pp. 1703, 1713–77, 1904–10: testimony of S. J. Benning; *Nashville Banner*, March 4, 6, 8, 1909.

33. *Nashville Banner*, March 9–12, 1909.

34. Ned Carmack all his life believed this interpretation of the state. "While the father attracted my father's attention in front, the son Robin shot my father through the back and the base of his head." Ned Carmack's comment on the killing appears in pencil notes at the biography of Henry Cooper in Carmack's copy of Kenneth D. McKellar, *Tennessee Senators as Seen by One of Their Successors* (Kingsport, Tenn.: Southern Publishing Company, 1942). This volume was loaned to the author by Dr. James High.

35. *Nashville Banner*, March 13, 15, 1909.

36. *Ibid.*, March 16, 1909.

37. *Ibid.*, March 17, 1909.

38. *Ibid.*, March 19, 20, 1909.

39. *Nashville Tennessean* and *Nashville American*, March 21, 1909.

40. Montell, *Killings*, p. 155.

41. J. C. Bradford, quoted in Waller, ed., *Nashville 1900 to 1910*, pp. 98–99.

42. *Nashville Banner*, April 15, 1909.

43. *Ibid.*, April 21, 22, 27, 1909; Rebecca Edwards Jones to Mary Wharton, letter, May 3, 1909, in the Cooper Family Papers.

Chapter Five

1. Katrina Williamson to Duncan B. Cooper, letter, April 2 [no year], in the Duncan Brown Cooper Papers, Manuscripts Section, Tennessee State Library and Archives, Nashville.

2. *Cooper, et al. vs. State*, 138 *Southwestern Reporter*, 830 (1911).

3. Paul R. Coppock, *Memphis Memoirs* (Memphis: Memphis State University Press, 1980), pp. 152–56; Arthur S. Pier, *American Apostles to the Philippines* (Boston: Beacon Press, 1950), pp. 37–49; Thomas B. Turley to Edward Carmack, letter, May 28, 1897, in the Edward Ward Carmack Papers; *Nashville Banner*, February 1, 1910; *Cooper vs. State*, p. 829. The Edward Ward Carmack Papers are located in the Southern Historical Collection, the University of North Carolina at Chapel Hill. Photocopies were consulted at the Manuscripts Section, Tennessee State Library and Archives, Nashville.

4. Cooper Frierson to Duncan B. Cooper, letter, December 30, 1908, in the Duncan Brown Cooper Papers.

5. *Nashville Banner*, December 7, 1910; John W. Green, *Lives of the Judges of the Supreme Court of Tennessee* (Knoxville: Archer and Smith, 1947), pp. 232–36; *Who's Who in Tennessee; A Biographical Reference Book of Notable Tennesseans of Today* (Memphis: Paul and Douglass, Publishers, 1911), p. 434.

6. Green, *Judges of the Supreme Court, pp. 247–48; Chat* (Nashville), reprinted in William Waller, ed., *Nashville in the 1890s* (Nashville: Vanderbilt University Press, 1970), pp. 239–40. Judge McAlister was father of Hill McAlister, governor of Tennessee from 1933 to 1937.

7. *Nashville Banner*, February 1, 3, 1910.

8. John W. Green, *Law and Lawyers; Sketches of the Federal Judges of Tennessee; Sketches of the Attorneys General of Tennessee; Legal Miscellany; Reminiscences* (Jackson, Tenn.: McCowat-Mercer Press, 1950), pp. 138–40; Moore and Foster, *Tennessee*, Vol. II, pp. 104–08; *Knoxville News Sentinel*, October 16, 1938.

9. *Nashville Banner*, February 3, 1910.

10. Kenneth McKellar, *Tennessee Senators as Seen by One of Their Successors* (Kingsport, Tenn.: Southern Publishing Co., 1942), p. 569.

11. *Nashville Banner*, March 29, 30, April 19, 1910.

12. *Ibid.*, March 31, April 1, 2, 1910; Joe Michael Shahan, "Reform and Politics in Tennessee, 1906–1914," Ph.D. dissertation, Vanderbilt University, 1981, pp. 212–14.

13. Frank Trigg Fancher, *The Sparta Bar* (Sparta, Tenn.: privately printed, 1950), p. 84.

14. *Nashville Banner*, April 13, 1910.

15. *Cooper vs. State*, pp. 837, 839, 841–42, 847, 850–52.

16. *Ibid.*, pp. 856, 858–59, 863, 865–67, 869–70, 872–76. This discussion is also indebted to Robert A. Lanier, "The Carmack Murder Case," *Tennessee Historical Quarterly* 40, no. 3 (Fall 1981), pp. 278–85.

17. *Nashville Banner*, April 14, 1910.

18. *Cooper vs. State*, p. 878.

19. *Nashville Banner*, April 13, 14, 16, 1910; Austin Peay to Duncan B. Cooper, letter, April 13, 1910, in the Duncan Brown Cooper Papers. (Peay's letter is apparently misdated 1909.) See also S. D. Wilson to Duncan B. Cooper, letter, April 15, 1910, W. L. McKee to Duncan B. Cooper, letter, May 19, 1910, and John B. McLendon to Duncan B. Cooper, letter, April 16, 1910, all in the Duncan Brown Cooper Papers.

20. *New York Times*, April 15, August 6, 1910. All the rest of these editorial opinions on Patterson's pardon of Cooper were reprinted in the *Nashville Banner*, April 18, 1910.

21. Joe Michael Shahan, "Politics and Reform in Tennessee, 1906–1914," (Ph.D. Diss., Vanderbilt University, 1981), pp. 216–17; Fancher, *The Sparta Bar*, p. 84; McKellar, *Tennessee Senators*, pp. 569–70.

22. *Nashville Banner*, April 26, 1910; *Nashville Tennessean*, August 3, 1910.

23. *Nashville Banner*, April 27, 1910; Shahan, "Politics and Reform," pp. 219–20.

24. J. W. Reid to Duncan B. Cooper, letter, July 30, 1910, in the Duncan Brown Cooper Papers.

25. Biographical notes on the justices-elect may be found in the *Nashville Tennessean*, August 5, 1910.

26. Everett Robert Boyce, ed., *The Unwanted Boy; The Autobiography of Governor Ben W. Hooper* (Knoxville: The University of Tennessee Press, 1963), pp. 18–25, 72–74.

27. R. M. Barton to Duncan B. Cooper, letter, September 10, 1910; Katrina Williamson to Duncan B. Cooper, letter, n.d., 1910?, both in the Duncan Brown Cooper Papers.

28. Paul E. Isaac, *Prohibition and Politics: Turbulent Decades in Tennessee, 1885–1920* (Knoxville: The University of Tennessee Press, 1965), pp. 185–94; Shahan, "Reform and Politics," pp. 238–48; Boyce, ed., Hooper, *Unwanted Boy*, pp. 78–85; *Nashville Tennessean*, August 3, 1910; Ben W. Hooper to Cobey D. Carmack, October 29, 1910, in the Edward Ward Carmack Papers.

29. *Nashville Banner*, February 7, April 26, 1910; *Nashville American*, July 15, 20, 1910; *Nashville Tennessean*, August 6, 1910; Shahan, "Reform and Politics," p. 318; Sandra M. Kopchick to James Summerville, letter, July 3, 1986; Moore and Foster, *Tennessee*, Vol. 4, pp. 103–04. In 1916 McCarn successfully defended C. C. Trabue, who had shot Harry Stokes to death. (John M. Anderson was another of the defendant's lawyers.)

30. *Nashville Banner*, September 5, 1910; *Nashville American*, September 5, 1910; *Nashville Tennessean*, September 5, 1910.

31. Boyce, ed., Hooper, *Unwanted Boy*, pp. 89–93.

32. Luke Lea to Cobey D. Carmack, letter, November 24, 1910; Cobey D. Carmack to Luke Lea, letter, n.d. (1916?), both in the Edward Ward Carmack Papers; *Nashville Banner*, June 24, 1914.

33. Cobey D. Carmack to "Mr. Craig," letter, n.d.; Boyce, ed., Hooper, *Unwanted Boy*, pp. 161–62; William D. Miller, *Mr. Crump of Memphis* (Baton Rouge: Louisiana State University Press, 1964), pp. 356–57; Cobey D. Carmack to S. W. Carmack, letter, August 23, 1915. These two letters of Mrs. Carmack are in the Edward Ward Carmack Papers, as is her short, undated summary of the campaign of 1908 bearing the slashes.

34. Boyce, ed., Hooper, *Unwanted Boy*, pp. 131–32, 135.

35. McKellar, *Tennessee Senators*, pp. 574–85; Green, *Judges of the Supreme Court*, pp. 244–46.

36. Paul Deresco Augsburg, *Bob and Alf Taylor; Their Lives and Lectures; The Story of Senator Robert Love Taylor and Governor Alf Alexander Taylor* (Morristown, Tenn.: Morristown Book Company, 1925), pp. 80–89; Robert E. Corlew, *Tennessee; A Short History*, 2nd ed. (Knoxville: The University of Tennesssee Press, 1981), pp. 449–51.

37. Malcolm R. Patterson to Duncan B. Cooper, letters, July 25, December 9, 1911; Katrina Williamson to Duncan B. Cooper, letter, n.d., all in the Duncan Brown Cooper Papers.

38. *Nashville Banner*, July 25, 26, 29, 1913; letter, author unknown, to Malcolm R. Patterson, April 24, 1932, in the Malcolm Rice Patterson Papers, Manuscripts Section, Tennessee State Library and Archives, Nashville; Malcolm R. Patterson to Duncan B. Cooper, letters, August 14, 1913; March 1, 1914, in the Duncan Brown Cooper Papers; Austin Peay to Malcolm R. Patterson, May 18, 1923, letter, in the Malcolm Rice Patterson Papers; Luke Lea, Jr., to Mary Gardner Patterson, letter, March 11, 1935, in the Malcolm Rice Patterson Papers. Patterson's column quoted here and the song lyrics from the campaign of 1932 are found in his papers. For the discussion of events surrounding the collapse of the Bank of Tennessee, the author is indebted to Corlew, *Tennessee*, pp. 465–67. On the historically important campaign of 1932, see David D. Lee, *Tennessee in Turmoil; Politics in the Volunteer State, 1920–1932* (Memphis: Memphis State University Press, 1979), pp. 130–49. For Carmack's teetotalist view, see Edward Ward Carmack, *Character; Or The Making of the Man* (Nashville: McQuiddy Printing Company, 1909), p. 40.

39. Washington *Evening Star*, March 10, 1936; Katrina Williamson to Duncan Brown Cooper, letters, December 8, no year; September 11, no year, in the Duncan Brown Cooper Papers; Peter Taylor, "Their Losses" in *The Widows of Thornton* (New York: Harcourt, Brace and Company, 1954), pp. 3–23; *Commercial Appeal* (Memphis), March 9, 1936; *Memphis News-Scimitar*, March 9, 1936.

40. Jim Stokeley and Jeff D. Johnson, *An Encyclopedia of East Tennessee* (Oak Ridge: Children's Museum of Oak Ridge, 1981), pp. 84–85; genealogy of the Cooper Family of Maury County, Tennessee, in the Duncan Brown Cooper Papers, Manuscripts Section, Tennessee State Library and Archives; "Grant A. LaFollette," *The National Cyclopedia of American Biography*, Vol. 40 (New York: James T. White Co.), p. 300; *New York Times*, March 19, 1924; *Colfax* (Washington) *Commoner*, September 26, 1929.

41. C. W. Maier to Duncan B. Cooper, letters, May 22, July 7, 8, August 10,

September 14, October 8, 1914; Charles P. Wofford to Duncan B. Cooper, letters, November 28, 1911, April 2, 1912, January 23, 1913; Duncan B. Cooper to Charles P. Wofford, December 11, 1914, all in the Duncan Brown Cooper Papers; Duncan B. Cooper to Theodore Roosevelt, letter, June 25, 1914, in the Theodore Roosevelt Papers, Library of Congress. In the letter to T.R., the account Cooper gives of his political history and his claim to have voted for Lincoln in 1864 — when he was a prisoner of war! — may be charitably doubted.

42. Robin J. Cooper to Duncan B. Cooper, letter, August 19 [no further date, presumed 1910], in the Duncan Brown Cooper Papers.

43. Albert Bramblett Neil, "My Great World," unpublished memoir, in the Tennessee State Library and Archives; Isaac, *Politics and Prohibition*, pp. 180–81. A. B. Neil served as a justice of the Supreme Court of Tennessee from 1942 to 1960.

44. *Nashville Banner*, November 15, 1910; *Nashville Tennessean*, November 15, 16, 18, 19, 1910; *New York Times*, December 13, 14, 1910.

45. William Waller, ed., *Nashville in the 1890s* (Nashville: Vanderbilt University Press, 1970), p. 186; Don H. Doyle, *Nashville in the New South, 1880–1930* (Knoxville: The University of Tennessee Press, 1985), p. 24.

46. Chancery Court of Davidson County, Tennessee, Rule Docket, Vols. 21–30, 1910–1919; Mrs. William M. Geraldton, *Social Directory, Nashville, Tennessee* (Nashville: Cumberland Press, 1915); Oscar Cromwell Tidwell, *Belle Meade Park* (Nashville: privately printed, 1983), p. 28; *Martindale's American Law Directory* (New York: G. B. Martindale, 1919).

47. William Klingaman, *1919; The Year Our World Began* (New York: St. Martin's Press, 1987), pp. 141–42, 340, 370; 388–92, 422.

48. *Nashville Banner*, September 1, 2, 5, 1919.

49. This account of Robin Cooper's whereabouts on the last day of his life relies on a story published in the *Nashville American* (a.k.a. the *Evening Tennessean*), September 3, 1919. The *Nashville Banner* of that same date characterized the meeting among Cooper and the men in the Stahlman Building lobby as an argument.

50. *Nashville Tennessean*, August 31, September 3, 1919; *Nashville American*, September 2, 1919.

51. *Nashville Banner*, August 30, September 1, 1919; *Nashville Tennessean*, August 31, 1919; *Nashville American*, September 2, 1919.

Chapter Six

1. *Nashville Tennessean*, August 31, 1919; *Nashville Banner*, September 5, 1919.

2. *Nashville Banner*, August 30, 1919; *Nashville Tennessean*, September 9, 1919.

3. *Nashville Banner*, August 30, 1919; *Nashville Tennessean*, August 31, 1919.

4. *Nashville Banner*, August 31, 1919; *Nashville Tennessean*, August 31, 1919.

5. *Nashville American*, August 30, 1919; *Nashville Banner*, August 31, 1919; *Nashville Tennessean*, August 31, 1919.

6. *Nashville Banner*, September 2, 1919; *Cincinnati Post*, September 2, 1919. Many years later Robin Cooper's coffin was disinterred and removed to Louisville, where it was buried in the same plot that would receive his wife's.

7. *Cincinnati Post*, September 2, 3, 1919.

8. Ed Huddleston, *The Bootleg Era* (Nashville: *Nashville Banner*, 1957), pp. 2–5.

9. *Nashville Banner*, September 2, 1919; *Nashville American*, September 3, 1919.

10. *Nashville Banner*, August 30, 31, 1919.

11. *Nashville Banner*, September 2, 1919; *Nashville American*, September 3, 1919.

12. *Nashville Banner*, September 3, 1919; *Nashville American*, September 3, 1919.

13. *Nashville Tennessean*, September 4, 1919; *Nashville American*, September 3, 4, 1919; *Birmingham* (Alabama) *Ledger*, September 3, 1919. The *Ledger*, the *Cincinnati Post*, and the Memphis *Commercial Appeal* were all examined for the foregoing discussion. From this time on, they reprinted material from the Nashville papers.

14. William Waller, ed., *Nashville in the 1890s* (Nashville: Vanderbilt University Press, 1970), pp. 91, 295; Nashville *City Directory*, 1899–1913.

15. *Nashville Tennessean*, September 5, 7, 1919.

16. *Nashville Banner*, September 1, 7, 1919.

17. *Nashville Banner*, September 1, 7, 1919; *Nashville Tennessean*, September 2, 1919.

18. *Nashville Tennessean*, September 2, 1919; *Nashville American*, September 3, 1919.

19. *Nashville Tennessean*, September 15, 1919.

20. *Nashville American*, September 5, 6, 8, 1919.

21. *Nashville Tennessean*, September 27, 28, 1919.

22. *Nashville American*, September 25, 26, 1919; *Nashville Tennessean*, September 26, 1919.

23. *Nashville Tennessean*, September 5, 27, 1919.

24. *Nashville Banner*, September 26, 1919; *Nashville Tennessean*, September 27, 28, 1919; *Nashville American*, September 29, 1919. Associate counsel with Bond on the case for the defense was Lurton Goodpasture, later a prominent member of the Nashville bar.

25. *Nashville American*, September 5, 26, 1919; *Nashville Banner*, September 26, 1919; *Nashville Tennessean*, September 27, 1919.

26. *Nashville Banner*, September 13, 26, 1919; *Nashville American*, September 26, 1919; *Nashville Tennessean*, September 5, October 9, 1919.

27. *Nashville Tennessean*, September 3, 5, 1919; *Nashville American*, September 26, 1919; *Nashville Tennessean*, September 27, 1919.

28. *Nashville Tennessean*, September 5, 1919; Memphis *Commercial Appeal*, September 7, 1919.

29. *Nashville Banner*, October 4, 1919; *Nashville American*, October 4, 1919; *New York Times*, October 4, 1919; *Nashville Banner*, October 5, 1919.

30. *Nashville American*, September 25, 30, October 8, 1919; *Nashville Tennessean*, September 27, 1919; *Nashville Banner*, October 8, 1919.

31. *Nashville Banner*, October 6, 8, 1919; *Nashville American*, October 8, 1919.

32. *Nashville Banner*, October 8, 9, 10, 11, 13, 23, 1919; *Nashville American*, October 10, 11, 13, 15, 1919.

33. *Nashville Banner*, March 12, 14, 18, 20, April 2, 5, 1919.

34. *Nashville American*, October 30, 1919; *Nashville Banner*, October 30, 1919.

35. Jenny Bell Yeatman to unknown correspondent, letter, n.d., Yeatman-Polk Collection, Manuscripts Section, Tennessee State Library and Archives, Nashville; *Birmingham* (Alabama) *Ledger*, September 2, 1919; Jordan Stokes, III, to Gary Blackburn and James Summerville, interview, August 12, 1985, Nashville. See also the interview with Dr. Lucius Burch in the *Cincinnati Post*, September 3, 1909,

in which he pointedly denies any connection between the killing of Edward Carmack and the murder of Robin Cooper. Soon after hearing of his son's death, Duncan Cooper was telling the press that reports connecting it with the Carmack case were "gratuitous and without foundation." *New York Herald*, August 31, 1919.

36. Hugh Walker, "Ned Carmack's Revenge a Fantasy," *The Tennessean*, May 24, 1981.

37. This account of Ned Carmack's college days is drawn from his letters to Charlotte Lockridge between 1918 and 1920, located in the Edward Ward Carmack, Jr., Papers, Manuscripts Section, Tennessee State Library and Archives, Nashville.

38. A copy of Ned Carmack's undated ruminations, written to Jordan Stokes, III, was provided by him to the author. Stokes' interpretation of the document he gave in an interview with Gary Blackburn and James Summerville, August 12, 1985. This discussion also relies on facts developed by historian Hugh Walker in his important investigation of the Cooper murder case, "Ned Carmack Claimed Revenge" and "Ned Carmack's Revenge a Fantasy," *The Tennessean*, May 10, 24, 1981.

39. Jordan Stokes, III, provided the author a copy of Carmack's harrowing poem, "You Again," from which these lines are taken. The original remains in Stokes's possession.

40. Among friends Ned Carmack renounced bankers and capitalists in the standard ideological rhetoric of the thirties left. To some he contrasted his father and the Coopers in terms of class differences. Mrs. Thomas Caruthers to Charlotte L. Carmack, letter, n.d., in the Edward Ward Carmack, Jr., Papers; Will Dunn Smith, "The Carmack-Patterson Campaign and Its Aftermath in Tennessee Politics" (M.A. thesis, Vanderbilt University, 1939), p. 82.

41. For this account of Ned Carmack's whereabouts on the evening of Robin Cooper's death, the author and all students of the case are indebted to Hugh Walker's investigative reports, which appeared in the Nashville *Tennessean* on May 10 and 24, 1981, as part of a larger series on the Cooper-Carmack affair. The story printed on the latter date quotes Carmack as claiming to have murdered Duncan Cooper and Lucius Burch, Jr.'s, reply. Burch repeated his comments about the circumstances of his grandfather's death in an interview with Gary Blackburn and James Summerville on October 29, 1985. See also the diary of Dr. Lucius E. Burch, volume two, October 29–November 4, 1922, where he describes the last illness and death of Colonel Cooper. The diary is in the Manuscripts Section, Tennessee State Library and Archives, Nashville.

In his copy of *Tennessee Senators*, next to the profile of his father, Carmack noted that "Robin Cooper, who assassinated my father, [lived] in Belle Meade. There, one August night (1919), he was killed." The author is indebted to Dr. Jim High for the loan of this volume from Carmack's effects: Kenneth D. McKellar, *Tennessee Senators as Seen by One of Their Successors* (Kingsport, Tenn.: Southern Publishing Company, 1942).

42. Lucius E. Burch, Jr., to Gary Blackburn and James Summerville, interview, October 29, 1985. The slip of paper may be examined in box thirteen, folder two of the Duncan Brown Cooper Papers, Manuscripts Section, Tennessee State Library and Archives, Nashville.

43. Nashville *City Directory*, 1884–1902; *Nashville Banner*, January 21, 1902; Albert W. Hutchison, Jr., to James Summerville, interview, August 16, 1986. Mr. Hutchison was Dr. Stonestreet's grandson.

44. William Waller, ed., *Nashville 1900 to 1910* (Nashville: Vanderbilt University Press, 1972), p. 351; Thomas W. Hutchison to Duncan B. Cooper, letter, May 17, 1909, in the Duncan Brown Cooper Papers.

45. The newspaper article is quoted in Waller, ed., *Nashville, 1900 to 1910*, pp. 15–16. This discussion also relies on the Nashville *City Directory* for 1918.

46. *Nashville Banner*, March 15, 1921; *Nashville Tennessean*, March 15, 1921.

47. Frances Jacobs Hooper to James Summerville, interview, August 6, 1988, Cookeville, Tennessee. The photograph of the Jacobs family is in Mrs. Hooper's possession.

48. County Court Clerk of Davidson County, Tennessee, *Wills and Inventories*, Vol. 36, p. 286, on microfilm in the Manuscripts Section, Tennessee State Library and Archives, Nashville; Nashville *City Directory*, 1895–1970; Frances Jacobs Hooper to James Summerville, interview; *Nashville Banner*, February 18, 1964.

49. *Confederate Veteran* 17, no. 9 (September 1909), p. 471; *Nashville Banner*, August 17, 1909, October 1, 1924; *Nashville Tennessean*, August 18, 1909; B. W. Collier, *Representative Women of the South 1861–1929*, Vol. 6 (n.p.; n.d., 1925?), pp. 243–44 (this excerpt may be found in the ephemeral file for Leslie C. Warner in the Nashville Room, Ben West Public Library of Nashville and Davidson County); William Waller, ed., *Nashville in the 1890s* (Nashville: Vanderbilt University Press, 1970), p. 256.

50. Nashville *City Directory*, 1890–1916; Frances Jacobs Hooper to James Summerville, interview; *Nashville Banner*, June 10, July 15, August 7, 1914; Chancery Court of Davidson County, Rule Docket, Book 24; Lee Douglas, United States Attorney to the Attorney General [Thomas W. Gregory], letter, May 25, 1915. The records of the United States Attorney for the Middle District of Tennessee, containing correspondence and memoranda related to the investigation of Empire Realty, are in the National Archives, Washington, D. C.

51. The complicated history of Empire Realty, its associated companies, and their collapse is traced in the *Nashville Banner*, September 5, 6, 7, 8, 9, 11, 1916. See also the case file from the records of the federal district court. Jacobs was listed as a mining engineer in the Nashville *City Directory* for 1918, the canvass for which was probably made the previous year.

52. Arthur Miller, *Death of a Salesman* (New York: Viking Press, 1967), p. 138; Nashville *City Directory*, 1896–1911.

53. G. N. Georgana, ed., *The New Encyclopedia of Motorcars, 1885 to the Present* (New York: E. P. Dutton, 1982), p. 125; Frances Jacobs Hooper to James Summerville, interview; Miller, *Death of a Salesman*, p. 138.

54. Nashville *City Directory*, 1893–1920–21; *Nashville Banner*, March 15, 16, 1921; *Nashville Tennessean*, January 17, 1922.

55. Nashville *City Directory*, 1893–1918; Fedora Small Frank, *Beginnings on Market Street; Nashville and Her Jewry, 1850–1900* (Nashville: privately printed, 1976), *Nashville Banner*, May 29, 1942. Leah Rose Werthan (daughter of Clarence Bernstein) to James Summerville, interview, June 3, 1988.

56. Nashville *City Directory*, 1918; *Nashville Banner*, May 11, 18, 1919; State of Tennessee, Office of the Secretary of State, *General Index to Charters*, Vols. 4 and 5 (1914–1919) and foreign corporations files.

57. *Nashville Banner*, July 25, December 17, 1918; *New York Times*, January 26, 1919. Graphite's importance in sustaining war industries is discussed by Arthur H. Redfield, "Foreign Graphite" in R. W. Stone, ed., *Mineral Resources of the United States, 1919; Part II — Nonmetals*, Department of the Interior, United States Geological Survey (Washington, D.C.: Government Printing Office, 1922), p. 181. War demands led to an overproduction of graphite on the world market, causing a marked depression of the industry by 1919. See Henry G. Ferguson, "Graphite," and L. M. Beach, "Graphite," idem, pp. 223–65 and 309–17.

58. *New York Times*, March 17, 1919; *Nashville Banner*, September 3, 1919; *Memphis News-Scimitar*, September 3, 1919.

59. Nashville *City Directory*, 1922; Chancery Court of Davidson County, Rule Docket, Vols. 21–30, 1910–1919, passim; Don H. Doyle, *Nashville in the New South, 1880–1930* (Knoxville: The University of Tennessee Press, 1985), pp. 104–06, 220–22.

60. The principal sources for this discussion are the surviving records of the United States Attorney of the Middle District of Tennessee relating to the Stahlman investigation and on file in the National Archives.

61. Diary of Lucius E. Burch, Vol. III, October 23, 1923. Katherine Burch Warner and E. B. Stahlman worked together in the campaign that led the Tennessee legislature to ratify the Nineteenth Amendment, adding it to the U. S. Constitution. See Rose Long Gilmore, *Davidson County Women in the World War, 1914–1919* (Nashville: Advisory Council of 25 Davidson County Women, 1923), pp. 450–51.

62. Nashville *City Directory*, 1902–1949; *Nashville Banner*, February 15, 1919.

63. Tennessee State Board of Health, Bureau of Vital Statistics, Certificate of Death for James Madison Jacobs, September 12, 1922. The Indianapolis *City Directory* for 1920 lists a "James Jacobs, repairman" living there; after that year's directory, the listing disappears. Also living in Indianapolis in this period was a Belle Jacobs, a public stenographer and lettershop proprietor. James Jacobs had a niece named Belle, but it is not certain that these are one and the same person. Sources for these notes on the life of Bibb Jacobs in the last years of his life include: State of New York, Department of Health of the City of New York, standard death certificate of George Bibb Jacobs, October 1, 1924; Lawrence R. Freedman, *Infective Endocarditis and Other Vascular Infections* (New York: Plenum Medical Book Company, 1982); *Nashville Banner*, October 1, 1924; Samuel T. McSeveney to James Summerville, letter, February 18, 1989.

64. *Stuart* (Florida) *News*, February 1, 1945; Grafton Green "to whom it may concern," September 29, 1930; John H. DeWitt "to whom it may concern," October 1, 1930. The news stories and these letters are in the Thomas E. Matthews Collection, Manuscripts Section, Tennessee State Library and Archives, Nashville.

65. Thomas E. Matthews to Mrs. Leonard G. Bond, letter, August 30, 1930, in the Duncan Brown Cooper Papers; *Nashville Banner*, January 29, 1945.

Epilogue

1. Senate Joint Resolution No. 39, *Acts of the State of Tennessee, Fifty-sixth General Assembly, 1909*, Part Three (Nashville: McQuiddy Printing Company, 1909), pp. 2238–39.

2. *Nashville Tennessean*, June 6, 1925.

3. *Ibid.*; *Nashville Banner*, January 5, 1919. See also the Nancy Cox-McCormack Scrapbook in the Manuscripts Section, Tennessee State Library and Archives, Nashville.

4. *Nashville Tennessean*, June 6, 7, 1925; *Nashville Banner*, June 6, 1925; Mary Louise Lea Tidwell, *Luke Lea of Tennessee*, (Bowling Green, Ohio: Bowling Green State University Popular Press, 1993).

5. *Nashville Banner*, August 23, 1931; Sandy Seawright, "Ten Greatest Tennesseans'—A Reappraisal," *Tennessee Historical Quarterly* 35, no. 2 (September 1976), pp. 222–24.

6. *Nashville Tennessean*, November 5, 1928; Murfreesboro (Tennessee) *Daily*

News Journal, June 15, September 11, November 21, December 23, 1934, and n.d., in box 8, folder 5 of the Edward Ward Carmack, Jr., Papers, Manuscripts Section, Tennessee State Library and Archives, Nashville.

7. *Nashville Banner,* March 4, 23, 26, 31, 1937.

8. *Nashville Tennessean,* May 31, 1942; *Commercial Appeal* (Memphis), July 26, 1942. McKellar's letters to Carmack, often attaching memoranda from military bureaucrats, reveal Carmack's persistent attempts to enlist. This correspondence is in the Edward Ward Carmack, Jr., Papers.

9. James N. Hardin, comp., *Official Returns, 1942; Democratic Primary, August 6; Regular Election, November 3* (Nashville: State Democratic Executive Committee, n.d., 1942?); Margaret Pouder and Malinda Jones, comps., *Tennessee Blue Book, 1947–1948* (Nashville: Joe C. Carr, Secretary of State), 1948. See also V. O. Key, Jr. (with Alexander Heard), *Southern Politics in State and Nation* (New York: Alfred A. Knopf, 1949), pp. 70–72. The author is grateful to Dr. Jim High for the loan of Ned Carmack's copy of Kenneth D. McKellar, *Tennessee Senators as Seen by One of Their Successors* (Kingsport, Tenn.: Southern Publishing Company, 1942).

10. Jordan Stokes, III, untitled paper, read by its author to the Freolac Club of Nashville, June 4, 1973, copy in the author's possession; *Nashville Tennessean,* September 19, 1972; Louise Davis, "What Am I Bid?" *Nashville Tennessean Magazine,* February 4, 1973.

11. A copy of Carmack's undated ruminations, written to Jordan Stokes, III, was provided to the author by him. Stokes gave his interpretation of the document in an interview with Gary Blackburn and James Summerville, August 12, 1985, in Nashville.

12. *Nashville Tennessean,* September 29, November 16, 17, 19, 22, 23, 1972; February 9, 1973.

13. *Nashville Tennessean,* January 12, February 9, 10, 11, 1973; *Nashville Banner,* February 10, 1973. For this account, the author is also indebted to Davis, "What Am I Bid?"

14. Edward W. Carmack, Jr., to Mrs. Paul Severence, letter, December 23, 1949, in the Edward Ward Carmack, Jr., Papers.

—— WORKS CITED ——

Manuscript Collections

Chapel Hill. Southern Historical Collection, University of North Carolina at Chapel Hill. Edward Ward Carmack Papers. (Photocopies at Nashville. Tennessee State Library and Archives. Manuscripts Section.)

Nashville. Ben West Public Library, Nashville Room, Biographical files.

Nashville. Jean and Alexander Heard Library, Special Collections. Alumnus files.

Nashville. Tennessee State Library and Archives, Manuscripts Section. Cooper Family Papers.

Nashville. Tennessee State Library and Archives, Manuscripts Section. Duncan Brown Cooper Papers.

Nashville. Tennessee State Library and Archives, Manuscripts Section. Edward Ward Carmack, Jr., Papers.

Nashville. Tennessee State Library and Archives, Manuscripts Section. James Douglas Anderson Papers.

Nashville. Tennessee State Library and Archives, Manuscripts Section. Lucius E. Burch Diaries.

Nashville. Tennessee State Library and Archives, Manuscripts Section. Malcolm Rice Patterson Papers.

Nashville. Tennessee State Library and Archives, Manuscripts Section. Nancy Cox-McCormack Scrapbook.

Nashville. Tennessee State Library and Archives, Manuscripts Section. Scrapbook—Prohibition, 1887–1940.

Nashville. Tennessee State Library and Archives, Manuscripts Section. Thomas E. Matthews Collection.

Nashville. Tennessee State Library and Archives. Manuscripts Section. William Henry McRaven Collection.

Nashville. Tennessee State Library and Archives, Manuscripts Section. Yeatman-Polk Collection.

Washington, D.C. Library of Congress. Theodore Roosevelt Papers.

Washington, D.C. National Archives. Records of the United States Attorney for the Middle District of Tennessee.

205

Newspapers

Birmingham (Alabama) *Ledger*
Chattanooga Sunday Times
Cincinnati Post
Colfax (Washington) *Commoner*
Commercial Appeal (Memphis)
Daily Herald (Columbia, Tennessee) [a.k.a. *Herald and Mail*]
Daily Times (Chattanooga)
Knoxville Sentinel
LaFollette Press (LaFollette, Tennessee)
Lebanon Democrat (Lebanon, Tennessee)
Memphis News-Scimitar
Murfreesboro (Tennessee) *Daily News Journal*
Nashville American [a.k.a. *The American, Daily American*]
Nashville Banner
Nashville Tennessean
The New York American
The New York Herald
The New York Times
The New York World
Stuart (Florida) *News*
Washington (D.C.) *Evening Star*

Public Documents

Acts of the State of Tennessee, Fifty-sixth General Assembly, 1909. Three parts. Nashville, 1909.

Acts of the State of Tennessee Passed by the Forty-ninth General Assembly, 1895. Nashville, 1895.

Chancery Court of Davidson County, Tennessee. *Rule Docket.* Vols. 21–30, 1910–1919.

Cooper, et al., vs. State. 118 *Southwestern Reporter* (1911).

County Court Clerk of Davidson County, Tennessee. *Wills and Inventories.*

Duncan B. Cooper and Robin J. Cooper, in Error, vs. The State of Tennessee. Trial transcript. Nashville, 1910.

General Index to Charters. Vols. 4 and 5 (1914–1919). State of Tennessee, Office of the Secretary of State.

House Journal of the 52nd General Assembly of the State of Tennessee, 1901. Nashville, 1901.

Mineral Resources of the United States, 1919. Part II—Nonmetals. R. W. Stone, ed. Washington, D.C.: Department of the Interior, United States Geological Survey/Government Printing Office, 1922.

1980 Census of Population, Vol. 1, Part 44. Population Characteristics—Tennessee. Washington, D.C.: Department of Commerce, Bureau of the Census, 1983.

Official Returns, 1942: Democratic Primary, August 6; Regular Election, November 3. James N. Hardin, comp. Nashville: State Democratic Executive Committee, n.d.

Senate Journal of the 52nd General Assembly of the State of Tennessee, 1901. Nashville, 1901.

Senate Journal of the 56th General Assembly, 1909. Nashville, 1909.
Senate Journal of the First Session of the Forty-ninth General Assembly of the State of Tennessee. Nashville, 1895.
Thirteenth Census of the United States, 1910. Vol. I, Population. Washington, D.C.: Department of Commerce, Bureau of the Census and Government Printing Office, 1912.
_____. *Vol. VI, Population—Occupation Statistics.* Washington, D.C.: Department of Commerce, Bureau of the Census and Government Printing Office, 1912.
[U.S.] *Senate Miscellaneous Document 9,* 46th Congress, 3rd Session.
William West, in Error, vs. The State, Brief and Assignment of Errors, by Sam E. Young for the defendant, in East Tennessee Division, Tennessee Supreme Court, January 1905.

Theses, Dissertations, and Unpublished Material

Bass, Frank Embrick. "The Career of Edward Ward Carmack in Congress." M.A. thesis, George Peabody College for Teachers, 1930.
Crutcher, Robert Franklin. "The Career of Edward Ward Carmack and the Cooper-Sharp Trial." M.A. thesis, Western Kentucky University, 1932.
Flamming, James Douglas. "The Sam Jones Revival and Social Reform in Nashville, Tennessee, 1885–1900." M.A. thesis, Vanderbilt University, 1983.
Goodpasture, Henry. "Memoirs of Henry Goodpasture." Mimeographed. Nashville: privately printed, 1979.
Hutton, Marilyn J. "The Election of 1896 in the Tenth Congressional District of Tennessee." Ph.D. diss., Memphis State University, 1976.
Neil, Albert Bramlett. "My Great World; or Fifty Years on the Bench." Mimeographed. Nashville: privately printed, n.d., 1964?
Shahan, Joe Michael. "Politics and Reform in Tennessee, 1906–1914." Ph.D. diss., Vanderbilt University, 1981.
Smith, Will Dunn. "The Carmack-Patterson Campaign and Its Aftermath in Tennessee Politics." M.A. thesis, Vanderbilt University, 1939.
Stokes, Jordan, III. Untitled paper read to the Freolac Club, Nashville, June 4, 1973.

Interviews and Letters

Burch, Lucius, Jr., to Gary Blackburn and James Summerville, interview, October 29, 1985, Nashville.
Deane, Roxanna, to James Summerville, letter, November 12, 1986.
Hooper, Frances Jacobs, to James Summerville, interview, August 6, 1988.
Hutchison, Albert W., Jr., to James Summerville, interview, August 16, 1986.
Kopchick, Sandra M., to James Summerville, letter, July 3, 1986.
McSeveney, Samuel T., to James Summerville, letter, February 18, 1989.
Roberts, Lesbia Word, to James Summerville, letter, July 9, 1989.
Stokes, Jordan, III, to Gary Blackburn and James Summerville, interview, August 12, 1985, Nashville.

Taylor, Albert, to James Summerville, letter, November 20, 1986.
Torres, Louis, to James Summerville, letter, August 12, 1986.
Werthan, Leah Rose Bernstein, to James Summerville, interview, June 3, 1988.

Articles

A. B. and C. D. [pseud.] "The True Story of the Cooper-Carmack Tragedy." *The Taylor-Trotwood Magazine* 9 (1909): 68–75.
Davis, Louise. "What Am I Bid?" *Nashville Tennessean Magazine*, February 4, 1973: pp. 8–11.
Faris, Clyde J. "Carmack v. Patterson: The Genesis of a Political Feud." *Tennessee Historical Quarterly* 38:3 (Fall 1979): 332–47.
Folk, Edgar Estes. "Senator Edward Carmack; A Life Sketch." *Baptist and Reflector* 20:21 (January 14, 1909): 2–4.
Grantham, Dewey W., Jr. "Goebels, Gonzales, Carmack: Three Violent Scenes in Southern Politics." *Mississippi Quarterly* 2:1 (Winter 1958): 29–37.
Inglis, William. "A Democratic Presidential Possibility; Edward Ward Carmack, Ex-Senator from Tennessee." *Harper's Weekly* 51:2636 (June 29, 1907): 942–43.
Lanier, Robert A. "The Carmack Murder Case." *Tennessee Historical Quarterly* 40:3 (Fall 1981): 272–85.
Seawright, Sandy. "Ten Greatest Tennesseans — A Reappraisal." *Tennessee Historical Quarterly* 35:2 (September 1976): 222–24.
Vietor, Richard H. K. "Businessmen and the Political Economy: The Railroad Rate Controversy of 1905." *Journal of American History* 64:1 (June 1977): 47–66.

Books and Pamphlets

Alexander, Virginia Wood, and Jill Knight Garrett. *Maury County, Tennessee, Marriage Records, 1838–1852.* Columbia, Tenn.: n.p., 1963.
Allison, John, ed. *Notable Men of Tennessee.* Two volumes. Atlanta: Southern Historical Association, 1905.
Ash, Stephen V. *Middle Tennessee Society Transformed, 1860–1870.* Knoxville: The University of Tennessee Press, 1988.
Augsburg, Paul Deresco. *Bob and Alf Taylor, Their Lives and Lectures; The Story of Senator Robert Love Taylor and Governor Alf Alexander Taylor.* Morristown, Tenn.: Morristown Book Company, 1925.
Baker, Thomas Harrison. *The Memphis Commercial Appeal; The History of a Southern Newspaper.* Baton Rouge: Louisiana State University Press, 1971.
Blocker, Jack S., Jr. *Retreat from Reform: The Prohibition Movement in the United States, 1890–1913.* Westport, Conn.: Greenwood Press, 1976.
Boyce, Everett Robert, ed. *The Unwanted Boy; The Autobiography of Governor Ben W. Hooper.* Knoxville: The University of Tennessee Press, 1963.
Brice, James M. *I Had a Real Good Time; The Making of a Country Editor.* Union City, Tenn.: privately printed, 1984.
Brownlow, Louis. *A Passion for Politics.* Chicago: The University of Chicago Press, 1955.
Bumpus, Paul Franklin. *Carmack; The Edward Ward Carmack Story.* Franklin Tenn.: privately printed, 1977.
Caldwell, James E. *Recollections of a Life Time.* Nashville: privately printed, 1923.

Caldwell, Joshua W. *Sketches of the Bench and Bar of Tennessee.* Knoxville: Ogden Brothers and Co., 1898.

Carmack, Edward Ward. *Character; Or, The Making of the Man.* Nashville: McQuiddy Printing Co., 1909.

"Center Shots in the Senatorial Campaign; Plain Truths Plainly Told" (pamphlet). Edward Ward Carmack Papers.

Century Review, 1805–1905, Maury County, Tennessee. Columbia, Tennessee, 1905. Reprint. Easley, S.C. Southern Historical Press, 1980.

Clark, Norman H. *Deliver Us from Evil; An Interpretation of American Prohibition.* New York: W. W. Norton, 1976.

Collier, B. W. *Representative Women of the South, 1861–1929.* Six volumes. N.p., 1925?

Connelly, Thomas L. *Civil War Tennessee; Battles and Leaders.* Knoxville: The University of Tennessee Press, 1979.

Coppock, Paul. *Memphis Memoirs.* Memphis: Memphis State University Press, 1980.

Corlew, Robert W. *Tennessee; A Short History.* Second edition. Knoxville: The University of Tennessee Press, 1981.

Davis, Richard Harding. *Three Gringos in Venezuela and Central America.* New York: Harper and Brothers, 1896.

DeTocqueville, Alexis. *Democracy in America.* Edited by J. P. Mayer and Max Lerner. New York: Harper and Row, 1966.

Doyle, Don H. *Nashville in the New South, 1880–1930.* Knoxville: The University of Tennessee Press, 1985.

Fancher, Frank Trigg. *The Sparta Bar.* Sparta, Tenn.: privately printed, 1950.

Frank, Fedora Small. *Beginnings on Market Street; Nashville and Her Jewry, 1850–1900.* Nashville: privately printed, 1976.

Freedman, Lawrence R. *Infective Endocarditis and Other Vascular Infections.* New York: Plenum Medical Book Co., 1982.

Garrett, Jill K., and Marise P. Lightfoot. *The Civil War in Maury County, Tennessee.* Columbia, Tenn.: privately printed, 1966.

Garrett, Jill K., comp. *Obituaries from Tennessee Newspapers.* Reprint. Easley, S.C.: Southern Historical Press, 1980.

————, ed. *War of 1812 Soldiers of Maury County, Tennessee.* Columbia, Tenn.; Daughters of the American Revolution, n.d.

Georgana, G. N., ed. *The New Encyclopedia of Motorcars, 1885 to the Present.* New York: E. P. Dutton, 1982.

Gilmore, Rose Long. *Davidson County Women in the World War, 1914–1919.* Nashville: Advisory Council of Davidson County Women, 1923.

Grantham, Dewey W. *Southern Progressivism; The Reconciliation of Progress and Tradition.* Knoxville: The University of Tennessee Press, 1983.

Graves, John P. *Northwest Davidson County; The Land — It's* [sic] *People.* Nashville: privately printed, 1985.

Green, John W. *Law and Lawyers; Sketches of the Federal Judges of Tennessee; Sketches of the Attorneys General of Tennessee; Legal Miscellany; Reminiscences.* Jackson, Tenn.: McCowat-Mercer Press, 1950.

————. *Lives of the Judges of the Supreme Court of Tennessee.* Knoxville: Archer and Smith, 1947.

Hamer, Philip M., ed. *Tennessee, A History, 1673–1932.* Four volumes. New York: American Historical Society, 1933.

History of the State of Tennessee from the Earliest Times to the Present. Nashville: Goodspeed Publishing Company, 1886.

"How Governor Taylor Tickled Republicans Under the Ribs" (pamphlet). Edward Ward Carmack Papers.

Huddleston, Ed. *The Bootleg Era*. Nashville: *Nashville Banner*, 1957.

Indianapolis *City Directory*, 1920.

Isaac, Paul E. *Prohibition and Politics: Turbulent Decades in Tennessee, 1885–1920.* Knoxville: The University of Tennessee Press, 1965.

Johns, C. D. *Tennessee's Pond of Liquor and Pool of Blood*. Nashville: C. D. Johns and Co., 1912.

Jones, Robert B. *Tennessee at the Crossroads; The State Debt Controversy, 1870–1883.* Knoxville: The University of Tennessee Press, 1977.

Key, V. O., Jr. (with Alexander Heard). *Southern Politics in State and Nation*. New York: Alfred A. Knopf, 1949.

Klingaman, William. *1919; The Year Our World Began*. New York: St. Martin's Press, 1987.

Lee, David D. *Tennessee in Turmoil; Politics in the Volunteer State, 1920–1932.* Memphis: Memphis State University Press, 1979.

McBride, Robert M., and Dan M. Robison. *Biographical Directory of the Tennessee General Assembly*. Two volumes. Nashville: Tennessee State Library and Archives and Tennessee Historical Commission, 1979.

McKellar, Kenneth D. *Tennessee Senators as Seen by One of Their Successors*. Kingsport, Tenn.: Southern Publishing Co., 1942.

Majors, William R. *Continuity and Change; Tennessee Politics Since the Civil War*. Macon, Ga.: Mercer University Press, 1986.

_____. *Editorial Wild Oats; Edward Ward Carmack and Tennessee Politics*. Macon, Ga.: Mercer University Press, 1984.

Martindale's American Law Directory. New York: G. B. Martindale Co., 1919.

Men of the South. New Orleans: Southern Biographical Association, 1922.

Miller, Arthur. *Death of a Salesman*. New York: Viking Press, 1967.

Miller, William D. *Memphis During the Progressive Era, 1900–1917*. Memphis: Memphis State University Press, 1957.

_____. *Mr. Crump of Memphis*. Baton Rouge: Louisiana State University Press, 1964.

Montell, William Lynwood. *Killings; Folk Justice in the Upper South*. Lexington: University Press of Kentucky, 1986.

Moore, John Trotwood, and Austin P. Foster. *Tennessee: The Volunteer State, 1769–1923.* Four volumes. Chicago: S. J. Clarke Publishing Co., 1923.

Nashville *City Directory*, 1884–1970.

National Cyclopedia of American Biography. Vol. 40. New York: James T. White Co., 1955.

Norton, Herman A. *Tennessee Christians; A History of the Christian Church (Disciples of Christ) in Tennessee*. Nashville: Reed and Co., 1971.

Painter, Nell Irvin. *Standing at Armageddon: The United States, 1877–1919*. New York: W. W. Norton, 1987.

Pier, Arthur S. *American Apostles to the Philippines*. Boston: Beacon Press, 1950.

"Regulations for the Primary of June 27, 1908 and the Convention of July 14, 1908. Prescribed by the Democratic State Executive Committee" (pamphlet). Manuscripts Section, Tennessee State Library and Archives.

Roberts, Lesbia Word. *Hugh Cooper (1720–1893) of Fishing Creek, South Carolina, and His Descendants*. Fort Worth: privately printed, 1975.

Robison, Daniel Merritt. *Bob Taylor and the Agrarian Revolt in Tennessee*. Chapel Hill: The University of North Carolina Press, 1935.

Schirmer, Daniel B. *Republic or Empire; American Resistance to the Philippine War.* Cambridge, Mass.: Schenkman Publishing Co., 1972.

Smith, Frank H. *History of Maury County, Tennessee.* Columbia, Tenn.: Maury County, Tennessee, 1969.

Snodgrass, Charles Albert. *The History of Freemasonry in Tennessee, 1789–1943.* Chattanooga: Masonic History Agency, 1944.

Speer, William S., comp. *Sketches of Prominent Tennesseans.* Nashville: Albert B. Tavel, 1888.

Stokeley, Jim, and Jeff D. Johnson. *An Encyclopedia of East Tennessee.* Oak Ridge: Children's Museum of Oak Ridge, 1981.

Taylor, Peter. *The Widows of Thornton.* New York: Harcourt, Brace and Company, 1954.

Tennessee Blue Book, 1947–1948. Margaret Pouder and Malinda Jones, comps. Nashville: Joe C. Carr, Secretary of State, 1948.

Tidwell, Mary Louise Lea. *Luke Lea of Tennessee.* Bowling Green, Ohio: The Popular Press of Bowling Green State University, 1993.

Tidwell, Oscar Cromwell. *Belle Meade Park.* Nashville: privately printed, 1983.

Timberlake, James H. *Prohibition and the Progressive Movement, 1900–1920.* Cambridge, Mass.: Harvard University Press, 1963.

Turner, William Bruce. *History of Maury County, Tennessee.* Nashville: Parthenon Press, 1955.

Wallace, Paul A. W. *Pennsylvania; Seed of a Nation.* New York: Harper and Row, 1962.

Waller, William, ed. *Nashville in the 1890s.* Nashville: Vanderbilt University Press, 1970.

_____. *Nashville 1900 to 1910.* Nashville: Vanderbilt University Press, 1972.

Weaver, John D. *The Brownsville Raid.* New York: W. W. Norton, 1970.

Welch, Richard E., Jr. *Response to Imperialism; The United States and the Philippine-American War, 1899–1902.* Chapel Hill: The University of North Carolina Press, 1979.

Who's Who in Tennessee; A Biographical Reference Book of Notable Tennesseans of Today. Memphis: Paul and Douglass, Publishers, 1911.

Woodward, C. Vann. *Origins of the New South, 1877–1913.* Baton Rouge: Louisiana State University Press, 1951.

Wyatt-Brown, Bertram. *Yankee Saints and Southern Sinners.* Baton Rouge: Louisiana State University Press, 1985.

Miscellaneous

Catalogue of the Officers and Students of Jefferson College for the Academical Year, 1859–60. Canonsburg, Pa.: the College, 1860.

"Members of the Open Letter Club, Nashville and New York." Unpublished document, in possession of the author.

INDEX

Numbers in **boldface** *refer to pages with photographs.*